To Kenny,
A damn good

THE
BLUE MOUNTAIN
LEGION

A History of the
Hamburg Unit
of the
Pennsylvania Army
National Guard

Master Sergeant (Retired)
Craig A. Kleinsmith

HERITAGE BOOKS
2005

HERITAGE BOOKS

AN IMPRINT OF HERITAGE BOOKS, INC.

Books, CDs, and more—Worldwide

For our listing of thousands of titles see our website
at
www.HeritageBooks.com

Published 2005 by
HERITAGE BOOKS, INC.
Publishing Division
65 East Main Street
Westminster, Maryland 21157-5026

International Standard Book Number: 0-7884-3282-6

DEDICATION

To all the soldiers of the Hamburg unit of the Pennsylvania Army National Guard, whose gallant and honorable deeds are recorded herein. Through the decades they never once faltered in the service to their community, the Commonwealth of Pennsylvania, or the nation. May those that now serve, and those who will serve in the future preserve what those before them so nobly defended with their very lives.

This book is also dedicated in the memory of Charles M. Eyer, Hamburg Armory custodian and maintenance repairman from September 24, 1958 to February 28, 1991. His thirty-two years of inspirational attitude, unselfishness, dedication, and loyalty to the soldiers of the Hamburg unit never once waned.

A hero in his own right, he served his nation as a staff sergeant in the Army Air Corps. As a ball-turret gunner on a B-17 Flying Fortress bomber in World War II, he flew fifty-nine combat missions over enemy territory in both the African and European theaters before his aircraft was shot down over Frankfurt, Germany, in May of 1944. He was taken prisoner by the Germans and held in Stalag Luft IV for almost a year before being liberated in April of 1945. His devotion to his nation and comrades never failed. He was decorated many times, including the Air medal with nine Oak Leaf Clusters, the European-African-Middle Eastern Service Medal with Three Bronze Stars, the Prisoner of War Medal, and the Pennsylvania Meritorious Service Medal, which is the highest Pennsylvania military decoration that can be awarded to a civilian in peacetime. His words and wisdom were often sought out by this author and many other soldiers who were fortunate enough to have known him. Thank you, Charlie.

CONTENTS

	Dedication	iii
	Introduction	vii
CHAPTER 1	The Frontier 1755 – 1763	1
CHAPTER 2	The Revolution 1774 – 1781	19
CHAPTER 3	The Militia 1782 – 1860	27
CHAPTER 4	The Civil War 1861 – 1865	35
CHAPTER 5	The Blue Mountain Legion 1875 – 1917	109
CHAPTER 6	World War I 1917 – 1919	127
CHAPTER 7	Between the Wars 1920 – 1940	161
CHAPTER 8	World War II 1941 – 1945	165

CHAPTER 9   Post World War II – Korean War   177
                   1946 – 1952

CHAPTER 10   Protecting the Peace   181
                   1953 – 1989

APPENDIX A   Lineage   209

APPENDIX B   Campaign Participation   213

APPENDIX C   Commanding Officers   215

APPENDIX D   Rosters   219

APPENDIX E   Awards   287

APPENDIX F   Annual Training   291

BIBLIOGRAPHY   295

INDEX   299

INTRODUCTION

Craig A. Kleinsmith

The student of history is no less diligent in his research than any other student, and should not be content with a general knowledge of events. As he goes through all of the avenues of the past to discover the truth, he is often saddened by the fact that so many important items of history are now buried in oblivion.

We desire to find the exact details, but they have lost some of their reliability, and many important facts are lost as they pass through time. We strive to learn more of the facts, but we ask in vain because many sources fail to give us the detailed information that we desire to learn. We search earnestly in books and old documents, but regrettably a large part of history was never written, and now it is gone far beyond our reach. We stand behind a curtain that divides the past from the present. We wish that the curtain could be raised so that we might rescue the unwritten history. But the past is unchangeable and our wishes cannot be granted.

Some years ago I became deeply interested in the history of the Hamburg Army National Guard unit. Immediately I started to gather information about the unit. My enthusiasm increased as rapidly as my collection of information was obtained, until I deemed it a subject worthy of a description in which others might be interested. My first plan was to give a mere description of the unit's history. However, the interest that I felt about it, and the desire I had to share this information with others convinced me to undertake the task of writing a more detailed history. Had it been written a few generations ago, it would most certainly contain much more interesting information then can be obtained today. If I succeed even partly in preserving the past of the Hamburg unit, I shall feel compensated for the time and energy in writing this history.

I hope this book will accomplish two objectives. First, to remind us all that we still live in a threatening world. A world in which our armed forces defend and protect this nation from those whose goal it is to eliminate us as a world power and defender of freedom. Second, I want those soldiers serving in the Hamburg unit to learn about, and appreciate the magnificent performance of those soldiers who preceded them on battlefields all over the world. Young soldiers should gain a sense of identity with a history most are unaware even exists, or have only heard through word of mouth. Older soldiers will find many changes in equipment, unit organization, tactics and pay scales, but the important characteristics such as esprit de corps, the desire to serve, and sense of purpose, never change.

CHAPTER 1

The Frontier
1755 - 1763

It is not within the scope of this chapter to analyze the reasons which caused the hostilities between the Native Americans and the white man in Pennsylvania. The policies of the government of Pennsylvania were normally of a peaceful character and based on the principle of fair dealing with the Native Americans. It is sufficient to say, that they saw themselves being pushed back by the onward march of the settlers. Their hunting grounds, teeming with game and streams filled with fish were being lost to them.

Regardless if their loss came about either through fair purchase or fraudulent action on the part of the settlers, it needed but a spark to ignite their anger. That spark came from the fields of Braddock's defeat in 1755 in western Pennsylvania. In its aftermath, hundreds of warring parties swarmed down upon the frontier settlements of the Province. These warring parties, carrying death and destruction with them everywhere didn't end until the year 1783. In early fall of 1755 the Delaware and Shawnee sent two especially troublesome war parties raiding eastward, harassing the settlements along the Blue Mountains in northern Berks County.

At that time the Blue Mountains north of Hamburg practically marked the limit of actual settlement. It was along this range that the storm burst forth in all its fury. Standing on the edge of civilization and forming a natural barrier, it was logical to occupy the mountains for the purpose of defense and there to halt any further attacks by the Native Americans. Keep in mind the fact that the attacks of the Native Americans were not made in large groups or numbers. Neither were the tactics of what was deemed civilized warfare followed.

Usually a party of three to ten or twenty Native Americans would creep quietly past sentries, suddenly fall upon their unsuspecting victims. Then just as suddenly disappear after their attack, and long before any alarm could be spread or the most alert troops could overtake them.

Unusual methods of defense were needed and required the building of forts. These forts which were not very far from each other would occupy prominent avenues of approach. They were situated on level ground to furnish the garrison with a view of the surrounding area. They were also meant to give convenient access to the settlers who might, and did constantly flee to them for refuge. Last, but by no means least, they were built in a location that provided plenty of water nearby.

After the first attacks and killing of settlers, blockhouses were erected by some settlers for protection. Sometimes a farm house was used for protection if it was located where the danger seemed most imminent. To say the least, the life of the early settlers in their new mountain home was not very peaceful. The Native Americans that lived in this region at that time displayed open unfriendliness, and the hostilities grew more intense until the settlers were driven out of their homes. Some early settlers built a stone fort in Windsor Township located near the Smoke Church.

In 1756 the government took the defense of the settlers into its own hands. Governor Morris proposed a chain of defenses along the line of the Blue Mountains from Easton to Mercersburg. These were to be sizeable stockades capable of holding a company of militia and many families, and erected at twenty-mile intervals. Smaller blockhouses for temporary shelter were also erected at five-mile intervals. Eventually, a chain of forts was established along the Blue Mountains reaching from the Delaware River to the Susquehanna River. The distance between the forts was approximately ten to fifteen miles apart. These were normally occupied, depending upon the location of the prominent gaps in the mountains.

Sometimes the chain of defenses ran on the south side of the mountain range, and sometimes on the north side. Frequently both sides of the mountain range were occupied as the needs of the population demanded. Some of the forts consisted of the defenses previously built by the settlers. They were available for the purpose intended and of which the government took possession, while others were newly erected.

Almost without exception, the forts were composed of a stockade of heavy planks. Each had from one to four blockhouses, pierced with loop holes for muskets, and occupied as quarters by the soldiers and refugee settlers. In addition to these regular forts, it became necessary at various locations where attacks were more frequent to have additional places of defense and refuge. These were also garrisoned by soldiers and generally consisted of farm houses selected for their strength and convenient location. Around these locations the usual stockade was built, or occasionally a blockhouse erected.

The soldiers who garrisoned these forts and defenses were Provincial troops. Almost without exception they were details from the 2nd Battalion of the Pennsylvania Regiment under the command of Lieutenant Colonel Conrad Weiser. The first companies formed to garrison the forts mustered from 30 to 75 men. The smaller forts had a captain and a lieutenant as officers and the larger forts also had an ensign. By the spring of 1756 the companies were reorganized to a uniform size of three officers and 50 men.

On April 15, 1756, the Assembly passed a law modeled on the then current version of the British Mutiny Act, which meant that the troops could be subjected to military discipline. With 1,400 officers and men on the rolls, the Province formed its companies into three battalions, and eventually into the 2nd Battalion, Pennsylvania Regiment, and a single battalion, the Augusta Regiment. Berks County was part of the 2nd Battalion.

One of the forts that protected the Hamburg area was Fort Lebanon. This fort was located six miles north of Port Clinton and a mile and a half east of Auburn. It was eleven miles from Fort Northkill located near Strausstown. The first mention of Fort Lebanon is in a letter of instruction sent by Governor Morris to Colonel Weiser on January 25, 1756. In this letter he speaks of having ordered Captain Jacob Morgan, "who is posted at a fort in the forks of the

Schuylkill River, named Fort Lebanon, to take 20 men and build Fort Northkill." The order itself, as sent to Captain Morgan begins, "As you are a captain of a company of foot in the pay of the Province, now posted in a fort in the forks of the Schuylkill, I think it necessary to give you the following orders and instructions for your better government and direction."

The date when Fort Lebanon was built is not given, but on January 25, 1756 it is already mentioned as in existence. We know that the Native American raids reached the Hamburg area about November of 1755, and also know that the fort was built by the government as one of the chain of defenses erected about November of 1755. We also know that the forts commander Captain Morgan, and most likely its first commander was not commissioned until December 5, 1755. I believe that the fort came into existence during the month of December 1755, and have every reason to believe that its construction was by Captain Morgan and his soldiers.

Following is a description of Fort Lebanon, 1756:

> One hundred foot square with stockades 14 feet high; a house within measuring 30 feet by 20 feet with a large store room; a magazine 12 feet square; located on a barren hill with not many trees around it; built in three weeks with the help of neighbors, and was probably one of the larger and more important forts.

On January 25, 1756, Captain Jacob Morgan, in command of Fort Lebanon, was ordered to leave 20 men at the fort and with the remaining 30 men proceed "to some convenient place about half way between that fort and Fort Henry at Tolihaio, and there to erect a stockade of about 400 foot square, where he is to leave 20 men under a commissioned officer and to return to Fort Lebanon, which he is to make his headquarters and from that staccato and from Fort Lebanon, his men are to range and scour the woods both eastward and westward." The fort to be erected is without doubt Fort Northkill.

Commissary James Young had this to say of the fort during his tour of inspection on June 21, 1756: "Accordingly we set out for Fort Lebanon from Fort Northkill, all the way from Fort Northkill to Fort Lebanon is an exceeding bad road, very stony and mountainous. About six miles from Northkill, we crossed the north mountain, where we met Captain Morgan's lieutenant with ten men, ranging the woods between the mountains and Fort Lebanon. We passed two plantations, the rest of the country is chiefly barren hills, at Noon we came to Fort Lebanon, which is situated on a plain, on one side is a plantation, on the other barren pretty clear of woods all around, only a few trees about fifty yards from the fort, which I desired might be cut down. This fort is a square of about 100 feet well stockaded with good bastians, on one side of which is a good wall piece, within is a good guard house for the people, and two other large houses built by the country people who have taken refuge here, in all six families. The fort is a little too much crowded on that account."

The soldiers were kept busy most of the time. By Captain Morgan's journal it appears that he sent a party to patrol the woods four or five times a week, and to also guard the settlers as they worked. Fort Lebanon was unquestionably of great importance to this area since it occupied and commanded the Schuylkill River gap. On July 11, 1756, Colonel Weiser writes to Governor Morris: "that his orders to Captain Morgan, with regard to the garrison at Fort Lebanon, are that fifteen men shall stay in Fort Lebanon, eight men will protect the people over the hill [Hamburg] during harvest time, and ten men will range constantly eastward and westward, and if the settlers return to their plantations thereabouts, to protect those that first join together to do their work."

Following are some letters of interest that will give the reader some good insight into the acts by the Native Americans, the suffering of the settlers, and the mission of the soldiers who garrisoned the fort.

THE BLUE MOUNTAIN LEGION

Captain Jacob Morgan to Governor Denny:

November 4th, 1756

Honored Sir,

Yesterday morning at break of day, one of ye neighbors discovered a fire at a distance from him; he went to the top of another mountain to take a better observation, and made a full discovery of fire, and supposed it to be about seven miles off, at the house of John Finsher; he came and informed me of it; I immediately dispatched a party of ten men (we being but 22 men in the fort) to the place where they saw the fire, at the said Finsher's house, it being near the Schuylkill River, and the men anxious to see the enemy if there, they came through the water and the bushes to the fire, where to their disappointment saw none of them, but the house, barn, and other out houses all in flames, together with a considerable quantity of corn; they saw a great many tracks and followed them came back to the house of Philip Culmore, thinking to send from thence to alarm the other inhabitants to be on their guard, but instead found the said Culmore's wife and daughter and son-in-law all just killed and scalped; there is likewise missing out of the same house, Martin Fell's wife and child about one year old, and another boy about seven years of age, the said Martin Fell was him that was killed, it was just done when the scouts came there, and they seeing the scouts ran off. The scout divided in two parties, one to some other houses near at hand and the other to the fort (it being within a mile of the fort) to inform me; I immediately went out with the scout again, (and left in the fort no more than six men) but could not make any discovery, but brought all the families to the fort, where now I believe we are upwards of 60 women and children that are fled here for refuge, and at 12 o'clock at night I received an express from Lieutenant Humphres, commander at Fort Northkill, who informed me that the same day about 11 o'clock in the forenoon, (about a half a mile from his fort) as he was returning from his scout, came upon a body of Indians to the number of twenty at the house of Nicholas Long, where they had killed two old men and taken another captive, and doubtless would have killed all the family, they being nine children in the house, the Lieutenant's party though seven in number fired upon the Indians and thought they killed two, they dropping down and started up again, one held his hand over his wound, and they all ran off making a hallowing noise; we got a blanket and a gun which he that was shot dropped in his flight. The Lieutenant had one man shot through the right arm and the right side, but hopes not mortal, and he had four shots through his own clothes. I this day went out with a party to bury the dead near there; we are all in high spirits here; if it would please his honor to order a reinforcement at both forts, I doubt not but we should soon have an opportunity of revenging the loss, from

> Honored Sir
> Your most humble servant to command
> Jacob Morgan

———————

Fort Lebanon, Wednesday, the 4th of November at 3 O'clock, post meridian

To the Honorable William Denny, Esquire, Lieutenant Governor and Commander in Chief of the Province of Pennsylvania and County of Newcastle, Kent, Sussex on Delaware.

The humble petition of Jacob Morgan, Captain, Commander, at Fort Lebanon, most humbly showeth:

That having two forts belonging to one company, and nine men to the November of 19 was drafted from me, being total but 53, your petitioner thinks himself too weak to be of any service to the frontier, seeing the enemy commits violent outrages near the fort;   as yesterday, the 3rd of November, I found three persons scalped and there is three more missing within a mile of Fort Lebanon, and two men killed and one took captive within a half mile of Fort Northkill, and dangerous it is to keep the forts if their was a superiority in numbers to besiege them, so your petitioner in humility begs that your honor would take the premising into consideration, and do as it shall seem meet or expedient to your honor, which is in distress from him that for your honor shall ever Pray.

Jacob Morgan

The letter above was sent by express carrier to Colonel Weiser who was in Philadelphia, requesting that he present it to the Governor. The express carrier passed through Reading and of course told the news, leaving at the same time a letter for James Read, Esquire, who happened to be away at Lancaster. Upon his return he also writes to the Governor giving him an account of the activities at Fort Lebanon. He writes:

What I can gather from a person who was near Fort Lebanon (where Captain Morgan is stationed) at the burial of the people killed thereabouts is, that on Wednesday last, about noon, a party of savages came to the farm of one Jacob Finsher, about six miles from that Fort, and set fire to his house, barn, barracks of corn and hay. Upon first notice whereof, Captain Morgan detached ten men from his fort, and soon followed with a few more, who, as they were returning from their pursuit, not having met any enemy, found Finsher's barn, etc. consumed, and at Martin Fell's house, about a mile from the fort, found Martin and his wife's sister and her mother scalped, the young women being not yet quite dead, but insensible, and stuck in the throat as butchers kill a pig; she soon died, and was buried with the others. Martin's wife, and two children, one about twelve months old the other about seven years old, were carried off captives. By a gentleman who left Fort Lebanon yesterday afternoon, I hear that sixty women and children have fled into it for refuge, and several families have come further into the settlements, with their household goods and stocks.

On June 24, 1757, Captain Morgan writes:

On Wednesday last we were alarmed by one of the neighbors that came to the fort, and acquainted us that one Jonathan Bushy had seen an Indian at his house, (which was about three miles from Fort Lebanon). I immediately went out with a party of men to the place where we found the tracks of three, but could not see any of them. Yesterday morning about 8 o'clock, the son of one Adam Drum, (whom the Indians had killed the night before in Allemingle, and took the son captive) found an opportunity to make his escape, and came to the fort; he informed me that the Indians (8 in number) had got a quantity of liquor out of his father's house, and came to a hill about seven miles from the fort, where they got a dancing, and made themselves drunk, he took the opportunity and escaped to the fort, the Indians followed him near a mile and half whom our men afterwards tracked; so as soon as the young man came I sent out a party to the place where the man left them, but when they came there they only found an old pair of moccasins, and a deer skin whom they had left, but the Indians were fled; they tracked them as far as they could but night coming, obliged them to return home. I have this day sent out a party to intercept them in the way, to the Gap of the second mountain (where the Schuylkill River comes through) being the place which I often found where they retreat back; the men will range about two days.

Following is the Monthly Journal for July 1757 of Captain Morgan:

1st – Sent a Corporal with eleven men on a scout to Clingaman Hausaboughs, at Allemingle, who stayed all night; sent Sergeant Matthews with several men to Reading, to be qualified and be supplied with necessaries.

2nd – The scout returned from Allemingle, and reported they had made no discovery of the enemy.

3rd – Sent a party to range Allemingle, same date came a scout from Northkill fort and returned again the same day, bringing no news.

4th – Our men returned from Allemingle, and reported, that some of the inhabitants that were afraid, near the mountains, were removing downwards; Sergeant Matthews returned with the men from Reading, the rest guarding the fort.

5th, 6th & 7th – Was exceeding heavy rain, and the water very high.

8th – Being a day of humiliation we applied ourselves thereto.

9th – Rainy weather, we could not scout.

10th – I sent out a party to range Allemingle; this day Sergeant Matthews returned from Colonel Weiser, with orders for me to station ten men in Windsor Township, and to keep ten men in readiness to go to Easton.

11th – The scout returned back, I prepared the men in readiness according to orders, and sent some men to guard the farmers in their harvest.

12th – I went with the ten men to Windsor Township and stationed them there, where I found the most proper. In the evening was very heavy rain and thunder, obliged me to stay all night; we sent some parties from the fort to guard the farmers.

13th – I returned in the morning to the fort, I received a letter from Lieutenant Colonel Weiser, to send ten men to Easton to guard at the Treaty; parties went to guard the farmers, and this day, in my return, I met the scout which I had posted in Windsor Township, ranging about the farmers houses.

14th – I sent Sergeant Matthews with nine men to Easton to the Treaty to guard, and sent out some parties to range and guard the farmers, who did return in the evening by reason of the heavy rain and thunder, which fell in the evening.

15th – Being all day very heavy rain, and the creeks so high that the Schuylkill River rose perpendicular 15 feet in about nine hours time, being considerable higher than ever was known in these parts; the guards could not return and we remained in the fort, with only eight men to guard.

16th – The rain continued but more moderate, our parties could not return, we stayed in the fort and guarded as usual; the party ranging up Long Run among the vacant houses, they found old tracks but none new.

17th – Some of our guards returned, being relieved by others in their lieu – the creeks fell very much this day.

18th – I sent a party to guard the farmers at their harvest, and left some at the neighboring houses, the rest to guard at the fort.

19th – I likewise sent a party to guard who returned in the evening, the residue guarding at the fort.

20th – I sent out two parties to range and guard the farmers, who both returned in the evening.

21st – I likewise sent out a party to guard, we were advised by Jacob Shefer that an Indian was seen near his house, we having two men ranging there they saw nothing of their tracks, and believe it was a mistake.

22nd – Sent out a party to range to the Fort, at Northkill, with Ensign Harry for ammunition, who stayed all night, the rest guarding at the fort and farmers.

23rd – The party from Northkill returned with a command of Colonel Weiser's men, with Lieutenant Colonel Weiser himself, who stayed here all night; sent out a party to guard the farmers, who returned in the evening to the fort.

24th – Lieutenant Colonel Weiser returned with his company, sent a party of ten men to relieve the party in Windsor Township; the rest to guard.

25th – The party returned from Windsor Township to the fort, when a party of them enlisted for three years.

26th – Sent Sergeant Robert Smith with a company of ten men to Reading to be qualified, and being but a few at the fort could not range; have two commands at the farmers.

27th – I went down to Windsor among the men to see whether they kept good orders; I found everything very well, and enlisted more men and stayed there all night, the command remaining at the farmers.

28th – I returned back to the fort, and found everything well; Sergeant Smith, with his party, returned from Reading, the guard still remaining with the farmers.

29th – Ensign Harry went out with a party to range among the farmers, and sent out two parties to guard the neighbors at the harvest; they returned without any discovery or signs of the enemy.

30th – I went over the hill to Windsor Township, in order to send some men to Reading to be qualified, I sent a Corporal with 16 men; I returned in the evening to the fort.

31st – The party returned from Reading; we had parties at the neighboring houses, who remained there on guard.

The following is taken from the journal at Fort Northkill:

June 27th, 1757 – Gave orders to Sergeant Smith to go scouting the woods between this and Fort Lebanon, and if Captain Morgan thought that it was serviceable, to range someway up the Schuylkill River, as the gap is their common rendezvous.

July 1st, 1757 – Sergeant Peter Smith returned with the scout, and reported that when he came to Fort Lebanon, Captain Morgan sent a detachment under Ensign Harry to the gap of the Schuylkill. And that on the 28th last past, they ascended the mountains, and when they came on the other side, they found an encamping place of the Indians, which, after Ensign Harry had surrounded with his party, he sent off Sergeant Smith with another party to lay in ambush on the Indian path all night, but as nothing was to be heard of the Indians, they met again the next day; the Indians, as he supposes, having left that place the day before. However, they found two match coats, one spear, one scalping knife, some vermillion, and 800 blank wampum, also a great variety of salves.

August 20th, 1757 – Sent a scout of fifteen men to range the wood towards the Schuylkill, into Windsor Township, and with orders to call in some detachments lying in Windsor Township, according to Lieutenant Colonel Weiser.

The following articles are from the Pennsylvania Gazette during 1757:

September 1st - We hear from Berks County that several Indians have lately been seen near Fort Lebanon; and that on Sunday the 21st of August, the house and barn of Peter Semelcke were burnt, and three of his children carried off; himself, wife and child, being from home at this time. This was done within two miles of the fort.

October 6th – The accounts from the frontiers are most dismal; that some of the inhabitants are killed or carried off; houses burned and cattle destroyed daily; that, at the same time, the people are afflicted with severe sickness and die fast, so that in many places they are neither able to defend themselves, when attacked, or to run away.

October 13th – We hear from Reading that three miles from Fort Lebanon, at the Schuylkill, the Indians came to Peter Conrad's house. He and another man in the house resolved to defend themselves. The Indians kept themselves concealed and shot whenever they saw a person. This lasted three hours. In the meantime Peter Conrad sent his hired man to the fort to Captain Morgan for help. No man came because they did not know how many Indians there were. He sent again and asked for only five men. At least several neighbors came. An Indian crept into the mill aside of the water wheel and set the mill on fire. Then they fled to the mountains and yelled joyfully. When Captain Morgan heard that there was only four, he sent a party after them but could not find them. They killed the wife of Balzer Neytong and shot David Hand through the arm and took a boy eight years old captive. Not far from the place they burned a small house. Small bones and a skull were found in the ashes and it was supposed that they burned the boy.

In February of 1758 the fort was called Fort William for the first time. Exactly when and why its name was changed is unknown. It was probably changed towards the latter part of 1757 or the beginning of 1758, but the reason for changing is not known. Fort William however, is without doubt one and the same as Fort Lebanon. The fort was also called Fort Schuylkill from time to time.

James Young, Commissioners of the Musters, and Adjutant Kern, made an inspection tour to the forts between the Susquehanna and Delaware rivers. The following is a report of their observations after having visited Fort Lebanon in February of 1758: At Fort William (Fort Lebanon), Captain Morgan, Lieutenant Humphreys and Ensign Harry were the officers. The report states that there were in the fort at the time of inspection 53 men, 23 of whom had their own weapons, and 30 had Provincial weapons. The fort contained 75 pounds of powder, 80 pounds of lead, 12 cartridges, and provisions for 14 days. Jonas Seely was the commissary at the fort. Also during this time, 28 men were stationed and on duty in Albany Township. Nothing could be found in regards to ammunition or provisions for those men, so I believe they were there on temporary duty.

———————

The following is from the journal of James Burd:

Friday, February 24th, 1758 – This morning set out from Reading to Fort William, arrived at Peter Rodermils at 2 PM, 15 miles from Reading, it snowed and blowed prodigiously. I stayed there all night.

Saturday, February 25th, 1758 – Marched this morning, the snow deep, for Fort William; arrived at Fort William at 12 Noon, here was Lieutenant Humphreys and Ensign Harry, ordered a review of the garrison at 2 PM; at 2 PM reviewed the garrison and found 53 good men, deficient in discipline, stores three-quarter cask of powder, 150 pounds of lead, 400 flints and 56 blankets, no arms fit for use, no kettles, no tools, nor drums, two months provision. Here I found a target erected ordered the company to shoot at the mark, set them the example myself by wheeling around and firing by the word of command. I shot a bullet into the center of the mark the size of a dollar, distance 100 yards. Some of them shot tolerable bad, most of their arms are very bad. Ordered Captain Morgan to continue to Northkill and Allemingle.

Sunday, February 26th, 1758 – Marched from hence at 10 AM, went over the mountains to Mr. Everitts, where Captain Weatherholt is stationed.

There seems to have been a period of quiet when no hostile acts were committed by the Native Americans. This lasted for a few short years between 1759 and 1762. In 1763 the Native Americans once again started their raids against the local settlers. Following are some reports sent to the Governor from Fort William (Lebanon):

September 10th, 1763
Honored Sir:

I am sorry I have to acquaint your honor of the following melancholy account which I received from Captain Kern last night; on the 8th instant a party of Indians came to the house of one John Finsher, about three-quarters of a mile distant from Captain Kern's men, commanded by Ensign Schaffer. They killed Finsher, his wife and two of his sons; his daughter is missing; one little boy made his escape from the savages and came to the Ensign, who immediately went to the place with his party. But the Indians were gone, and finding their tracks which way they went, pursued them to the house of one Nicholas Miller, where he found four children murdered. Our party still pursued and soon came up with the enemy and fired on them. They returned the fire, but the soldiers rushed on them so furiously that they soon ran off and left behind them two prisoners, two tomahawks, one hanger and a saddle; the Indians were eight in number and our party seven; three of the enemy were much wounded. The two prisoners that our party recovered were two of said Miller's children that they had tied together, and so drove them along. Miller's wife is missing; in all there are eight killed and two missing in the neighborhood.

I am, honored sir, your most obedient humble servant,
Jonas Seely

Jonas Seely wrote again to Governor John Penn on November 25, 1763, telling him that the Native Americans killed three men on Tuesday, November 15th. This attack took place about 22 miles from Reading, on the north side of the mountain, in the forks of the Schuylkill River. These unfortunate people were returning to a farm which they had previously deserted. Captain Kern upon learning of this attack immediately marched after the enemy and pursued them for two days. A very heavy snow fell and the Native Americans fled a considerable distance, so Captain Kern ended the pursuit.

This was the last raid by the Native Americans in Berks County during the French and Indian War. However, there were some problems with the Native Americans in the area during the American Revolution, which will be covered in a later chapter. Mention is made to a number of killings in Berks County in the Pennsylvania Archives, but no names and dates are given, and have been therefore omitted in this history. There were no railroads, no telegraphs, and even no mail coaches and post offices. Consequently, many trials and hardships of the settlers were only partly reported, while others were never brought to the attention of the government.

Our history of Fort Lebanon ends here. I regret that a more detailed report of the events of this important fort cannot be provided. Many settlers were killed during the French and Indian War in this area of the country. Many were taken captive by the Native Americans, and few of those ever returned home or were heard from again after the war. Many of the captives were either adults or children who could have told the story of their capture. However, many are believed to have either been killed or perished from the harsh environment.

It may seem hard to believe, but during the same time only a few Native Americans were actually killed in the County by either the soldiers or settlers. The question arises as to what are the reasons that the Native Americans killed and captured so many settlers. Also, the question naturally arises as to why the new inhabitants of this land, with all their vigilance, weapons, military skill and forts, killed only a few of their enemy.

Reflecting for a moment will explain the reasons. The Native Americans were robust, active, and cunning. They could endure physical exertion to a much greater degree then that of the settlers or soldiers. Or as someone once said, "they run so swift that if a deer does not fall upon the first shot, they throw off their blanket and seldom fail to overtake him."

Remember, the forts along the frontier were from ten to twelve miles apart. The fleet of foot Native Americans would quietly cross the mountains and attack unexpectedly, and then escape quickly. They would stealthily approach a field were a family of settlers was working tilling the soil, kill or take captive the settlers, and be gone before an alarm could be given. So swiftly that most times they were long gone before any soldiers could even reach the place of the attack. Even when soldiers were in sight of the enemy they often easily escaped due to their agility. Making their escape through the woods and rocky places and over the mountains, they disappeared without receiving a wound. The failure to capture more Native Americans was not for the lack of watchfulness and determination on the part of the settlers or soldiers. Rather, it was due to their cunning and ability to avoid danger. Whenever they were met or pursued by the settlers or soldiers, their quickness enabled them to escape even when they were pursued on horseback.

I believe that this chapter in our history was the beginning of the Hamburg unit. Many of the soldiers that manned the fort and patrolled the area were recruited from this immediate area, just as is the case today. One must remember that during this time, the nation of the United States of America did not exist. We were still a colony of the British Empire, and therefore those soldiers served the Crown. But in reality they served their neighbors, just as is the case to this very day.

CHAPTER 2

The Revolution
1774 – 1781

The Battle of Lexington was fought on April 19, 1775. When the news of this battle reaches Berks County, each township resolves to raise and train its own company. On July 28, 1775 the Assembly approves the resolution that Congress passed on July 18, 1775 which, recommends that all able bodied men between the ages of 16 and 60 in each Colony immediately form themselves into regular companies. Each company was to consist of one captain, two lieutenants, one ensign, four sergeants, four corporals, a clerk, a drummer and fifer, and 68 privates.

All officers in each company were to be chosen by their respective companies. It should be noted that the persons chosen to be officers represented the upper class of citizen and taxpayer. Most officers were prominent men and were the heads of business, political, and social affairs within the community, township, or county. Officers above the rank of captain were appointed by the Assembly or by the Committee of Safety. Companies were formed into battalions, with each battalion having a colonel, lieutenant colonel, two majors, and an Adjutant or Quartermaster as its officers.

Each soldier was to be equipped with a good musket that will carry an ounce ball, with a bayonet, steel ramrod, worm priming wire fitted with a brush. They were also to be furnished a cutting sword or tomahawk, a cartridge box capable of holding 23 cartridges, 12 flints, and a knapsack. The musket barrels were three feet and eight inches long, and the bayonet 16 inches long. The barrel bore of sufficient size to carry 17 balls to the pound.

Each soldier was required to take the following Oath of Allegiance: "I have this day voluntarily enlisted myself as a soldier in the American Continental Army, for one year, unless sooner discharged, and do bind myself to conform in all instances to such rules and regulations as are or shall be established for the government of the said army."

During the Revolution the British never invaded Berks County, and no battles or skirmishes took place within the County. Not a single British unit crossed the county boundary lines anywhere while carrying on military movements from one colony to another. Geographically, the county was fortunately situated. The inhabitants were thankful that their families and properties were spared from the cruelties and sufferings of war. However, they did realize the possibility of great loss if the county were to be invaded, and appreciated the perilous situation of the neighboring counties of Chester and Philadelphia. Because of this, they responded promptly to the numerous calls for troops, and willingly furnished large quantities of supplies of all kinds to sustain the Continental Army.

By looking over the names of the men from this area who participated in the fight for independence, you will find that they are mostly of German extraction. The population of the local area was then, as it is today, largely of German extraction, and they used the German language in their daily affairs. It was natural for them to sympathize with the independence movement, because it was in accord with their ideas of political life and social existence. The colonists had a firm belief in local government and desired to carry it on successfully without unnecessary restrictions or burdens. Taxation without representation was to them a very unreasonable and unjust policy.

The colonists or their fathers had emigrated from Germany and settled in the area during the previous 50 years. They did this for the purpose of enjoying civil rights, and of conducting their business, social and political affairs with as little interference as possible. They felt compelled to oppose any extra taxes placed upon them without their consent for the benefit of the King of Great Britain, and that was not for their own improvement or convenience. The militia system provided for by the Assembly was appreciated greatly. The colonists sincerely cooperated in its establishment throughout the county, and responded to the call for troops willingly and promptly.

The appearance of the men is of special interest, being that they were remarkably stout and hardy. Most dressed in white frock coats or rifle shirts, and wore round hats. Each man carried a musket and a tomahawk or a small axe. The soldiers also carried a long knife, usually called a scalping knife, which served many purposes while campaigning. Their under-dress was by no means of military style. It was normally a deep ash colored hunting shirt, leggings, and moccasins if they could be procured.

Apparently the fashion of that time was for these riflemen to mimic the manners and style of the Native Americans. The men were also noted for their accurate marksmanship, and could hit a target with certainty up to 200 yards away. A well trained soldier while advancing quickly could fire his rifle and hit a seven inch diameter target at a distance of 250 yards. Their shooting frequently proved fatal to British officers and soldiers who exposed themselves to view, even at more than twice the distance of a common musket shot.

In 1775 the records show that the northern section of Berks County made up the 4th Battalion, under the command of Lieutenant Colonel Baltzer Geehr, with Michael Lindenmuth as major. Captain George May of Windsor Township was an officer in this battalion. This battalion appears to have been in service at New York and Long Island from June 1776 to January 1777. The full battalion of six companies is supposed to have gone into the field with an estimated strength of 300 men.

Local units most likely took part in the Battle of Long Island in August of 1776. General George Washington was in doubt as to the intentions of the enemy on Long Island. The British force was estimated to be 8,000 soldiers, but they were actually somewhere around 16,000 strong. Washington ordered reinforcements over to the Brooklyn side and among these were troops from Berks County. The Battle of Long Island was fought on August 27, 1776, and the command was stationed on the coast road near the Red Lion Tavern on Long Island, New York during this engagement.

The British troops outnumbered the American troops by three to one. The British advance guard marching up the Narrows Road between 38th and 40th Streets, struck the American pickets in the vicinity of the Red Lion Tavern at about 2:00 AM. The pickets retreated before the enemy without checking the enemies advance. There was hardly more than an exchange of fire before many Americans were taken prisoner. The Americans were defeated because the British completely outflanked and surprised them on the Jamaica Road. The Americans suffered many casualties, including many taken as prisoner.

On September 1, 1776, the 4th Battalion of Berks County Militia, under the command of Colonel Baltzer Geehr arrived in Bethlehem, Pennsylvania. The entire battalion was in attendance at a religious service conducted by Reverend Ettwein that afternoon. In 1777 the northern section of Berks County made up the 3rd Battalion, with Colonel Michael Lindenmuth of Bern Township in command and the following officers: Lieutenant Colonel George May of Windsor Township, and Major Martin Kaercher (founder of Hamburg) of Windsor Township, with the following companies:

1st Company: Pine Grove – Captain Jacob Wetstein (Whetstone)
2nd Company: Brunswick Township – Captain Conrad Minnich
3rd Company: Bern Township – Captain Jacob Shraedel
4th Company: Bern Township – Captain Sebastian Emrich
5th Company: Bern Township – Captain John Soder
6th Company: Windsor Township – Captain Jacob Shadle
                     First Lieutenant Charles Siegfried
                     Second Lieutenant William Williamson
                     Ensign George Reber
                     Court Martial Men: George Hower and
                                     Eberhard Schappell
7th Company: Bern Township – Captain Daniel Will

8th Company: Windsor Township – Captain Ferdinand Ritter
First Lieutenant Michael Smith
Second Lieutenant George Adam
Ensign Jacob Stapleton
Court Martial Men: Jacob Tenant and
John Brobst

Captain Jacob Wetstein's company and Captain Conrad Minnich's company were mustered into service on August 7, 1777. Both companies participated in the campaigns around Philadelphia from August to December of 1777 under the command of General George Washington. During this time period the battles of Brandywine and Germantown were fought. The company of Jacob Hill (Windsor Township) with 41 men was mustered into service on October 25, 1777, and ordered to guard the Windsor Powder Magazine. I have been unable to determine the exact location of this powder magazine. The remainder of the battalion under the command of Michael Lindenmuth was mustered into service on September 27, 1777. They were engaged in service in the Schuylkill Valley area from that time until the American forces went into winter quarters at Valley Forge on December 18, 1777, at which time the men returned to the county.

In 1778 the records show the northern section of Berks County still comprising the 3rd Battalion. The battalion's strength was 722 men and Colonel Lindenmuth was still in command, with the following company commanders: Jacob Wetstein, Sebastian Emrich, Daniel Will, Conrad Minnich, George Souter, Ferdinand Ritter, Jacob Shraedel, and Jacob Shadle. During 1778, after some attacks by the Native Americans, the battalion served on the frontier. It appears that in July of 1778 the Torries and Native Americans conducted attacks in the Wyoming Valley, and thus companies from Berks County were sent to reinforce the Northumberland County Militia. On July 14, 1778, the Council thought it necessary to send one-half of the battalion to Sunbury and the other half to Easton.

In 1780 the records show the northern section of Berks County, comprising the 4th Battalion, under the command of Colonel Michael

Lindenmuth, Martin Kaercher as major, and the following company commanders: Jacob Frantz, Daniel Will, Ferdinand Ritter, Jacob Wetstein, Jacob Shartel, Francis Umbenhacker, Christian Balty, and Jacob Strabel. In May of 1780, 60 men were taken from the battalion for frontier service.

On May 6, 1780 Colonel Lindenmuth sent a letter to Council in regards to the killing of some inhabitants beyond the Blue Mountains. The letter speaks about moving families to the Little Schuylkill River, about 15 miles from Ganadenhuth (Lehighton). The letter also states that near the Susquehanna River in Northampton County that some Native Americans had invaded and attacked local inhabitants. Since they were likely to be attacked again, he asked for arms from the stores at Reading to be provided for self defense.

On August 30, 1780, John Negman who lived at a saw mill on the road from Reading to Shamokin, about three miles above Conrad Minnich's, and 33 miles from Reading was killed, along with his three children by the Native Americans. A group of five Native Americans had been seen on the same road a few days before. A day after this attack a house and barn on the Little Schuylkill River were burned by the Native Americans. No people were killed in this attack, but a boy named Shurr was taken captive.

These attacks alarmed the people living in that area so much that many fled. Scores of wagons were sent to the area to move the possessions of the inhabitants, and unless assistance was given in a hurry it seemed possible that the entire settlement on the other side mountain would be evacuated. Conrad Minnich lived in Brunswick Township along the Schuylkill River, several miles south of Sharp Mountain.

Captain Dennis Leary immediately marched to the location of the attack and buried Negman and two children. The third child, a girl, was carried off by the Native Americans. The next day, accompanied by ten men he went in pursuit of the attackers. He was joined by Captain Balty, and on the following day by Colonel Lindenmuth with 50 men. After searching the woods and area until August 30th, he and his men returned to Reading. They left 60 men there to defend the settlements. One interesting note is that Captain

Leary was in this area for the purpose of cutting trees to be used as masts for the American Navy.

On May 9, 1781, Colonel Valentine Eckert of Berks County was directed to order out one class of Colonel Lindenmuth's battalion of militia for the purpose of defending the frontiers of the county. In May of 1781, 64 men were sent once again to render service on the frontier. In October of 1781 when fear that the British in New York might move to aid Cornwallis who was besieged at Yorktown, the Berks County Militia was called up and went to Newtown in Bucks County. Also during this time British prisoners of war were being held in Reading.

When the British surrendered at Yorktown there was no longer a need for a large standing army, and most soldiers returned to their homes. In order to avoid the difficulty of discharging a large number of soldiers at the same time, furloughs were freely granted. By doing this a large part of the unpaid army was disbanded and dispersed without much commotion or disorder. As they were easily and quickly formed out of farmers, mechanics and laborers in 1775, they just as easily threw off their military nature and returned to their former lives. They had taken up arms earnestly for political freedom. But, when their services were no longer required, they laid down their arms peaceably to again become good and industrious citizens.

CHAPTER 3

The Militia
1782 – 1860

In 1783 the northern section of Berks County comprised the 2nd Battalion of the Berks County Brigade. It was commanded by Lieutenant Colonel Baltzer Geehr, with Martin Kaercher as major. The following companies were from the Hamburg area:

<u>Windsor Company No. 3</u>
Captain Godfrey Seidle
Lieutenant Simon Kreusher
Ensign Anthony Billich

<u>Windsor Company No. 5</u>
Captain Jacob Schappell
Lieutenant George Reber
Ensign Andrew Smith

Following is an extract from the *1st Volume, 6th Series, Pennsylvania Archives, Muster & Pay Rolls, Pennsylvania Militia 1790-1800.* Windsor Township was part of the 3rd Regiment of the Berks County Brigade.

3rd Regiment, Berks County Brigade, Lieutenant Colonel William Wheeler commanding, with Casper Hiell and John Wollison as majors, and companies organized as follows:

<u>1st Company</u>
Captain Frantz Umbenhacker
Lieutenant Abraham Stoudt
Ensign Philip Strouse

<u>2nd Company</u>
Captain Nicholas Bader
Lieutenant Andrew Miller
Ensign Daniel Stoudt

3rd Company
Captain Frederick Moyer
Lieutenant John Dries
Ensign Jacob Hill

4th Company
Captain Jacob Epler
Lieutenant Valentine Brown
Ensign George Machemer

5th Company
Captain Jacob Wetstone
Lieutenant George Orwig
Ensign Peter Kutz

6th Company
Captain George Poh
Lieutenant Henry Glick
Ensign Peter Fries

7th Company
Captain Henry Noecker
Lieutenant Daniel Kercker
Ensign Henry Hartzell

8th Company
Captain Philip Waggoner
Lieutenant George Retschler
Ensign Michael Nunemacher

Cavalry
Captain William Moore
1st Lieutenant Collinson Read
2nd Lieutenant Mark Biddle
Cornet Conrad Feger

During this time period, men between the ages of 18 and 45 were compelled by law to be a member of an enrolled militia unit. Each man had to provide his own weapon and uniform. Units were required to muster twice per year for one day of training. Drill days were set apart in the Spring and Fall for military exercise, on the last Monday of April and the first three Mondays of May, and also the last two Mondays of August, the last two Mondays of September, and the third Monday of October. Pay and rations were the same as what the Regular Army received, with the pay being as follows: captain - $20 per month, lieutenant - $13.50 per month, sergeant - $8 per month, corporal - $7.33 per month, drummer - $7.33 per month, and privates - $6.66 per month.

Pensions were allowed for incapacitating injuries not exceeding one-half the pay received, and for persons who died from wounds, or were killed in the line of duty. The Orphans Court was authorized to allow for support to the families in amounts not to exceed one-half the pay of such persons. Some men were exempt from military service in the militia and excused from bearing arms. They were delegates to Congress, members of the Executive Council, judges of the Supreme Court, masters and faculty of colleges, ministers, and legally purchased servants. Charles Shoemaker (founder of Shoemakersville) was the justice who administered the Oath of Allegiance to the men in the northern party of the County. In 1807 the unit was part of the Sixth Division.

War of 1812

After the Revolutionary War, the United States Government passed laws whereby foreigners could become naturalized citizens. However, the British government contended that a British subject could not be naturalized and claimed the right to stop all United States ships and search for British seaman. It is said that within a period of eight years that they captured 900 vessels and forced over 6,000 seamen into the British navy. This continued until it finally got to a point where it could no longer be endured, and war was declared.

Governor Schneider of Pennsylvania issued an order requiring 4,000 troops to be raised to support the war. On May 12, 1812, the Governor ordered the 1st, 2nd, 3rd, 4th, 5th, 6th and 7th Divisions to make up the 1st Division under the command of Major General Isaac Worrell. He also directed that the 8th, 9th, 10th, 11th, 12th, 13th, 14th, 15th and 16th Divisions should form the 2nd Division under the command of Major General Adamson Tannihill. The Divisions were ordered to assemble at Meadville, and Adjutant General Reed was ordered to take command.

When the news of Perry's victory on Lake Erie reached the county, the citizens celebrated the event with fireworks. However, on August 21, 1814 Washington fell into the hands of the British. Fearing the same fate might happen to some of Pennsylvania's cities, Governor Schneider issued a general call to arms. In a short amount of time 5,000 men under the command of Major General Watson were assembled and ready for service in York. When the British attempted to capture Baltimore some of these troops bore the brunt of the attack and forced the British back.

After Washington was taken by the British, 18 companies were organized in Berks County and left in August of 1814 for York. After six months of service they returned home, and not participating in any engagements. Daniel Udree of Oley was the commanding general of the 2nd Brigade; and eight companies served under Lieutenant Colonel Jeremiah Schappel of Windsor Township.

From 1834 to 1842, Hamburg's contribution to the State Militia, or National Guard, officially consisted of one unit. The Hamburg Artillery (Artillerists) commanded by Captain John F. Reeser, with First Lieutenant Simon S. Fister, and Second Lieutenant Frederick A. Beitenman as officers. However, mention is made of another unit in Hamburg during this same time period, and this unit was the Hamburg Light Dragoons, a cavalry outfit. According to official records, *Military Commission Book (Militia Book) 1842 – 1845, Volume B,* the Hamburg Light Dragoons unit does not appear on the State records until 1842. However, during my research I found a letter to all members of the unit dated February 6, 1838, as follows:

Mobilizing for the parade in full uniform on Thursday, February 22, 1838, in front of the restaurant of William Shomo, in the city of Hamburg, morning at 10 o'clock each trooper to bring twelve blanks.

By order of the Captain,
J. D. Barnet, O.C.

M.B. At the same time and place there will be a court of appellation for some of the last parades.

Although known as the Hamburg Artillerists they were really an infantry unit, and an assorted bunch that was both poorly equipped and trained. In fact, there was no organized training, and only one day per year designated as Battalion Day being used for training in warfare. As their compensation, all men that participated in these training days were exempted from paying taxes for that year. No equipment was furnished by the state. The men used any kind of weapons they happened to posses such as old muskets, flintlocks, and even canes being utilized.

In those days, Benneville Derr and Brigadier General Jeremiah Schappell, one of the original settlers of the area east of Windsor Castle, known as "Schappell's Valley", were the leaders of the militia in this district. The first record of the Hamburg Artillery is in *Order Book A, Issue of Ordnance and Quartermaster Stores, Pennsylvania Militia,* which shows an organization date of May 30, 1840. This was the same date of a requisition for a 6-pounder artillery piece for the company. The cannon order was placed with H. E. Simon of Lancaster. The unit was attached to the 2nd Brigade, 6th Division, as part of the Hamburg Volunteer Battalion.

The *Military Commission Book (Militia Book) 1842 – 1845, Volume B,* shows the existence of the Hamburg Volunteer Battalion. This was commanded by Major John Alfred Beitenman, with John Seiberling as Adjutant, and Thomas Seiger as Quartermaster. Two companies comprised this battalion and it was part of the 2nd Brigade. The Hamburg Artillery was commanded by Captain John F. Reeser, with Simon S. Fister as captain (later), and Frederick A. Beitenman as lieutenant. The Hamburg Light Dragoons was commanded by Captain Arthur S. Fesig, with William Shomo Jr. as first lieutenant, and John Talbot as second lieutenant.

The Hamburg Volunteer Battalion attended a military encampment in Reading City Park from May 18 to May 24, 1842. The following units from this battalion were in attendance at this encampment: the Hamburg Light Dragoons, commanded by Captain William Miller, with 30 men; the Hamburg Artillerists, commanded by John F. Reeser, with 52 men; and the Berks County Rifle Rangers, commanded by Captain Heinly, with a strength of 54 men. Brigadier General William High was in command of the Berks County Brigade during this encampment, and General Winfield Scott reviewed the troops.

The daily duty at the encampment was similar to Army regulation during actual war, and was as follows:

Morning gun at daybreak
Reveille
Roll-Call
Morning Parade
Breakfast
Detail of Guards
Inspection
Grand Parade – 10 AM
Dinner – 12 Noon
Regular Parade – 4 PM
Evening Gun – 6 PM
Tattoo and Countersign – 10 PM
Lights Out – 11 PM
From 11 PM to daylight the sentries walked their lonely rounds.

The *Military Commission Book (Militia Book), 1845 – 1848, Volume 9,* shows the Hamburg Artillerists still in existence. Lieutenant Frederick E. Beitenman as commander, Daniel M. Stambach as lieutenant, and still part of the Hamburg Volunteer Battalion, attached to the 2nd Brigade, 5th Division. Some references show the unit as part of the 2nd Pennsylvania Volunteers during the War with Mexico, under the command of Major H. A. Muhlenberg, but I have been unable to authenticate this.

The *Military Commission Book (Militia Book) 1848 – 1853, Volume 10,* shows the Hamburg Volunteer Battalion in existence, with Major John A. Beitenman commanding, and companies as follows: Hamburg Artillery commander by Captain John A. Beitenman, First Lieutenant Benjamin E. Shollenberger, and Second Lieutenant Benneville Derr as officers; Windsor Cavalry, commanded by Captain William Shomo, First Lieutenant Peter Krause, Second Lieutenant William R. Miller, and Cornet Joseph M. Miller as officers; also the Windsor Rifles, officers unknown. The Battalion was part of the 1st Brigade, 5th Division. During this time period the units paraded and trained in May of each year. This training occurred on the first Monday in May by companies, and then on the second Monday by battalions.

The *Military Commission Book (Militia Book) 1854 – 1858, Volume 10, Part 2,* shows the organization of the Hamburg Artillery. The commander was Captain John A. Beitenman, with First Lieutenant Benneville Derr, Second Lieutenant Samuel Foust, Second Lieutenant Benjamin R. Wagner, and Second Lieutenant William S. Deisher as officers. The Windsor Cavalry was also in existence under the command of Captain William Shomo, with First Lieutenant William R. Miller, Second Lieutenant John S. Seidel, and Joseph M. Miller as officers.

In 1856 there were 24 companies of militia in Berks County, and these were arranged into six battalions, and comprised the 1st Brigade of the 5th Division, Pennsylvania Volunteers. The 2nd Battalion (Hamburg Volunteer Battalion) was commanded by Major J. A. Beitenman, and consisted of the following: Windsor Cavalry, commanded by Captain William Shomo, with a strength of 54 men; the Hamburg Artillery, commanded by J.A.Beitenman, with a strength of 55 men; the Pleasant Valley Artillery, commanded by Captain Jonathan S. Herbein, with a strength of 40 men; and the Berks County Rifle Rangers, commanded by Captain George Heinly, with a strength of 57 men. Total strength of the Battalion was 206 men.

The *Military Commission Book (Militia Book) 1859 – 1861, Volume 11,* shows the existence of the 2nd Battalion (Hamburg Volunteer Battalion), commanded by Major John A. Beitenman, and attached to the 1st Brigade of the 5th Division, with companies as follows: Hamburg Artillery, commanded by Captain Benneville Derr, with First Lieutenant Edward Moll, First Lieutenant J. P. Stalnecker, First Lieutenant Levi Williamson, Second Lieutenant John Stitzel, and Second Lieutenant William R. Smith as officers; Windsor Cavalry, commanded by Captain William Miller, with First Lieutenant John S. Seidel, Second Lieutenant J. Machemer, and Cornet Levi Dumon as officers.

CHAPTER 4

The Civil War
1861 - 1865

In 1861 President Abraham Lincoln called for a force of 75,000 men. His request was mainly directed towards the governors and adjutant generals of each state, with specific quotas given to each for men and units. However, many units such as Hamburg's were already in existence before the outbreak of hostilities between the north and south. They volunteered their services even before being ordered to do so, and the unit traveled to Pottsville to enlist.

Captain Benneville Derr was in command of the Hamburg unit at the time, had lost vision in one of his eyes and was barred from military service. As a result of this, the unit was split in half, with some unit members forming Company G, 96th Pennsylvania Volunteer Infantry Regiment, and some going into Company D, 48th Pennsylvania Volunteer Infantry Regiment. Since men from Hamburg were members of both units, an account for each Regiment is given.

Company G, 96th PA Volunteer Infantry Regiment
(Hamburg Light Infantry)

The 96th PVI Regiment was recruited mainly in Schuylkill County, with some men from the Hamburg area, and others from Berks County. The Regiment was mustered into service on September 23, 1861 at Pottsville, under the command of Colonel H. L. Cake. Company G was under the command of Captain James M. Douden. The Regiment established a camp at Lauton's Hill overlooking Pottsville, and remained there recruiting men to fill the ranks.

The Company was mustered into the United States service on November 6, 1861. It embarked by rail for Washington, D.C. on November 8, 1861, and was one of the first units from Pennsylvania to arrive there. It was attached to Slocum's Brigade, Franklin's Division, Army of the Potomac till March of 1862; 2nd Brigade, 1st Division, I Corps, Army of the Potomac till April 1862; 2nd Brigade, 1st Division, Department of the Rappahannock till May 1862; 2nd Brigade, 1st Division, VI Corps, Army of the Potomac, and the Army of the Shenandoah till October 1864.

The Regiment went into camp outside of Washington at a place called Kendall Green, and became part of the 1st Provisional Brigade. Later the Regiment crossed the Potomac River and established a camp along the Leesburg Pike. This was a short distance past Fort Ellsworth which was a fortified defensive position in front of Washington. At this time the Regiment was assigned to Brigadier General H. W. Slocum's Brigade of Major General William B. Franklin's Division. They went into permanent quarters near the Hampshire Railroad near the crossing of Four Mile Run, and remained there on picket duty.

While in this camp they lived in tents, and the weather was nice until January of 1862 when it turned extremely bad with much rain and mud. Their training here included squad and company drill in the mornings, and battalion and regimental drills conducted in the afternoons. Drilling seemed to be the order of the day, which included bayonet training. Diseases started to spread rapidly while in this camp. Typhoid, pneumonia, and diphtheria were the most prevalent. By the end of 1861 many men were unfit for duty. Two men from the company died in camp, most likely from disease. Five other unit members were also medically discharged by the Surgeon, and the unit had its first deserter while in this camp.

In March of 1862 the weather improves and the unit receives orders to be prepared to move. They are to move to Manassas, but later this order is rescinded. They tear down their camp, are issued rations for two days, and for the first time issued dog (pup) tents. Up until this time the men lived in roomy Sibley or wedge tents. During the first night of movement the men try to make themselves comfortable in their new tents but, few sleep in them that first night. The ground is wet from recent rains and most of the men stay up all night talking around the campfires.

Peninsula Campaign

On April 4, 1862, the 96th Regiment begins the march towards Fredericksburg, Virginia. It reaches Catlett's Station where it goes into camp, remaining there until April 21 when they return to Alexandria. There they board transports for the upcoming Peninsula Campaign. Major General George B. McClellan commander of the Army of the Potomac had been ordered by the President to move on the Confederate capital at Richmond. The Union force of approximately 120,000 soldiers board boats outside of Washington. They are then transported to the Virginia Peninsula and disembark at the junction of the James and York Rivers. McClellan's plan is to use siege tactics to move up the peninsula and onto Richmond.

The 96th Regiment disembarks on April 23, 1862 along with the rest of General Franklin's Division in the vicinity of Cheeseman's Creek. The Confederates evacuate Yorktown on May 4, 1862. The unit again embarks and sails up the York River arriving at Brick House Point on May 6, 1862. Here, along with the 27th New York Regiment they form a battle line of skirmishers, and advance to protect Union pioneer (engineer) troops who are engaged in cutting down trees and building roads.

The following day the 96th along with the 95th Pennsylvania Volunteer Infantry Regiment, and three New York regiments advance in line of battle, driving off Confederates who are firing on Union pickets. Afterwards the unit remains on the extreme left of the Union line near Brick House Point to prevent a flanking movement by the Rebels. After this engagement the Regiment is assigned to the VI Corps, with General Franklin commanding, and General Slocum commanding the 1st Division. The Regiment is assigned to the 2nd Brigade under the command of Brigadier General Joseph J. Bartlett.

Gaines Mill

On May 25, 1862, the 1st Division moves past Gaines Mill and goes into camp near the Hogan House. A few days later it moves up to Mechanicsville and performs picket duty along the Chickahominy River until June 6, when it returns to its earlier position. On June 27, 1862 the unit enters the battle of Seven Days, at Gaines Farm. The 1st Division of the VI Corps, which the unit is part of is ordered to the relief of the V Corps, and arrives at 4:00 PM.

The Division is sent into the fight immediately. Each brigade is ordered separately to strengthen weak points along the line. The VI Corps is placed on the extreme right of the Union Army. The 2nd Brigade went to the aid of Sykes, who is struggling to hold a line against Confederate forces under D. H. Hill and Jackson, and with this help, pushes them back. The Rebels charge with great courage but, under withering fire and floundering through the swampy terrain, find the Union position too strong and soon flee. Company G has one man wounded during this action. Meanwhile, the left flank of the Union Army gives way. The VI Corps is pulled out of the line of battle and acts as the rear guard for Porter's Corps. They become engaged with the Confederates at Charles City Crossroads while performing their rear guard duties.

Malvern Hill

At the Battle of Malvern Hill they again occupy the right flank of the Union Army, but are not actively engaged. In a wheat field they remain in line of battle all day, changing position that night just enough to deprive the men of rest. On July 2, 1862 in a pouring rain, they depart this location for Harrison's Landing. The roads become very muddy and the men are exhausted, barely being able to drag themselves along. At 4:00 PM they arrive at Harrison's Landing, where they halt. Here under the covering fire of gunboats in the river, they camp, the men laying down in the mud and falling asleep.

They remain here for six weeks. Camp life is extremely dreary, sickly, and monotonous. They build strong entrenchments in the event the Confederates decide to attack. Sickness is very bad and very widespread. The men are worn out from constant hard work, sunburned, pestered and bit by the insects, and forced to drink impure water. However, the men did not simply sit by, and they work to improve their conditions. They dig wells for good water and bring small pine trees into the camp, setting them among the tents for shade. While at Harrison's Landing, the company loses three men who are medically discharged, probably because of illness or disease.

On July 8, 1862, President Lincoln reviews the troops at Harrison's Landing. The only other excitement while they are stationed there takes place on July 31st, when the Confederates make a demonstration against their position, but it is of no significance. On April 16, 1862 they depart Harrison's Landing. After two days of marching under a scorching sun they arrive at the Chickahominy River, which they cross on August 17, 1862. The crossing is made using a 2,000 foot long pontoon bridge, and they camp on the east side of the river that evening. The next day they pass through Williamsburg and camp there for the night. At dawn on August 19th they move out and after a very tiring march reach Yorktown, Virginia. On August 21, 1862, they march to Hampton, were they board transports and steam up the Potomac River.

There is quite a contrast in the appearance of the men now, compared to when they sailed down the river in April of 1862. At that time the ranks were full, the men healthy, uniforms new, and their equipment sparkled. Now they are fewer in number and can hardly be recognized as the same men who left the Washington defenses just four months ago. Their faces are now bronzed from the scorching sun and their uniforms worn and dirty. At sunset on August 23, 1862, the transport anchors off of Alexandria, Virginia. The men are not allowed to go ashore, and are required to sleep below decks in crowded conditions, breathing the very foul air. On August 24th they finally disembark and march through Alexandria to Fort Ellsworth, where they remain quietly until the afternoon of August 29, 1862.

The 96th Regiment along with the rest of the VI Corps is dispatched to join in the Second Battle of Bull Run. On Thursday afternoon, August 28, 1862 they receive their marching orders. The camp is torn down and the men made ready to move. At sunset no further orders being received, they pitch their tents again to sleep for the night. On the morning of August 29 they quietly and slowly march six miles to Annadale, Virginia, where they halt and camp for the night. On August 30 they again move at a leisurely pace, making frequent halts while listening to the battle raging at Bull Run.

They pass Fairfax Court House and proceed to Cub Run. Two miles past Centreville they encamp for the night. On September 1, 1862 they return to Fairfax Court House, and on September 2 return to Centreville and take possession of the heights. They are in line of battle until 3:00 PM and not being engaged, march back to Alexandria, reaching it at 10:00 PM. In a single evening they marched a distance that had earlier required two full days and part of another day in moving to Centreville.

On September 5, 1862, Confederate General Robert E. Lee crossed the Potomac River into Maryland. On the evening of September 6 the VI Corps was ordered to move. They leave Alexandria, move through Washington, and camp at Tanleytown for the night. On September 7 they resume the march at 5:00 PM and travel only six miles. At daybreak on the 8th they move six miles through Rockville and on the 9th march an easy three miles to Johnstown. At 9:00 AM on September 10th they move, driving small detachments of Rebel cavalry before them, and reach Barnesville, ten miles away, where they remain until September 12, 1862. On the 12th, they resume the march, going ten miles and halting near Urbana. After marching another ten miles they reach Jefferson on the 13th, driving a small force of Rebels through the pass.

Cramptons Pass

On September 14, 1862 they move at 10:00 AM to the foot of South Mountain, having marched 50 miles in eight days. The Confederates are holding Cramptons Pass through the mountain, and the VI Corps is ordered to push through the enemy position there. The unit forms a line of battle about a mile and a half from Cramptons Pass, and advances. Before them is the small village of Burkettsville, and beyond that the South Mountain. The mountain summit is teeming with Rebel artillery batteries and gray lines of Rebels, while the heavily wooded slopes conceal large numbers of the Confederates.

A winding road leads up the mountain side and through the narrow opening known as Cramptons Pass. The Confederates have planted artillery batteries and troops behind barricades to dispute the Union advance. At the foot of the mountain is a stone wall, behind which is posted the first Confederate line of battle. Rebel skirmishers hold the ground in front of the wall. Their position is a strong one, perfectly suited for defense, and can be held by a small force against a much larger one.

The time of day is late when the attack is ordered. As soon as the Union lines emerge from the cover of some woods, the Rebel batteries on the hill top open fire. The earth shakes beneath the Union troops. The air filled with the howling of shells which fly over their heads and dig up the earth all around them. At the same time the Rebel line behind the stone wall opens a fierce rifle fire upon the Union men. In the face of this the unit presses forward, moving at the double quick. Over the plowed fields and through corn fields they advance, halting for a few minutes at the village. When they reach the village the citizens welcome them, bringing water to fill their canteens, and even some food. Before long the advance is ordered again, and they push ahead in the face of a murderous fire, peering into a storm of lead.

The 1st Division was on the right side of the road during this attack. After severe fighting, and driving the enemy back from point to point, they seize the Gap at about 3:00 AM. The Confederates flee down the west side of the mountain. As the unit advances, they wonder not that their foe had offered such stubborn resistance, but that the position had been taken at all. The ground around them is scattered with dead Rebels, and the fire so furious that trees were cut to pieces.

The unit moves to the western side of South Mountain and sleeps with weapons at the ready all night, expecting the battle to be renewed at dawn. When the morning arrives they discover that the Confederates have departed. The unit remains in Pleasant Valley at rest on September 15th and 16th. Early on the morning of September 17, 1862 they depart in haste for Sharpsburg, Maryland, where the Union Army is now engaged in a fierce fight.

Antietam

The 96th PVI Regiment arrives at Antietam on September 17, 1862. They are placed on the Union right flank just as the tide of battle is sweeping across the cornfield, on what has been called the bloodiest day of the Civil War. The Company suffers two casualties during the fighting at Antietam. Both men struck by the same cannon ball. As they are securing the right flank of the Union Army, the Confederate artillery harasses them until nightfall. The Confederate Army retreats on September 18, 1862. The unit also falls back, finally giving the men a chance to cook some coffee and meals.

The men are awestruck by the total destruction that is everywhere. They are ordered forward again the same day, passing over the recently departed battlefield, which is strewn with hundreds of bodies. When they enter Sharpsburg they find homes riddled, burned, and battered into shapeless piles of rubble. The streets are filled with disabled wagons, rider-less horses, all types of equipment, and many wounded Rebels. They pass through the town and camp for the night.

On September 20, 1862 they retrace their steps and again pass over the battlefield. The stench is unbearable by this time. The unit reaches Williamsport at daylight where it remains until the morning of September 23rd.   They then march to Bakersville on the Hagerstown Turnpike and remain there for about three weeks. While near Bakersville, President Lincoln reviews the troops on October 3, 1862, and they receive some replacements.

Soon after Midnight on October 11, 1862 they are ordered to move to Hagerstown, Maryland. They march in a heavy shower and reach Hagerstown soon after daylight.   While stationed near Hagerstown, they perform picket duty along the river and have few other duties. The camp is a pleasant one, and the men need this time to recover since many of them are suffering from a severe shortage of clothing. The civilians are loyal to the Union cause here and provide them with some comfort items, making their lives a bit easier and enjoyable.

On October 28, 1862 they receive orders to move from Hagerstown. On October 30 they start a night march and reach Williamsburg where they camp for two days. They then march through Boonsboro, halting at Berlin, and re-crossing the Potomac River into Virginia on pontoon bridges. Their route then takes them through Lovettsville, Purcellville, Union Town, Upperville, and White Plains, not far from Thoroughfare Gap. On November 9th they reach New Baltimore where they stay for a week. They then spend another week on the banks of the Aquia Creek, not far from Stafford Court House.

Fredericksburg

About this time General Ambrose Burnside takes command of the Army of the Potomac, consolidating it into three Grand Divisions of two corps each. The VI Corps is part of the Left Grand Division. Again the march resumes and they reach Brooks Station, where they remain for a day. The weather is bitterly cold at this time. Then it is on to Falmouth Station, a hike of six miles, which puts the unit just opposite of Fredericksburg, Virginia. While here the men have a hard time trying to keep warm. It is too cold to sleep and many of the men stand around campfires all night to keep warm. Here they wait for three weeks; waiting for the pontoons to arrive so they can cross the Rappahannock River.

On December 11, 1862 they march to a point two miles below Fredericksburg. This move is easier then previous marches because the ground is frozen from the cold weather. They move down from Stafford Heights into the valley of the Rappahannock River. A dense fog obscures the far side of the river, which they can not see until about Noon. The engineers are busy laying pontoon bridges, and as soon as the fog lifts the Rebels fire upon them. Before long the Union artillery comes into action and silences the Rebels.

Fredericksburg sits upon the south bank of the Rappahannock River. On the north side of the river is a steep bluff called Stafford Heights and this is where the Union forces are posted. Behind the town the ground rises in several successive terraces until it reaches an elevation called "the mountain." Each terrace commands all below it and is ideal for the defense. Between the two high grounds is a level plain on both sides of the river which is about a mile wide. The Union artillery is posted on the heights north of the river. The Confederate forces are entrenched on the south side of the river on each terrace.

The unit pushes across the river just below Fredericksburg using the pontoon bridges. It is placed into line of battle on an open plain south of the town, with the intention of making the Confederates believe that a full scale attack is about to be launched there. The VI Corps advances through the town with ten regiments, including the 96th. They then cross the Fredericksburg plain towards Maryes Heights, where the Rebels are located in a sunken road.

The Union forces charge the sunken road twice and are repulsed twice before it is finally taken. The leading division attacks gallantly and for a few short minutes has everything going their way. Before long the Union troops find themselves in a precarious position. They are outnumbered and taking a severe beating, and soon forced to retreat.

When night came, the VI Corps finds itself drawn up in a ragged square near Banks Ford. The Rebels are on three sides of them and with the river to their back, it is a very gloomy night. The losses had been very heavy that day, and the lanterns of the stretcher bearers can be seen through the woods and across the fields for many hours. One soldier remembered that the night was indescribably gloomy. One of the men had been killed while climbing over a rail fence, and for some awful reason, remained balanced upright astride the top rail all night. The body slowly rocks back and forth in the breeze. The men nearby are able to see his white face distinctly in the light of the full moon. Rebel pickets held the line of this fence, and when they fired the flash from their guns put a garish light on the ghostly figure.

After the battle at Fredericksburg the Army went into camp on a line from Falmouth to Belle Plain. The VI Corps occupying nearly the center of the line at a place called White Oak Church on December 16, 1862. The men build huts and they make themselves as comfortable as possible. Disease soon spreads rapidly through the camp. The units are crowded closely together on low, wet ground. The men having never before erected winter quarters from shelter tents are not the experts that they become later on in the war. They suffer from their inexperience, as well as from the low and wet ground in the crowded camp. Also during this time desertions become alarmingly frequent.

In spite of the hardships the men endure, and with the coldest months yet to come, the weather is fair. The sun and the mild weather dry the roads and indications of a general movement are widespread. On January 20, 1863 the order came to move. The entire Corps breaks camp and moves toward Banks Ford, which is two miles up the river from White Oak Church. They halt at 5:00 PM in some woods near Banks Ford, which is the point selected for crossing the river. The men are soon camped out of sight of the Confederates on the opposite side of the river.

Barely had they settled themselves for a night's rest, when the clouds which had been thick since morning break with rain. The wonderful Indian summer gives way to rainy weather, which pours all night and all of the following day. By morning the roads are so softened by the rain that the horses can not pull the artillery or pontoons into position. The men are busy all day long, pushing and pulling the guns and pontoons by hand, sometimes in mud up to their knees. Some men are also detailed to return to Falmouth, a distance of five miles, to carry back additional rations. By the end of the day they are totally exhausted.

During the night a decision is made to abandon the attempt to cross the river. The Confederate army is now well aware of the Union intentions. This could have resulted in many Union casualties and perhaps even a defeat. At sunrise the unit is back on the road to their old camp, and this time for permanent winter quarters. All along the road are many dead horses and mules, which died during the tremendous efforts of the day before. Much of the artillery and wagons are still stuck in the mud, with the teams still working to free them.

The mud is deep, the day gloomy, and the men are discouraged and straggle badly as they press on to their old camps. One unit can not be distinguished from another, and the column becomes an unorganized mob. Even though the men are tired and discouraged, they keep up their lively talk and jokes, as though everything is easy. Toward evening they arrive at their old camp, which now will be their home until spring. They immediately begin the work of restoring the comforts of their abandoned camp. Unfortunately when they left the camp, not thinking they would return, had burned everything and hardly any building materials can be found. Nevertheless, quarters are soon erected and the routine of drills and picket duty are resumed once again.

General Burnside was relieved after the infamous "Mud March" and was replaced by General Joseph Hooker. General Hooker immediately began to reorganize the Army of the Potomac. He abolished the Grand Divisions of the Army, reorganized the cavalry, and renovated the support departments. The changes in the medical, quartermaster, and commissary departments brought up their standards higher then ever before. During the winter the men are well supplied. Bread, potatoes, vegetables of all type, fresh beef, flour, sugar, and coffee make up the regular rations issued to the men. The improvements in the quartermaster department are nearly as great, with abundant supplies being furnished.

The men however, have great difficulty in finding wood, and must carry the wood needed for cooking and heat on their backs for more than a mile. They endure their hardships, the weather and the constant picket duty, and are for the most part happy. The sounds of guitars and accordions can be heard almost every evening and on pleasant afternoons. Parties of men assemble in the company street to dance to the music. When snow covers the ground, mock battles with snowballs are a frequent form of amusement. Another favorite pastime is baseball. There are many good players in the Regiment and the regiments challenge each other to games, with the games drawing large crowds of soldiers. As the warm weather of spring approaches the men decorate their camps with evergreen trees. They also make beautiful arches that make the camps take on a very pleasant appearance. But they have little time to enjoy these, for as soon as the roads become passable, preparations start for the spring campaign.

During this time the command of the VI Corps passed from Major General Smith to Major General John Sedgwick. One of the major events of the winter was the review of the entire Army of the Potomac by President Lincoln. It must have been quite a sight and one the men never forgot. The President, in civilian dress and tall hat, accompanied by General Hooker, is followed by a large group, and is welcomed by the thundering of artillery firing a salute. The different corps' are assembled in line on a flat stretch of land within sight of each other. The President rides in front of each corps with a huge procession following him. He passes along the entire line carefully inspecting each regiment and then returns in the rear. After the inspection is complete, the President and staff position themselves and the entire Army of the Potomac passes in review before him.

Following the Union defeat at Fredericksburg, the Army of the Potomac is reorganized under the command of Major General Joseph Hooker. Preparations for the Chancellorsville campaign soon begin. On Tuesday, April 28, 1863 the unit receives orders to break camp and to be ready at a moments notice, and rations for eight days are issued to the men. The morale of the men at this time is high, having forgotten all of the former discouraging events, and they are now anxious to fight the Rebels.

Chancellorsville

A violent rain storm during the morning of April 28 makes the march difficult. But they march for six miles through thickets and bogs, bringing them to the rear of Falmouth Station and just a short distance from the river. The men work from dust until nearly dawn carrying the pontoon boats on their shoulders to the river where they launch them. They conduct this operation so quietly that the Rebels are completely surprised. Suddenly the Confederates see the 1st Brigade, 1st Division, VI Corps which the Hamburg unit is part of, as they approach in boats at daybreak. The astonished Rebels fire a few volleys at the men, but the Union artillery fires canister shot into them and they soon take off to a safer area.

By sunrise on April 29, 1863 the unit is across the river. They hold a plain with the pickets forming a half circle about three quarters of a mile in diameter. This is the very same spot where the unit had fought during the First Battle of Fredericksburg. The bridge is also in the same place at a point known as Franklin's Crossing. The men immediately begin preparing entrenchments, with the Rebels doing the same. The Confederates shelling of the Union position ends at nightfall and the men camp where they stand. About Noon on April 30, 1863 the troops are massed by brigades, and a message of congratulations from General Hooker is read. "The enemy," said Hooker "must now come out and fight us on our ground, or retreat ingloriously," to which the men cheered. Nothing else of interest occurred during the day.

On May 1, 1863 at sunset, Hooker ordered Sedgwick to use the VI Corps to assume a threatening posture. This included making a thorough demonstration, but not to make any attack at this time. There is much marching and getting into position. The units march and counter-march in a manner to make an impression to the Rebels that an attack is to be made at that point. The Confederates are deceived by these maneuvers, and heavy columns of gray infantry form into lines of battle. While our men stand in line of battle one of the Union bands near the skirmish line starts playing the tune "Dixie." When the Rebels hear this, they start cheering defiantly, to which our men answer with volleys of tremendous fire into the Rebel positions. Nothing else happened that day and the men retired when the sun went down.

With evening drawing near on May 2, 1863, the Union skirmishers attack and drive back the Confederate skirmish line. It is a gallant feat and finely executed. The men stay in line perfectly as if on drill, advancing and firing rapidly, pressing the Rebels at the "double quick." Our men do not halt until they cross the entire width of the plain and reach the base of the hills. The men remain in line all night, sometimes lying down on the ground where they stand to catch a few moments of sleep.

They finally advance at 4:00 AM on May 3, 1863. Straight across the plain they go, until they come to the base of the heights where the Rebels are waiting for them. Taking the Bowling Green road they turn to the right and proceed to the rear of Fredericksburg. As they approach the town, Confederate artillery batteries fire upon them, along with masses of Rebel infantry firing volleys into the Union ranks. In the meantime, the large formations of Union artillery on Stafford Heights positioned on the north side of the river are firing. They fire large shells across the wide valley and river into the Rebel positions. A couple of Union batteries near the head of the Union column also get into position and open a vicious cannonade.

The line of battle of the VI Corps extends from the pontoon bridge at Franklin's Crossing to the right of the town of Fredericksburg. The 1st Division is on the left holding the area in front of the river crossing. General Sedgwick finds that the heights can only be taken by a direct attack. So he orders storming columns to be formed and this is immediately executed. At 10:30 AM all dispositions are complete in preparation for the attack, and the Union artillery open fire upon the Confederate positions in front of the unit. The VI Corps advances toward the heights, which is barren of any trees, as is the plain below. This affords the Rebels an excellent view of all the Union movements. A railroad track traverses the plain near the bluffs, and in a deep cut through which it passes are the Rebels. As the Union forces approach this cut the Rebels fire into the line. Federal batteries soon send them retreating, and for a moment the Union troops halt as the artillery on both sides fires into each other.

It is a moment of conflicting emotions. The men feel pride, hope, and sadness, as these gallant soldiers stand face to face with those heights, ready to charge them. At the double quick, and impressively, they cross the plain. Their line so perfect, that it looks as if they are on drill. Union artillery is firing on the rebel positions as they advance. However, the Confederate batteries on the heights above continue to pour destructive fire into the advancing line. The unit continues advancing and taking the rifle pits at the base of the hill. They continue to push forward to capture the heights.

A more magnificent scene is hard to imagine. There are the hills, enough to tire any man in climbing them without a load and with no one opposing them. At the foot of the hills are thousands of Confederates firing in volleys. All the while their artillery firing grape and canister shot in a frightful storm into the Union ranks. But the men push on gallantly as the Rebels steadily retreat. They press undauntedly against the murderous storm of iron and lead. Men are falling, but the lines quickly close ranks and they continue to press forward. Finally with shouts and cheers, bayonets fixed, they mount the heights and force the Rebels to retreat in confusion, and the heights won. It was a glorious day for the 96th Pennsylvania Volunteer Infantry Regiment. Never was a charge more bravely made. But it was also a sad day, as many brave men are killed taking those heights.

However, the fighting for the day is not yet finished. Upon the heels of this brilliant success by the Union, lurks disaster. Hooker now orders Sedgwick to advance the VI Corps toward Chancellorsville to link up with the rest of the army. The VI Corps which had so nobly won the heights pushes on for further achievements. The division the Hamburg unit is part of takes the lead and advances as far as Salem Church on the Chancellorsville Pike. When, instead of meeting the rest of our army, shells from some hidden guns warn the unit of the presence of the Rebels.

A dense thicket is in front. The brigade is in the advance, deployed in a line of skirmishers to determine the position of the concealed Rebels, which they soon find. The brigade is quickly formed into a battle line. The 27th New York is on the right, the 5th Maine and 121st New York in the center, and the 96th Pennsylvania on the left. The 16th New York holds the skirmish line in front. General Bartlett advances the brigade into the woods, the 16th New York driving off the Rebel skirmishers, with the rest of the brigade following closely. At the edge of the woods the brigade halts, but is soon rapidly advancing again.

Advancing through the woods the brigade suddenly finds itself face to face with the Confederates. The Rebels are lying down in a road which passes through the woods. When the Union line is within 20 yards, the Rebels suddenly fire a volley which, had it been well aimed would have almost annihilated the brigade. The brigade returns fire with devastating effect. The Rebels are forced to abandon the road with many dead and wounded and seek shelter behind some rifle pits. These rifle pits are only a few yards to the rear of the road, and here a very strong Rebel force is positioned.

The Union force occupies the road now and fires against these rifle pits. But the Rebel fire is now intense and accurate, cutting down the troops in the unprotected Union ranks. For 15 minutes the brigade withstands the deadly fire before falling back in good order, having lost nearly 700 men. In the meantime the rest of the division and other parts of the corps are brought into action. The Rebels force the division to retire and are advancing against the Union line when the artillery repulses them. Darkness comes to the relief and the men sleep soundly on their arms after the grueling duties of the day.

While the men are resting, the Confederates bring up reinforcements from Richmond, Virginia. Early on the morning of May 4, 1863 the Federal artillery on Stafford Heights opposite the town, sends shells screaming across the valley to Mayre's Hill. This alarms those in the town and those that so recently departed. Long lines of Confederate infantry are seen all along the outskirts of the town and on the crests above. Before the men know what is happening, 15,000 Confederate troops position themselves between the VI Corps and the Fredericksburg Heights. The Union force is now in a precarious position, with lines of communication cut off, and surrounded by the Rebels.

The VI Corps is sandwiched between the Rebels on the heights and Lee's entire army. On the left is a strong force of Confederate infantry and on the right an impassable river. Dispositions are immediately made to meet this emergency. The Division is being drawn back, and another division changing its position, quickly extending the Union line of battle to the river. This line includes

Bank's Ford, six miles above the city, over which communications are at once reestablished.

Confederate General Early's Division occupies the crest of Marye's and Cemetery Hills; the divisions of Anderson and McLaws are on the Union flank; and the brigades of Hays, Hoke, and Lawton, supported by Lee's entire army are behind us. The unit is in the vicinity of Salem Church, and their only line of retreat is the road leading to Bank's Ford.

The Confederates make a demonstration during the morning of May 4, 1863 against the positions held by Neill's brigade. They are repulsed, losing 200 men as prisoners along with the colors of the 58th Virginia Regiment. The rest of the day wore away with little fighting until 5:00 PM, at which time the Rebels attack with a force of three divisions. The 3rd Brigade, 2nd Division, holds the line and stubbornly resists the attack, thus enabling the rest of the VI Corps to cross the river at Bank's Ford. The 96th falls back to Bank's Ford at dusk and occupies rifle pits there and keeps up a constant skirmish with the Rebels.

Toward morning the Corps crosses the Rappahannock River on pontoon bridges. This is done with much difficulty since one bridge has been destroyed by Rebel artillery. The other bridge is barely saved from destruction long enough to allow the troops to quickly pass over. The unit has passed through a fearful ordeal, and has shown itself to be made of brave material. No two more brilliant feats had been performed then the storming of the heights at Fredericksburg, and the resistance when surrounded and attacked by overwhelming forces. The men came out of this fight not demoralized, but as ready to scale those terrible heights again, just as they had been called upon on the 3rd of May.

The army now returns to its old position. They occupy a location one mile behind the old camp at White Oak Church. Here the ground has been unoccupied and a growth of pines and oak trees afford far better surroundings then the old quarters. The wounded are taken to an immense field hospital at Potomac Creek. At that location are hospital tents to accommodate 8,000 casualties. This location also provides pure water. On May 9, 1863 many of the Union wounded are brought to the river at Fredericksburg, and sent over to our side by the Confederates on pontoon boats under flags of truce. In time, nearly all our wounded are returned to us, and are sent to either Potomac Creek or Washington.

An interesting note is the fact that just before the Chancellorsville campaign, Hooker issued an order assigning each corps and division its own badge, which was to be worn by all officers and soldiers. The 96th Pennsylvania wore a red Greek cross, designating the 1st Division of the VI Corps. All wagons and ambulances were also marked with the appropriate badge. Wounded soldiers who fell to the rear to the ambulances had little difficulty in finding their own supply train. The quartermaster and others connected with the trains were greatly assisted in their duties by the badge system of identification.

The men enjoyed a pleasant month at this camp and were eager in spite of their comfortable quarters, to begin active campaigning. The health and morale of the men had never been better, and in spite of the failure at Chancellorsville they feel very confident. When they receive orders to move again, they receive it with pleasure and depart their camp willingly.

They leave camp on the morning of June 5, 1863. It is a lovely day and they take the road already traveled on two previous occasions. They halt in the valley of the Rappahannock River on the very spot where they rested during the first and second battles of Fredericksburg. Now they prepare for the third time in six months to cross the river. Pontoons and artillery batteries form long lines behind a small ridge which runs parallel with the river. The infantry march and counter march in order to get into the correct positions. Here, behind the little ridge they rest until about 5:00 PM. The men climb the small ridge and peer across the river to see that the Rebels have turned the rifle pits that the Union had made early to their own use.

Before long the engineers draw the pontoons to the edge of the river as the Rebels fire briskly at them. But the Rebels soon draw their heads behind the earthworks as the Union artillery fires into their positions. The Rebel fire is sporadic and annoying, and it is evident that the safest way to cross the river is in boats. This is done and the Confederates scatter before a rapid charge made by the 26th New York and 5th Vermont Infantry Regiments. This accomplished, the engineers proceed in completing the bridge. On the following morning the 2nd Division of the VI Corps crosses over, but there is very little fighting except for occasional artillery duels.

Early in the morning of June 12, 1863 the Regiment is sent out on picket duty in the area between the Rappahannock and Potomac Rivers. On Saturday night, June 13, 1863 they withdraw from Fredericksburg and start on the Pennsylvania Campaign. Lee's forces are now moving north. The Army of the Potomac is also moving, keeping their forces between the Confederates and Washington. The VI Corps is assigned as the rear guard to the army, starting their march sometime around 10:00 PM.

The darkness is intense, and a thunderstorm hits them just as they start. For some distance their route is through a thick forest, which shuts out the little bit of light that might have penetrated the clouds. The column marches in complete darkness. The road is muddy and many of the artillery pieces frequently get stuck in the mire. As the rain pours down upon them in torrents, the men stumble over rocks and fallen trees. Later in the night the rain ends and the roads become more passable, but it is still very difficult to see the road clearly.

At one point they pass over a corduroy road which is very slippery from the rain. The men heavily burdened with knapsacks, rifles, and cartridges sometimes fall headfirst. Many of them fall off the side of the road and tumble down the steep embankments. A laugh is heard from the comrades of the unfortunate soldier, and at one point someone calls out, "Have you a pass to go down there?" The men march on until about 3:00 AM, when they finally halt along the Potomac Creek. There they sleep soundly upon the wet ground until daylight.

The following day was Sunday and the VI Corps does not march until evening. This gives the men a chance to rest from the tiring march of the previous night. All day long they watch the immense army supply trains hurrying by on their way north. At 9:00 PM that night they take to the road again and march rapidly. It is at this time that the men hear the news of Lee invading the north, and they now become anxious to move on and engage the rebels. The dark column pushes on through the entire night. Occasionally there is a halt, but not for rest, and the men expecting to move at any moment remain standing in the ranks. Faint and weary, yet with determination, the men march along.

As the morning turns to afternoon the heat of the sun is almost intolerable, and the dust kicked up by the thousands of marching soldiers is suffocating. As a matter of fact, the dust is so thick that one can not see half the length of the regiment. Eventually some of the men begin to drop from exhaustion. In every corner of rail fences and under every tree and bush, groups of men are strewn. The sight along the roadside is appalling, as regiments become like companies, and companies losing their identity as the units become intermingled. Men are dying from heat stroke, but still the march goes on.

This can not go on much longer. The men still marching are starting to fade fast, and soon there won't be any troops capable of moving. At 3:00 PM they arrive at the small village of Dumfries, and there to the enjoyment of all stop in a field. When they halt there is no cheer or any expression of gladness. The tired men, with blistered feet which are worn out by 17 hours of constant marching, just throw themselves down on the ground. They rest for a short time before waking just long enough to make coffee and eat some pork and hardtack. All who participated in this march remembered it as one of the most trying marches ever made by the Army of the Potomac.

The men are very grateful for the sleep they get that night. At 2:00 AM the shout passes all along the line, "fall in! fall in!" Without having the chance to make coffee, they roll out of their blankets and fall into line. But as often happens when an entire army moves, some units have to wait a long time before moving because other units are in the way. The VI Corps waits till 4:00 AM, and the men finally have their coffee before having to move. It proves to be another hot and dusty day, but not quite as bad as the day before. At about 2:00 PM they arrive at Occoquan Creek, where they cross at Wolf Run Shoals and rest for two hours. No sooner has the column halted when the men plunge into the stream, and soon the creek is alive with swarms of men.

Although they already made a long march, at 4:00 PM they are again on the road, marching six miles and reaching Fairfax Station before dark. This is a more cheerful march than the others since the men are refreshed from their bath, a good dinner, and two hours rest. Now they talk, sing and laugh, as though the marching is play to them. On this day they get the news that Lee is in Pennsylvania! The Pennsylvania men are extremely anxious now to go forward and chase the Rebels from their home State. That night they camp in a grove alongside the road from Fairfax to Manassas, and remain there the following day.

On June 19, 1863, at 5:00 AM, they are again marching and reach Fairfax Court House before Noon. Then on June 20 they pass through Centreville on their way to Bristow Station. In this location they remain for five days, guarding the passes from the Shenandoah Valley. The weather is good and the men enjoy the much needed rest. On the night of June 26 the VI Corps leaves Bristow Station.

The night is dark and a drizzling rain makes the march unpleasant. The pace of the march is quite fast and some of the men fall behind. Before daylight the column halts at Centreville and the men lie down upon the soggy ground and sleep for two hours, with the rain falling on them. At 6:00 AM they are awakened and prepare for movement once again. This march is another severe one and the men are glad when they arrive at Drainsville before dark, where they camp. Early the next morning they reach Edwards' Ferry along the Potomac River, where they cross on a pontoon bridge into Maryland. On Sunday they leave Edwards' Ferry, and march through Poolesville and Barnestown to Hyattstown. It is there that the men learn that Major General George Meade has replaced Hooker as the commander of the Army of the Potomac.

The movement of the entire army is now being done by several columns on nearly parallel roads. The VI Corps is on the extreme right marching towards Manchester. At 5:00 AM, Monday, June 28, 1863 they are marching again, passing through Monroeville, New Market, Ridgeville, and Mount Airy Station, and halt for the night at

Sam's Creek. As they pass through Westminster on June 29, the people welcome them with much joy, especially since some Rebel cavalry had left there just two hours before. By evening they arrive at Manchester, but still 20 miles from the rest of the army. Here they rest until the evening of the next day.

In the last four days they have marched over 100 miles, and all that under a burning sun and carrying a heavy load. The men have endured and kept up, but the greatest march of all was yet in store. In Manchester the inhabitants are well supplied with whiskey. Soldiers have a way of finding out about these things, and of getting some for themselves. It wasn't long before a considerable number of the men are drunk. At 9:00 PM on July 1, 1863 they are on the road again. Those men, who had indulged in the whiskey during the day and were unable to stand in line, are quietly laid by the roadside. They are later gathered up by the squads of cavalry scouring the area for stragglers.

Gettysburg

On July 1, 1863 while the unit is held at Manchester, Maryland, General Meade alerts General Sedgwick to be ready to move in any direction at a moments notice. Meade sent this dispatch to Sedgwick after receiving Buford's message to Reynolds the night before warning of a strong Confederate concentration near Gettysburg. At 4:30 PM Meade orders Sedgwick to bring the VI Corps to Taneytown that evening. However, shortly after issuing those orders they are changed. Instead of going to Taneytown, Meade instructs the VI Corps to immediately head for Gettysburg by the shortest route. Without the VI Corps, the Union army is outnumbered.

In order to hasten his movement, Meade authorizes Sedgwick to stop all supply trains which might be in his way or force them off the road. The first order at 4:30 PM calls for a stiff march of 20 miles from Manchester to Taneytown by way of Westminster. The second leg is a forced march of 30 miles. They use the Baltimore Pike to get to Gettysburg. Once they arrive, they are only to rest long enough to revive the men, and then to form a line of battle at some strong point to cover a retreat. The unit arrives at Gettysburg between 2:00 and

3:00 PM on July 2, 1863. Initially the VI Corps replaces the V Corps as a reserve on the right flank of the Union army.

Though other units made marches during the campaign which may have been equally as grueling, the circumstances surrounding that of the VI Corps made it famous. The word came that they were needed and needed in a hurry. So they marched from 10:00 PM until 5:00 PM the next afternoon, with only a few breaks for coffee or now and then a short rest. On and on they trudged, endlessly it seemed, at first through the darkness and then in the heat of the July sun, 34 long miles to Gettysburg.

One veteran recalled hearing strains of band music. Catching the beat of "Old John Brown's Body," he noted that the men immediately strode along more briskly. Then a hundred, a thousand, and then ten thousand voices sang out the battle cry of "Glory, Glory, Hallelujah, His Soul Is Marching On." All night long they march at an incredible pace to the sounds of bands which alternate with the shrill of fifes and the roll of drums. Never before have their bands played on the march except when they entered a town, and their performance this time is a happy inspiration.

By mid-morning the heat of the day has wilted the men into complete silence except for the rhythmic slap, slap of their feet on the stony road. Some men reel and stagger as if drunk, and every now and then a soldier collapses in his tracks. His comrades quickly drag him to the grass along the side of the road, place his rifle next to him, and then resume their places in the ranks. Thoughtful farmers and their families keep others from dropping out by bringing to the roadside tubs and pails of cool water. Some are even more generous and feed the men cherries, milk, and a great variety of cooked food.

Finally the men can hear the distant boom of cannon which, as they come closer, serves as a guide for them to follow. When they arrive at Gettysburg, and without any rest, they immediately head towards the heaviest firing. Arriving just in time to help turn back the last desperate attack by Confederate General Longstreet on the Union left. The Brigade is then pushed forward along the right of the road leading to the Peach Orchard near the northwest slope of Little Round Top.

The 96th holds a position there along a stone wall until the close of the battle. Today monument stands in that location marking the exact spot of the Regiment during the battle. Despite some savage fighting on the Union left flank, the regiment suffers only one casualty on July 2, 1863. With the exception of some scattered firing, the Union left is relatively quiet on July 3rd. The major fighting that day takes place further up the line as Lee attempts to smash the center of the Union line on Cemetery Ridge. The Confederate assault is severely repulsed and ends the fighting at Gettysburg. The battlefield is quiet on July 4 as the Confederates start their retreat south amid a driving rain storm.

The Regiment holds its position near Little Round Top until the morning of July 5, 1863 when it joins the rest of the VI Corps in the pursuit of Lee's army toward the Potomac River. The hardship of the pursuit is intense as the Regiment crosses the Cotactin Mountains at night in the midst of a thunderstorm. The VI Corps spends all of July 6 and until Noon of the following day getting its artillery over South Mountain. When they are finished the horses are unfit for further use. The infantry marches ahead without their artillery support until the horses are either rested or replaced. The 96th skirmishes and advances along the Funkstown Road and helps drive the Rebels across Antietam Creek at Claggert's Mill, near Fairfield. The 1st Division of the VI Corps presses on towards Williamsport on July 14, but the Confederate army escapes safely into Virginia.

During the latter part of July 1863 the Brigade is detached from Wright's Division and is sent to New Baltimore, Virginia. That area is plagued by John Mosby's famous rebel raiders. The unit is employed in picketing and guarding along with the usual drill and parades. On the night of September 4, 1863, rebel guerillas stage a raid on General Bartlett's headquarters at New Baltimore. However, the 96th Pennsylvania which is on picket duty at the time routes the raiders, suffering three wounded. The Regiment spends most of September and October of 1863 in camp near Warrenton, Virginia, moving with the brigade to Rappahannock Station on November 7th.

General Meade issues orders for a march at dawn to seize Confederate bridgeheads at Rappahannock Station and Kelly's Ford on the north bank of the Rappahannock River. By securing these bridgeheads, General Meade hopes to move against the bulk of the Confederate army positioned south of the river. Kelly's Ford is taken in a surprise attack by the III Corps, but the forces at Rappahannock Station, protected by strong fortifications, hold on tenaciously. The V and VI Corps attack the Rebels on both flanks, but are unable to dislodge the defenders. The 1st Division is hotly engaged and takes the brunt of the fighting as they are called upon to perform unusual feats of valor. The Rebels are posted in strong positions behind extensive earthworks, forts, redoubts, and rifle pits. Their artillery posted so as to sweep the plain and sloping grounds before them.

The gray lines of Confederate infantry pour out from behind their earthworks and meet the Union troops at the edge of the plain. As the Union line of battle appears on the crest of a hill, the Rebel batteries open fire. The air is filled with shrieking projectiles which explode above and just behind the troops. Fortunately the Rebel aim is high, and many of the shells plow the ground to the rear or explode near the Union hospitals.

The unit is pressing toward the Rebel works at the double quick under terrible rifle and artillery fire. But the soldiers push everything before them. As they near the Rebel works the Union skirmishers along the whole line throw themselves to the ground and wait for the line of battle to come up. The Rebel skirmishers do the same. Confederate infantry crowds the opposite side of the plain, the slopes of the hills and the rifle pits. The entire line is ablaze with the fire of rifles and the roar of the battle steadily increasing.

Near sunset, Brigadier General Russell proposes a surprise night assault on the Rebel works. Colonel Emery Upton, who replaced General Bartlett as the 2nd Brigade commander the day before, would support Russell's men. The 3rd Brigade of the 1st Division, consisting of the 6th Maine, 5th Wisconsin, and the 49th and 119th Pennsylvania Regiments are ordered forward.

First the Maine and Wisconsin regiments rush forward. At Russell's order to charge the two regiments quicken their pace to a run, and with fixed bayonets, never stopping to fire, run forward. They seize the fort but the Rebels rally and drive them out. Again they charge with hand to hand fighting resulting. The men leap into the fort using their rifles as clubs, and when the fighting is too close for that, drop their weapons and beat their adversaries with fists. Russell immediately calls forth the remaining regiments of the brigade. But in the ten minutes it takes for the Pennsylvanians to come up on the run, half of the 6th Maine and nearly as many of the Wisconsin regiment have fallen.

None the less gallant is the charge of the 2nd Brigade, led by the young and ambitious Colonel Upton. His regiments are the 5th Maine, 95th and 96th Pennsylvania, and the 121st New York. The 2nd Brigade occupies the left flank of the VI Corps. Under the cover of darkness the courageous Upton leads his brigade to within a few yards of the Confederate rifle pits, when the order to charge is given.

Instantly the rifle pits are ablaze with a destructive volley fired into the men. Rapidly the men leap into the rifle pits and clear everything before them. All this while not a shot is fired by the men but, charging with the bayonet, capture the rebel defenses. The Rebels start running away and attempt to flee to the other side of the river. However, their pontoon bridge is now in the possession of Union troops, and hundreds of panic stricken Rebels jump into the rapidly flowing river and attempt to swim across. Some succeed, but many drown in the attempt. The credit for this victory belongs mainly to the 1st Division of the VI Corps. They captured 1,600 prisoners, 6 pieces of artillery, 4 battle flags, and more then 2,000 rifles. The 96th Pennsylvania which was part of Upton's Brigade suffered several casualties in this assault.

After this the unit goes into winter quarters along the Rappahannock River along with the rest of the Union army. The winter months pass quietly with the exception of an aborted movement upon Lee's positions at Mine Run. On May 4, 1864, Colonel Upton's Brigade breaks their quarters and crosses the Rapidan River at Germanna Ford to join in on what would become the Battle of the Wilderness. For the next five days, the 96th will be engaged in almost constant fighting.

The Wilderness

After crossing at Germanna Ford, the unit camps about two miles beyond on the Plank Road. On May 5, 1964 the march is resumed on the Plank Road to Wilderness Tavern. Enroute the brigade is placed on one of the many winding roads to cover the right flank of the Union column; later moving to the left and forming a line with the rest of the VI Corps. On the evening of May 7 the unit moves out from Wilderness Tavern via Chancellorsville, to Piney Branch Church. There they halt for some breakfast. Resuming the march on the Spottsylvania Road, the brigade meets enemy units engaging the V Corps. Upton's brigade is positioned on the right of the road to support an attack. They hold this position overnight and are relieved by a division of the V Corps on the morning of May 9, 1864. Upton then moves the brigade to the left side of the Spottsylvania Road and fortifies a new position.

The VI Corps faces the center of the Confederate line, where the Rebels are firmly entrenched behind seemingly impenetrable breastworks of a protruding salient. The enemy entrenchments are solidly built of logs and earth with heavy traverses built at frequent intervals. About 100 yards to the rear of these trenches is a second line, not yet completed, but also manned. All along the line are artillery emplacements so that any attacking force will face both rifle and cannon fire.

Spottsylvania

Colonel Upton believed that an attack spearheaded by hand picked troops, could break and hold the enemy line if the assaulting column could get a solid mass if infantrymen onto the parapet rapidly. He would soon get a chance to test his theory, and on May 10, 1864 the 96th Pennsylvania would play an active part in this experiment in warfare. At 5:00 PM the men are ordered to drop their knapsacks and rid themselves of anything that might slow them down in a charge.

Colonel Upton who is commanding the 2nd Brigade, 1st Division, VI Corps, is directed to take 12 hand picked regiments from the Corps, and lead them in a charge against the right center of the Confederate line. The regiments which share the honor of this magnificent charge are, in the first line, the 121st New York, 5th Maine, the 96th Pennsylvania, and the 119th Pennsylvania. The second line is made up of the 77th New York, 43rd New York, 5th Wisconsin, 6th Maine, and the 49th Pennsylvania. The third line consists of the 2nd, 5th, and 6th Vermont regiments. It is indeed an honor to be selected for this assault, but it will be an honor paid for by a terrible cost in lives.

The 12 regiments assemble in an open space in front of the Union positions, then, silently enter a strip of woods between the two opposing lines. Passing through to the further edge of the woods, the 12 regiments form in columns of three lines, each consisting of four regiments. As soon as a regiment is in place, the men in it lay down upon the ground. All orders are given very quietly because the Rebels are only a hundred yards away across an open field, and bullets fired by their skirmishers whistle among the trees and bushes.

At 6:00 PM everything is ready and the Union artillery opens a terrific fire. The artillery sends shells howling and shrieking over the heads of the charging column into the rebel positions. This is the signal for the attack, and Colonel Upton's voice rings out, "Attention, Battalions! Forward, Double-Quick! CHARGE!" In an instant every man is on his feet. Their tremendous cheers are answered by the wild yells of the Rebels as the column rushes forward from the cover of the woods.

Lightning quick a sheet of flame bursts from the Rebel line and a hail storm of lead sweeps the ground over which the column is charging. The Rebel artillery sends canister rounds crashing through the Union ranks at every step. Hundreds of our brave soldiers fall, literally covering the ground. This does not discourage the men as they rush upon the defenses, leaping over a ditch in front, and climbing the breastworks. The Rebels make a determined stand and hand to hand fighting ensues until with their bayonets, the men fill the rifle pits with dead and wounded Rebels. About 2,000 Confederates are captured and immediately taken to the rear under guard.

Without stopping to catch their breath, the column rushes toward the second line of Confederate defenses, which is as equally strong as the first. The resistance here is less stubborn than the first line, yet the Rebels in their rifle pits refuse to flee until forced to do so at the end of a bayonet. The Union ranks are now fearfully thinned, yet the brave men move on to a third line of rebel defenses, capturing them also. It is but a shattered remnant that rushes from the woods against the Rebel defenses that reaches this advanced point. Now finding that reinforcements are reaching the Confederates, while the Union force is melting away, a retreat is ordered. There is not even time to bring away the six artillery pieces captured, so the barrels are filled with earth and abandoned. What remains of the 12 regiments' retreats to the cover of our rifle pits, leaving the dead and most of the wounded in the hands of the Confederate force.

During this famous charge only the men in the three leading regiments were allowed to place the percussion caps on their rifles. The others were allowed to load their weapons, but not cap them until they reached the rebel defensive positions. Since an uncapped rifle could not be fired, the men in the second, third and fourth lines couldn't stop in the open field to fire and delay the full impact of the charge.

When the first three regiments reached the trench they were to fan out and drive the defenders down the line in both directions. The second wave was to open fire on any reinforcements coming up from the Confederate second line. The men in the remaining lines were to lie down just short of the trench for use as needed. All officers were instructed to urge the men on by repeating the command "Forward" constantly, from the start of the charge until the defenses were taken.

The men carried out their assignment perfectly. However, General Mott's division of the II Corps, which was to exploit the breakthrough and relieve Upton's men failed to cross an open field. That field however, was covered by 22 rebel cannons. The men are left hanging three-quarters of a mile beyond friendly lines, and being severely shot up, are forced to retire. Colonel Upton, finding his position untenable, supervises an orderly withdrawal. Colonel Upton's report of the action describes the scene:

"Twenty minutes lapsed before all the preparations were completed, when at command, the lines rose, moved noiselessly to the edge of the wood, and then, with wild cheer and faces averted, rushed for the works. Through a terrible front and flank fire the column advanced, quickly gaining the parapet. Here occurred deadly hand-to-hand conflict. The are enemy sitting in their pits with pieces upright, loaded and with bayonets fixed, ready to impale the first who should leap over, absolutely refused to yield the ground. The first of our men who tried to surmount the works fell pierced through the head by musket-balls. Others, seeing the fate of their comrades, held their pieces at arms length and fired downward, while others, posing their weapons vertically, hurled them down upon the enemy, pinning them to the ground."

The first fight for the unit at Spottsylvania is over, for the time being. Although Upton's attack failed to make a permanent breach in the enemy line, the assault demonstrated what a force of determined men could do against an entrenched enemy. Union commanders would borrow a page from Upton's book two days later, but on a much larger scale.

On May 12, 1864 the VI Corps is withdrawn from its position, and marches along the rear of its works to join in an attack with the II Corps. The Rebel defenses are taken by the II Corps and occupied by the VI Corps, and the Rebels make desperate attempts to retake them. Forming their troops in heavy columns, they hurl themselves against our line with tremendous force. The 96th Pennsylvania, along with the rest of the 1st Division holds the center of the line of the corps at a point known as the "Angle", and later referred to as the "Bloody Angle."

This angle is the key to the whole position. Our forces hold the rebel works from the left as far as the angle, with the Rebels still holding the rest of the line. Whoever can hold the angle will be the victor. With the angle either party can possess the entire line and for this reason the desperate efforts by the Rebels to drive the Union from the position. The 1st Division is unable to hold this position alone, so the 2nd Division is sent to assist, and as they take their positions the battled turns into hand to hand combat.

Only a breastwork of logs separates the combatants. The men reach over this partition, firing their rifles in the very face of the Rebels, with the Rebels doing the same. Finally the men begin to use their rifles as clubs, and then rails are used. The men are willing to fight from behind the breastworks. But to rise up and attempt a charge in the face of the opponent so near and so strong in numbers requires unusual bravery. Yet they do charge and drive the rebels back, holding the angle.

The trees in front of the position during this remarkable struggle are literally cut to pieces by bullets, with trees more than a foot in diameter cut down by the constant firing. A section of one of the trees is in the Smithsonian Institute in Washington, D.C. The fighting becomes more and more vicious and lasts until 11:00 PM. Eventually the second line of Confederate defenses is taken, with great loss on both sides. The unit has now fought non-stop at close range for eight hours. Behind the defenses the Rebel dead lay piled one on top of another, with wounded men groaning under the weight of the bodies of their dead comrades.

It now begins to rain and the men in the trenches stand up to their knees in bloodstained water. The ground outside the trenches trampled by the massed soldiers turns into a stiff gumbo in which bodies of the dead and wounded are trampled out of sight. Never before had so many rifles been fired so fast, on such a narrow front, and at such close range. About all that kept the two opponents from completely annihilating each other was the fact that most men were firing too rapidly to aim.

The logs of the breastworks are splintered. The bodies of dead and wounded men, hit over and over again until they simply fall apart, becoming unrecognizable remnants of bloody flesh rather then corpses. There are big charges and little charges with bayonet fighting when the men come to close quarters. At times Union and Confederate flags wave side by side on the parapets, as bullets shred them into tattered streamers.

The men fire at one another through gaps in the logs, or stab through them with their bayonets, and sometimes reach over the top and swing their rifle like a club. Some men jump on top of the logs and fire down on the Rebels as fast as their comrades can pass loaded rifles up to them. Each man gets off a few rounds before being shot, and when he falls someone else clambers up and take his place. Dead men fall on top of wounded men, and the men coming up to join the fight have to step on this dreadful writhing pile.

Colonel Upton is riding his horse back and forth just behind the line. The only mounted man in sight, going unhurt by some miracle, while every man on his staff is either killed or wounded. He is proud of the way his men are fighting, but he feels that they can even do better if they have some help from the artillery, so he sends back for a section of guns.

In a few minutes two cannons come splashing through the rain, wheel about and unlimber within point blank range. Artillery charging infantry, all roles reversed in this mad fight. The gunners' fire double charges of canister into the Confederate ranks, and at that close range the effect is incredible. The gunners' inspired by the effect, run their pieces forward until they touch the parapet and resume firing. They keep this up as long as the guns can be manned, which is not very long. When the guns fall silent they can not be removed because all of the horses are dead, and of the 24 men who came with the guns, only two remain unwounded.

There had been hand to hand fighting before, but it usually reached a quick climax and then ended with one side or the other breaking contact. Here nobody broke and ran. The fighting did not stop for a moment. Details are sent to the rear to clean the rifles since the men are firing so continuously that their weapons become fouled and can not be reloaded. As the day wears on, from time to time exhausted men stagger a few feet away from the firing line; fall down unhurt into the mud and go to sleep. Now and then men have to stop fighting and lift the bodies of dead and wounded comrades out of the wet ditch and drop them in the mud outside. There are so many bodies that they interfere with the fighting.

This was the Bloody Angle, and it was here that the war came down to its darkest moment. It could never be any worse then this because men could not possibly imagine or do anything worse. This fighting was not planned or ordered. It was unstructured, horrible, something no General could will. It grew out of what the men were and what the war had taught them; the cruel knowledge of killing, wild contempt for death, and furious rage.

There is frenzy on both sides, as they grapple in the driving rain with the smoke and the wild shouting and the great shock of gunfire all about them. This one muddy ditch with a log wall running down the middle becomes the center of their entire world. Nothing matters except to possess it completely or to clog it breast high with corpses. There is neither victory nor defeat in all of this.

The fighting goes on all day long and continues after dark. Some men said later that they fired more then 400 cartridges apiece. Finally somewhere around midnight the fighting ends and the exhausted Union soldiers fall asleep in the rain. In the morning they cautiously go forward to take a look at the ground they have won. In places the trenches hold corpses piled four and five deep. Sometimes at the bottom of such a pile, a living wounded man is found. Many bodies are mutilated beyond any chance of recognition. The 96th Pennsylvania is severely weakened by the fighting, losing more men at Spottsylvania than in any other battle of the war.

Cold Harbor

The next battle for the unit would be at Cold Harbor, Virginia. The VI Corps leaves the trenches at Spottsylvania during the night and early morning. It slogs along through choking dust which raised a foul, strangling cloud and makes it impossible to see the length of a company. The men remembered this march as about the worst they ever made.

When they reach Cold Harbor in midmorning of June 1, 1864, they are dirt caked and completely worn out. They form a line of battle with most of the men dropping were they stand and falling into a drugged sort of sleep. It was remembered later that the men seemed brainless from their weariness as they formed the line of battle. The feverish excitement that normally ran through a body of men lining up for an attack is missing.

At 4:00 PM an advance is made against the Rebels. The skirmishers advance first and prepare the way for the main body of infantry and the artillery. The firing of the skirmishers becomes more and more frequent, until a sharp rattle of rifle fire tells of the actual presence of the Rebels. The artillery is run out and opens a rapid fire upon the Confederate positions, who in turn reply with their own guns.

The unit is placed in the center of the line. In front is an open space two-thirds of a mile wide, beyond which is a strip of pine woods. In those woods is entrenched a strong Rebels force. The order to charge is given and the men weary and exhausted from many days and nights of hard labor, and also from the tiresome march of the day, dash across the plowed field with shouts and cheers. The storm of battle seems suddenly to have started without the usual warning; our troops only arriving shortly before, and already a bloody struggle is in progress.

The 1st Division advances. Where the ground begins to rise up they come upon an entanglement of felled trees and sharpened saplings which the rebels have put 30 yards in front of their firing line. This type of obstacle is called abatis, and is normally trees that have been cut down with the brushy tops pointing towards the enemy. The butts are embedded in shallow trenches to hold them in place, and the branches sharpened and tied together making it almost impossible to get through them. Often the abatis is supplemented by heavy logs laid end to end and bound together with chains, with six foot long stakes sharpened to a point and projecting in such a way that a man who tries to scramble over is certain to find himself or his clothing snagged and held fast. The men clear the abatis in short time and seize the Rebel defenses.

The entire line thunders with the nonstop volley of rifle fire, and the shot and shell of the artillery shriek and howl. Many good men are falling and the stretcher bearers are very busy removing the wounded from the field. After a stubborn resistance of a few minutes, the unit is forced to give up the defenses it has captured and falls back. Darkness comes at last and the fighting dies away. The men dig in where they are and count their losses, but overall the days action has been a success.

On June 3, 1864 at 6:15 AM the Union skirmishers advance again, and as soon as they are engaged our artillery fires upon the Rebel positions with the conflict again commencing. The men advance but the Confederate defenses are too strong, the abatis too troublesome, and the rebel forces too numerous. Their line can not be taken. The boys in blue find themselves caught in what seems to be a semi-circle of rebel entrenchments. Confederate guns a mile away shell their flanks, while the rebel infantry in front fire as if they are equipped with repeating rifles.

The VI Corps by this point in the war was credited as the best fighting corps in the army, but it can not move the Rebels from these defenses. Not more than ten minutes have elapsed from the moment they began their advance to the moment when those who have been hit start to look for shelter. The dense thickets, impassable briar patches, and little bogs break the Union lines into fragments.

At 8:00 PM the Rebels rush the Union line as their artillery fires. The Rebels come on with determination, but their attack is met by volley after volley of effectively aimed rifle fire. The well directed fire from the Union artillery creates huge gaps in their advancing lines, and the attack is repulsed, thus ending the Battle of Cold Harbor.

Washington

The 96th Pennsylvania is moved to Washington in July of 1864 when the capital is threatened by the Confederate forces under General Early. The VI Corps marches into Washington on Seventh Street. It is a solid column of soldiers with the Greek cross on their caps and their banners. Slouching along casually without bothering about alignment and seeming to be in no hurry at all but, somehow covering the ground very rapidly. They are indifferent and unemotional as they march behind their tattered and faded flags. As they tramp along they look cynically at the people on the sidewalks, and make mental note of the locations of saloons. The people on the sidewalks look at them and with a sudden elated cheer to each other, "The Sixth Corps! That's the Sixth Corps!"

From time to time the column halts for a rest, and every time it halts some of the veterans slip away and head for a barroom and a glass of something cold. The men who do not fall out make sarcastic remarks about militia, and quartermaster clerks, and well fed civilians. In mid afternoon they arrive at Fort Stevens where they are to be posted. The "amateurs" who had been manning the fort could relax now; the "professionals" were taking over. Most of the Corps is held in reserve at first, but they do relieve the picket line.

Several hundred VI Corps soldiers go out beyond the trenches to exchange shots with the Rebel skirmishers. The rifle fire seems hot and heavy to the clerks and 100 day militia, but the men in the company consider it light and scattering as they go about with cool competence. One of the men remembered with amusement that the troops being relieved were "astounded at the bravery displayed by the worn torn veterans in going out beyond the breastworks, and caringly volunteered most earnest words of caution." The Confederate skirmishers are 600 yards away and supported by artillery as the veterans move out and spar with them. After awhile darkness falls and the two opponents settle down for the night.

The following morning the Confederates press harder, just to make certain that the reinforced defenses are as solid as they appear. The VI Corps sends a brigade out to meet them, and in Fort Stevens and nearby Fort DeRussey the long range cannon come to life. The artillery plows the slopes where the Rebel skirmishers are in line, and knock down the houses where the sharpshooters are hiding. The noise echoes and rolls across the open country north of the city, a blanket of white smoke drifting into the hollows. Before long a trickle of wounded men start flowing back to the rear.

Shortly a carriage pulls up by a barracks that is located just behind Fort Stevens. A tall man in a frock coat and stovepipe hat gets out of the carriage. An unmilitary figure among all the soldiers, but moving nonetheless with a manner of one used to exercising command. It is President Lincoln, out to see for himself a little of the death and destruction which he has been living with for more than three years.

General Wright is in the fort and he greets the President. Without stopping to think and never imagining the invitation will be accepted, he asks Mr. Lincoln if he would like to get up on the parapet with him and watch the battle. The President said he would like that very much, and while Wright earnestly wishes he could recall his thoughtless words, the President clambers up on top of the parapet. He is tall and lean, towering over everybody, an obvious target, standing right there where rebel sharpshooters are peppering the place with bullets.

General Wright begs him to get down but Lincoln refuses, the idea of personal danger seeming not to enter his mind. A surgeon who has gotten up on the parapet is struck just a few feet from where Lincoln is standing. Bullets kick up the dirt near Lincoln, and Wright in desperation moves around to stand between the President and the Rebel fire. His pleading has no effect and Wright at last bluntly tells the President that he, General Wright, is in charge of operations at the fort and that it is his order that the President get down out of the danger. When Lincoln still fails to move Wright threatens to get a squad of soldiers and remove him by force. This seems to amuse Lincoln, and while Wright gulps at his brashness in threatening to arrest the Commander In Chief, Lincoln obediently gets down and sits with his back to the parapet.

Meanwhile the fight is getting heavier. The infantry going forward, taking losses, as Lincoln sees men killed and watches as the wounded are carried to the rear. The Confederates realize that the situation is hopeless and after awhile call in their skirmishers, and at dusk retreat. It had been a brisk fight while it lasted, but one of the Union veterans confessed that he supposed the Confederates had retired "more we think from the sight of the VI Corps flag than from the number assailing them."

The VI Corps pursues the Rebels, and the pursuit is extremely vigorous. The first nights march out of town is one of the worst ever made. The weather is hot and the roads are dusty, clogged with numerous stragglers and with obstructions which the Rebels had thoughtfully left in their wake. By the time the unit has seen the Confederates out of Maryland they are ready to call it quits and take a little rest.

For the unit the next two weeks are a nightmare. The men ford the Potomac River and travel through Leesburg and Snicker's Gap to the banks of the Shenandoah River. While there, General Grant concludes that the danger from General Early's raid is over and sends orders for the VI Corps to march to Petersburg, Virginia. The march is a hard forced march, with much straggling due to the heat and the general exhaustion of the men and as one surgeon confessed to, "bad whiskey from Washington." The Corps had no more then started when orders are again changed, ordering the Corps back into Maryland.

Unit morale now hit its all time low of the war. Originally the men had been delighted to leave the Petersburg area and come up to Washington. Their appearance as saviors of the capital, the only troops who had ever fought under the eye of Lincoln himself, made them think very highly of themselves. But the marching since then has been harder than anything before in all their experiences. Even worse than the marches they made during the Gettysburg campaign, which they always supposed were the absolute worst. When the unit arrives at Monocacy the men are totally exhausted.

Shenandoah Valley

The VI Corps transferred to the Army of the Shenandoah and participated in the Battle of Winchester on September 19, 1864. The 2nd and 3rd Divisions were hit hard by the Confederates and were falling back when the 1st Division same to the rescue. The division pushed straight on, nothing withstanding their advance, and they regained the lost ground.

The unit participated in the Shenandoah Valley until its term of service expired. It was mustered out of service in Philadelphia on October 21, 1864. However, many of the veterans reenlisted and transferred to Company G, 95th Pennsylvania Volunteer Infantry Regiment, where they remained till the end of the war.

Company D, 48th PA Volunteer Infantry Regiment

Recruiting for this regiment began early and enlistments were made so quickly that by early September 1861 the regiment was ready. Camp Curtain at Harrisburg was selected as the place to assemble and form the regiment. The Regiment was officially mustered into State service on September 19, 1861, and into Federal service on October 1, 1861. Colonel James Nagle was the first commanding officer of the Regiment. Some sources show that Hamburg comprised Company A of the Regiment, but other sources and grave markers give more convincing evidence that Hamburg made up Company D of this Regiment. The 48th was the first of Schuylkill County's 3-year units to march off to war.

Prior to the men being sworn in and accepted into the US service, each underwent a thorough physical examination. Any small physical defect prevented a man from enlisting. At the muster into State service two stands of colors were presented to the Regiment. One stand was presented by Governor Andrew G. Curtain on behalf of the Commonwealth. He made a very moving speech to the soldiers, who vigorously cheered at its end. The second stand of colors was presented by John T. Werner of Pottsville.

On September 24, 1861 they receive orders to proceed to Washington, D.C., and on September 25th they depart Harrisburg for Fortress Monroe, via Baltimore. Saboteurs attempted to derail the train between Harrisburg and Baltimore. Luckily only two cars are thrown off the tracks, and other then a few bruises, none of the men are seriously injured. Upon arrival at Baltimore they embark upon the steamer Georgia, a boat not really suitable to carry troops, to Fortress Monroe, Virginia. They sail all night long, land at Fortress Monroe, and go into camp near Hampton. The camp is called Camp Hamilton.

On October 22, 1861 they are furnished with clothing and equipment, and armed with Harper's Ferry muskets and using buck and ball cartridges. Their first uniforms are poor quality and it takes only a few weeks before they wear out. During their stay at Camp Curtain they did very little drilling except for squad drills and company drill once or twice a day, and regimental drill only twice during their stay there. However, at Camp Hamilton much attention is given to drilling at all levels and the Regiment is soon considered the best trained unit at the Camp.

At Camp Hamilton rations are plentiful and luxuries are abundant. Fish, oysters, clams, and crabs can be had with little effort. Despite a few rain storms accompanied by winds which blew down the tents, requiring the men to sleep in a few inches of water, they are for the most part comfortable and happy.

On November 10, 1861 they receive orders to prepare for a trip to Hatteras, North Carolina, and they immediately begin packing and cooking rations for the journey. The next morning they embark on the steamer S.R. Spaulding. They disembark on the 12th at about 9:00 AM and go into camp. They have some difficulty as their camp is about a half mile from the wharf, and part of the distance is waist deep with water, through which they must wade with all their equipment.

Their first night on the bleak island is very dreary. The coffee they cook is unfit to drink because the water is brackish and salty. The next day they dig new wells to obtain water which can be used for cooking and drinking. Occasionally Rebel tugboats appear in the Sound and fire a few shots at the forts, but cause no damage. A detail of men is sent a few miles up the island to build barracks, and by December 14, 1861 the unit is quartered in wooden buildings. The following is from the Miners' Journal:

Camp Winfield, Dec. 11, 1861

There are two volunteer regiments and a few regular troops here, in the fort. We have enough to keep our enemies at bay. They show themselves sometimes, but don't come within gun shot, and a few shells are enough to send them on the back track. Our boys are, with a very few exceptions, enjoying good health, and progressing in the drill.

The weather, since our arrival here, has been delightful; we have had but two showers since the 12th of November. Some nights have been very cold, and others quite summer like. Drills and dress parade are suspended at present, while we are building barracks for winter quarters. They will be fine quarters when completed for soldiers to live in. Each company will have its own house. With three rows of bunks. We are also building a fort, which will be called Fort Williams. We are hard at work every day, fixing up the camp around the fort, some are shoveling sand, some carrying boards, some doing carpenter work, and others rafting lumber. The water is better here than it was at Fort Clark, and the camp is very much more pleasant.

Yours truly, Benj. G. Otto

The Company Commander, Captain Daniel Nagle, is promoted to Major and transferred to Regimental Headquarters. At Hatteras Inlet the Company presents him a sword, inscribed as follows:

MAJOR DANIEL NAGLE

By the members of Co. D, 48th Regiment, Penn. Vols., Hatteras Inlet, N.C., December 25th, 1861, as a mark of their esteem for their former Commander.

Newberne

On March 10, 1862 the Regiment is ordered to accompany General Burnside's expedition to capture Newberne, North Carolina, and they depart on the steamer *Peabody*. Although the Regiment does not fire a shot in the action to reduce the Rebel stronghold, they do carry ammunition for miles through the sand to keep the troops that are engaged well supplied with cartridges. General Burnside is so impressed with their service in this capacity that he orders Newberne to be inscribed on the Regimental colors. Soon after this expedition they exchange their Harper's Ferry muskets for Enfield rifles.

The following article was published in the Miner's Journal in June of 1862:

Charles Arndt, a private of Co. "D", 48th P.V., is quite an illustration of what is being done by some of the older citizens of the Union. "Charley," as he is familiarly termed by the boys, is sixty-seven years of age, and is quite an active man, having never missed a day's duty while in the service. He says he can stand as much as one-half of the young men. He is a native of Germany, but has resided in the State of Pennsylvania for the last twenty-one years. He has seen service in the German army, having been in the cavalry branch of the service for seven years. He has been blessed with good health all his life, never needing the advice of a physician. Mr. Arndt lives in the vicinity of Ashland, Schuylkill County, and says he has warm blood tingling in his veins, and is willing to sacrifice his all for a free government like ours and to do his very utmost to preserve the old flag that has been trampled upon by traitorous rebels. He is a fine old gentleman, scholar and soldier, and stands high in the estimation of the men of the Regiment.

They unit goes to Newport News, Virginia, reaching that place on July 9, 1862. They depart Camp Lincoln at Newport News on August 2, 1862 aboard a steamer for Fredericksburg, Virginia. On the way a member of the Company committed suicide by shooting himself.

At Aquia Creek on the Potomac River they disembark, taking a freight train to Falmouth, which is just across the Rappahannock River from Fredericksburg, where they camp. On the evening of August 12, 1862 they begin a march over very muddy roads. The march is easy because they are in light marching order, having left their tents in storage at Aquia Creek. When they arrive at Bealton Station on the Orange and Alexandria Railroad they load on to freight cars for Culpeper Court House, arriving there too late to join in the battle at Cedar Mountain.

About this time General John Pope issues orders that the troops should subsist on the country and the soldiers take great liberties in doing so. The troops make most of the turkeys, chickens, geese, sheep, pigs, calves, potatoes, and cabbage disappear, and they are eating very well. However, the nights are very cold and the men really miss the tents they left behind at Fredericksburg.

On the night of August 18, 1862 they receive orders to quietly leave camp, because the position they are currently in is becoming dangerous. They march all night long, and the next day, passing through Stevensburg, stopping only for a few minutes for dinner. At one point during the night march they pass between Rebel outposts and their main column. The men secure their equipment and accoutrements so as not to make any noise, load their rifles, and pass by silently. They cross the Rappahannock River at Kelly's Ford and camp on its banks at a place called Whitleyville. Here they camp in a large wheat field, making themselves houses and beds from the stacked wheat.

On the morning of August 20, 1862 the artillery shells the woods on the opposite side of the river. The men stay in line of battle all day and late into the night. On the morning of the 21st they march without having breakfast to Rappahannock Station, where they eat both breakfast and dinner together. Here they support the artillery as it rains very hard, continuing into the night.

The following morning on the August 22 they start the march very early, continuing all day and late into the night on roads ankle deep with mud. It is very hard for the artillery and wagons to travel through the mud and the soldiers assist them in moving during the night. They halt twice to cook rations. The first halt they have nothing to cook, and the second halt doesn't give them enough time to cook the chickens they have borrowed along the route. At White Sulphur Springs the Confederate artillery fires on them from the hills on the other side of the river. They are shelled quite briskly until the Union batteries fire back, forcing the Rebel batteries to limber up and leave the area.

Second Bull Run

At Manassas Junction they arrive just as the Rebels depart, with rail cars burning from the Confederates hasty retreat. The unit moves to some high ground and is ordered to un-sling their knapsacks, which they will never see again because soon after moving the Rebels occupy that portion of the field. They now pass through a battery that is busy shelling some woods to their front. As they pass through and beyond this battery, the shells from the guns whistle over their heads, causing them to jump for fear of being hit by one of the shells.

It is now discovered that the rebels have moved in on the Regiment's left rear. They are ordered to move to their right rear to avoid being surrounded. However, some of the men get lost in the woods, move to the left, and are captured by the Confederates. The 48th Pennsylvania Regiment is part of the 1st Brigade, 2nd Division, IX Corps at this time.

On August 29, 1862 at about 3:00 PM the Regiment is formed, along with the 6th New Hampshire and 2nd Maryland into a line of battle. They march across an open field and into the woods, all the time through a very heavy fire from Rebel infantry. They reach an old abandoned railroad cut and are busily engaged with the Confederate troops to their front, when suddenly heavy firing erupts to their left and rear.

At first the men think it is coming from other Union forces, so they display the colors more clearly. But this only increases the hail of lead coming at them and now seeing they are partially surrounded, receive orders to fall back. At first the line moves slowly and orderly, but it is soon evident that they are flanked. Men begin to drop dead and wounded fall all around. As the Rebels appear closer the line finally breaks and the men flee in confusion to the woods, where they again form. By the time the regiment is reformed it is dark, and the field becomes quiet.

Early the next morning, August 30, the battle resumes. They are ordered to the left of the position of the previous day and remain there all day without becoming heavily engaged, although under fire the entire time. The men lay flat on the ground in front of a Union battery, supporting it in case the Rebels attack the guns. This exposed position is a very trying one, since the men are exposed to the shelling from rebel batteries, and also in danger from bad shells from our guns.

During the afternoon the battle is terrific, charge and counter-charge until towards evening, when the Union lines are broken and the field won by the Confederates. The Regiment is ordered into some dense woods and remains there until 9:00 PM, when they leave the field in good order. They ford Bull Run and reach Centreville, Virginia on the morning of August 31, 1862 in a heavy rain storm.

Up to this time they had 16 successive days of hard campaigning on short rations, without tents, and had been living in the open since leaving Falmouth on August 12. They were a pretty rough looking bunch of soldiers. The Company lost many men during the fighting at Bull Run, to include eight wounded and eleven missing in action. At Centreville they exchange places on the picket line with the 96th Pennsylvania Volunteer Infantry Regiment.

It is now discovered after the Union repulse at Bull Run that the Confederates intend to move themselves between the Union position at Centreville and Washington. The division the unit is part of moves to prevent this from happening, and a sharp fight ensues at Chantilly.

The fighting begins at 5:00 PM on September 1, 1862 at Chantilly. The Regiment forms on the right of the Brigade, which occupies the far right of the entire line of battle. It is exposed to heavy fire during the engagement, but luckily escapes with only a few casualties. The battle ends amidst rain and darkness, and ends as a victory for the Union because the Rebel plans are entirely upset.

The Union Army now falls back to Washington. The 48th Regiment is stationed for part of a day at Fairfax Court House to prevent straggling. The march of 13 miles is made without halting to rest. Their condition is shocking. The men are hungry, footsore, almost starving, and so dirty that it is almost impossible to recognize them as soldiers. However, a few days accomplish wonders. They are given new clothes, throwing away all of their old and tattered uniforms. Shelter tents are also furnished now, the first they have used.

They soon begin on the Maryland campaign. Marching rapidly they pass through Washington, Leesboro, Brookville, Haymarket, Kemptown, and Frederick City, reaching Middletown, Maryland on September 13, 1862.

South Mountain

After passing Middletown they proceed up the road leading to Fox's Pass. When they near the top of the mountain they turn left off of the road and into a corn field. Now they advance in a line of battle through some woods until reaching a low rail fence. They are positioned on the right of the Brigade and here begin a brisk exchange of fire with the Rebels, and soon exhaust their 40 rounds of ammunition. Fortunately the losses are light because of the protected position the unit held.

Sometime during the night the Confederate force retreats. In the morning when the Company passes over the ground previously occupied by the Rebels, they find a lane immediately in their front that is full of dead rebels. The dead are piled two and three deep in the lane. One Confederate soldier is found hanging across a fence, an arm and a leg on either side and riddled with bullets. In a log house they find another dead rebel in a sitting pose with his eye pressed against a chink between the logs, a bullet through his head. A burial detail is formed to bury the dead because the hot weather tends to make the bodies unfit to handle within a few hours. The Company suffers one man wounded in this engagement.

Antietam

The Battle of Antietam is fought on Wednesday, September 17, 1862, and made the small town of Sharpsburg, Maryland unforgettable in our national history. It is situated on the Antietam Creek. General Burnside is ordered to take the stone bridge that crosses the creek in a deep ravine. The Brigade is formed in a corn field near the creek and a little below the bridge, and receives the order to take the bridge.

The hill on the other side of the creek is very steep. Too steep to be ascended by horse, and must be literally climbed to be surmounted. The roadway on the other side of the bridge turns abruptly to the right and the left, and rises gradually along the hillside in both directions. On this steep hill and commanding the bridge is a Confederate battery, stone walls, rifle pits and earthworks filled with rebel infantry.

The Union line now advances, exposed to a withering fire from the rebel infantry and artillery form the heights on the other side of the creek. They push on until the 2nd Maryland Infantry Regiment reaches the bridge. At this point the men are stopped by the intense and fearfully destructive fire and lay down. Finding that there is no escape from this obstacle, they shift to the right and gain some cover opposite the bridge. In the meantime, the 2nd Maryland has cleared the roadway and carried the bridge. The 48th Pennsylvania now rushes across the bridge and takes the road to the left and captures a large number of prisoners. The Rebels had exhausted their ammunition, but still held the hill against every assault. They eventually make it to the top of the hill and stop there. The Company losses one man killed and eight wounded during the battle.

On September 26, 1862 they pack up and march two miles to their new camp. On October 3 President Lincoln and General McClellan review the troops near Sharpsburg. On October 7 they march to Harper's Ferry, where they stay until October 27, when in a heavy rain and wind storm start on the next campaign.

They cross the Potomac River on pontoon bridges at Berlin, Maryland, and go into camp at Lovettsville, Virginia. Soon again they are on the march, passing through Union, Bloomfield, and Upperville, Virginia, and camp at Oak Hill Station on the night of November 5, 1862. On November 9 they reach Amisville and reinforce the cavalry who are skirmishing with the rebels. The next morning the Confederates fire on the men, and the unit advances, driving them back. At 1:00 AM on November 10 they start a march to Sulphur Springs. They are very short on rations with very little to eat but persimmons, and some corn feed meant for the mules. They are short of rations for several days before finally receiving some bread.

On November 15, 1862 the Rebel artillery fires upon the men from the south side of the Rappahannock River. The Confederate artillery fire falls into the wagon train, killing and wounding many men until the Union batteries get into position and silence the Rebel guns. This is the very same spot where, during the previous August, they received a similar warm reception from the Rebels. After two days of marching they reach Falmouth, Virginia on November 19, opposite the city of Fredericksburg. Here it is expected that pontoon bridges will be ready for them to cross the river and occupy the city. But there are no boats to make a bridge, and no effort is being made.

Fredericksburg

Finally on December 12, 1862 they cross the river and occupy the city all that day and night. The Rebel shells are exploding all around them while they occupy this position, and some men are hit. On December 13 they are ordered to make an attack at 2:00 PM.

They advance and then halt, lying flat on their stomachs behind a frame house and long fence, while grape and canister artillery rounds are fired at them by the Rebels. They now move slightly to the left of the house and rush forward for some shelter under the brow of a slight rise in the ground. Here their advance is stopped by a large group of soldiers from other units also seeking to use this sheltered position. Here they remain, sniping and picking off officers and gunners in the rebel batteries until nightfall, when they withdraw under the cover of darkness.

Then marching a short distance to the right until they reach a position opposite of Marye's Heights, they advance in line of battle. Their objective is to occupy the high point of a knoll south of the railroad cut. Their right rests near a small house, and in front of the steepest part of Marye's Heights. Ten men from each company are detailed to pick off the rebel artillerymen immediately in their front, which are sweeping the Union ranks with deadly effect.

All efforts to dislodge the Confederates are unsuccessful, and the Union losses are very heavy. Night finally puts an end to the fight, and having exhausted all of their ammunition, the Regiment is relieved by the 12th Rhode Island Infantry Regiment, and they march back into the town. The men are soon asleep in the streets of the town, completely exhausted after ten hours of continuous fighting.

On December 15, 1862 the men are busy building rifle pits on the edge of the city. Later that night they quietly leave the city by the same route used coming into the town. The pontoon bridges have been covered with brush and dirt to prevent the Rebels from hearing their movement across them. After all troops are safely across the river, the pontoon bridges are removed and the men settle back into their old camp on the heights above Falmouth. The Company losses two men killed and two wounded during the battle.

The unit is involved next in "Burnside's Stuck in the Mud" campaign during January of 1863. It was a complete disaster and they got nowhere. It was very cold with frequent severe snow storms, and the troops suffered considerably. The Company held drills almost every day just to keep warm. At this time the Regiment received orders transferring it to the Department of Ohio Theater of Operations.

On February 6, 1863 they receive orders to move to Newport News, Virginia. They travel by rail in freight cars to Aquia Landing on the Potomac River, where they board the *US Steamer North America*, remaining at the wharf all night. At 5:00 AM they proceed down the river and into the Chesapeake Bay, and anchor at Fortress Monroe at nightfall. The next morning they sail again and arrive at Newport News and go into camp. From the 15th through the 23rd it rains almost every day, and since the men are living in shelter tents, their living conditions are not very pleasant or comfortable. On the 25th they receive some wedge tents which are much more comfortable.

On February 25, 1863 the 2nd Division, which the unit is part of, is sent by the transport *John A. Warner* to Baltimore. They remain aboard the steamer until early the next day when they are put ashore. They now march to the Northern Central Depot, taking the railroad through York, Harrisburg, and Altoona to Pittsburgh. While passing through Harrisburg, the temptation to go home for a few days is so strong that a few soldiers take "leave" to visit their folks back home.

When they arrive in Pittsburgh the citizens have prepared a huge dinner for them, and likewise in Cincinnati, where they are treated to an elegant meal. At Cincinnati they cross the Ohio River on the boat *Queen City* to Covington, Kentucky. There they board a train for an all night long ride to Lexington, Kentucky. On April 1, 1863 they go into camp near the fair grounds. They receive four months back pay and the boys go into town for some fun and relaxation, with some ending up in jail for several days.

The Regiment is detailed in the city as the provost guard. The men are quartered in comfortable wooden buildings, but on April 13 they are moved to an abandoned hemp warehouse just on the outskirts of the city. The change was a good one because it kept the men from frequenting the saloons as often. Lexington was a very appealing city that contained many people loyal to the Union cause, and the units stay there is very pleasant.

Near the end of April 1863 General Ulysses S. Grant was active in the Vicksburg, Mississippi area, and sent for the IX Corps as reinforcements. On April 30 the unit receives the dreaded order to leave Lexington the next morning, and on May 1 the Regiment is relieved by the 1st East Tennessee Regiment. While this is taking place the citizens of Lexington draw up a petition to keep the 48th Regiment in the city as the provost guard and take the petition to General Burnside in Cincinnati. The following day the 48th relieves the 1st East Tennessee, making our men very happy to be staying.

Their duties consisted of guarding the railroad stations, ordnance depots, jails, and patrolling the city to maintain order. They perform their duties very well as is evidenced by the citizens petition to keep them there. The men love this duty because there is plenty to eat, very little hard duty, and amusements of all kinds to keep them healthy and happy.

Other then a scare in July of 1863 because of some rebels operating in Kentucky, their stay is uneventful. On September 8, 1863 they receive orders to leave Lexington and join the 9th Corps, which had just returned from the capture of Vicksburg and was on its way to East Tennessee. They are relieved on September 10 and take the railroad to Nicholasville, Kentucky, and from there march to Camp Parke. As the regiment is leaving Lexington the entire town turns out to bid them farewell. A band accompanies the regiment as it parades out of town to the tune of Auld Lang Syne, while the girls wave handkerchiefs and cry sentimentally. Some of the soldiers said it was harder leaving Lexington then it was leaving home.

On September 12, 1863 they reach Camp Dick Robinson amidst a very heavy rain storm. Now they are marching every day, and by the time they reach Knoxville, Tennessee on September 28, they have marched for 19 days and covered 221 miles. They remain in Knoxville until the morning of October 4. At Noon they load into railroad cars and go to Morristown where they camp for the night. The following morning they march to Lick Creek and remain there until October 10, on which day they move to Blue Springs, where they find rebels.

They immediately go forward at the double quick. Coming upon some woods they charge and drive the Rebels back, killing and wounding quite a number and also taking prisoners. Having driven the Confederates from the field, and with the area being hilly and thickly wooded and night falling, all action halts for the time.

The next morning the Union pickets advance and find that the Rebels have left during the night. A pursuit is ordered immediately and the Regiment follows the rebels for 20 miles, stopping to rest just twice for a few minutes. This is probably the fastest marching the regiment ever experienced. At night they go into camp a few miles above Reamtown, and since they could not catch the rebels, they are ordered back to Knoxville. They march back to Morristown and take the railroad to Knoxville, having in 11 days marched over 70 miles and riding the train for another 90 miles.

Siege of Knoxville

On October 22, 1863 they are sent by rail to Loudon, below Knoxville, and remain there until the 28th. There it is learned that Confederate General Longstreet and a large force is moving from Chattanooga to attempt to capture General Burnside's entire army. The Confederate forces here outnumber the Union troops by a 3 to 1 ratio.

Orders are given to fall back to Knoxville. On the morning of October 27, 1863 some rebels occupy Louden on the south side of the river as our forces withdraw upon their approach. The Union forces remove the pontoon bridge across the river, and run at full speed a train engine and four freight cars into the river. This is at a location where a bridge had been destroyed and is done to prevent them from falling into rebel hands.

On the morning of October 28 they continue to fall back towards Knoxville, and reach Lenoir Station the following day. Here they remain in camp until November 14, awaiting the movements of the Confederates, and then moving back to Loudon on November 15. This day they start skirmishing with the rebels, with orders to hold and delay them as long as possible. This is required because the roads are in such bad condition due to the heavy and sustained rains, that the artillery and wagon trains are having a difficult time in moving. About 6:00 PM the unit reaches Lenoir, and from there they march by night and fight by day.

At Campbell's Station the supply and ammunition trains are very slow moving over the muddy roads. The Rebels seeing this press forward and a line of battle is formed to check their advance until the supply trains are a safe distance away. The fighting continues the entire day and only ends when darkness makes it impossible to distinguish friend from foe.

The Union losses are slight and the retreat resumes after dark, and they reach Knoxville on the morning of November 17, 1863. Upon arriving at the city they immediately begin to fortify the place, and soon the city is encircled with a strong line of earthworks. They remain under siege until December 5, 1863, when General Sherman arrives with a corps and forces the Rebels to flee into Virginia.

During the unit's encampment at Blaine's Cross Roads from December 7, 1863 to January 13, 1864, the condition of the men is awful. Most likely no other troops in the Union Army during the entire war, except for prisoners of war, suffered so much from the lack of supplies. Only two ears of corn or eight ounces of flour generally make up the daily ration for a man. Occasionally, when a drove of cattle shows up, they are quickly slaughtered for the meat. Other then that the only variety in their diet came from a little hard tack and some salted meats.

Most of the men in the wintry camp are tent-less, blanket-less, many without overcoats, and only a few with a change of underclothing. For shelter they use two heavy logs placed slightly apart, which support inclined fence rails that are thickly covered with pine boughs. Underneath the shelter they use additional pine boughs for bedding. To keep warm at night they lay heavy logs in front of the shelter forming a fire-bed, which is kept burning by one soldier while the others sleep.

The lack of clothing and the inability to even change clothing is a great annoyance to the men. There is no soap in the camp and many of the men try to wash their clothing in the mountain streams using clay as a substitute, but with poor results. Their feet are in no better condition than the rest of their bodies, and many soldiers have only cloth to wrap around their feet. When rawhide is available, they make moccasins to protect their feet from the cold. Yet only a few complain, since it was useless to complain because there was nothing better in sight.

Now they begin the long march back to Hickman Bridge in their awful condition. They march for nine days, covering 20 miles a day, over rough roads that are frozen at night and covered with slushy snow during the day. Hope alone sustains the men as they trudge along, footsore, hungry, and tired. Dead mules, broken down wagons and complete desolation mark every mile.

Nowhere along the road are fence rails or other wood suitable for making a fire, because it has all been used up by the passing troops. There is little wood for cooking fires and little food to cook. Only with great effort do they find enough wood to cook their coffee. In their condition it is impossible for the Regiment to move as a cohesive unit. At times they are strung out on the road for miles, and many men straggle into camp hours after the main body.

When they finally reach Lexington, Kentucky, the citizens greet them warmly. The men are glad to see a familiar place, and here they find plenty of food, shelter and supplies. Through all of this many of the men reenlisted on January 1, 1864.

On January 25, 1864 they start the long journey home. All along the route in Pennsylvania people turn out to welcome them home. They arrive in Pottsville on February 3, 1864. When they reach Pottsville they march in a parade through town, and afterwards they are presented with a flag and a fine meal. After this the ranks are broken and each soldier departs for his home and loved ones.

The mining areas of Pennsylvania were supposed to be full of strong "Copperhead" sentiment. Coal miners demonstrated against the draft so violently in some cases that troops had to be sent in to keep order, but the 48th had no trouble in getting new recruits to fill its ranks. It mustered more than 400 enlisted men for duty, and about one fourth of these were coal miners.

Their furlough ends on March 4, 1864 and the Regiment assemble in Pottsville on the 5th to go to the front again. Their ranks now full again with new recruits enlisted during the furlough, they depart on March 14. On March 18 they reach Annapolis, Maryland and go into camp at Camp Parole, assigned to the 1st Brigade, 2nd Division, 9th Corps, still under the command of General Ambrose Burnside. While in this camp they exchange the Enfield rifles for the more modern and better Springfield rifle.

When in camp a soldier tends to make things as comfortable as possible, and will collect everything imaginable to make his life more enjoyable. When camp is broken he does not want to let anything behind, believing he cannot get along without these luxuries. He thinks he can carry it all, and will at least try to take all of his possessions.

Usually at the start he has his rifle, a cartridge box with 40 rounds of ammunition, cap box, body belt and bayonet scabbard, a canteen full of water, haversack with five days rations, tin cup strapped to the haversack, and a frying pan or skillet thrown over his knapsack. The knapsack at the least holds one pair of socks, one pair of drawers, a few handkerchiefs, needles and thread, writing materials, sometimes a Bible, overcoat, dog tent, gum blanket, and wool blanket, and a picture or two of family members.

Now, after marching for five or more miles in the hot sun, he begins to wonder what items he can live without, because the load is feeling very heavy. The days are hardly cold enough for the need of an overcoat, and except for guard duty at night, he can probably borrow one or do without, and he tosses his away. His load feels lighter now, and he marches along very nicely for the next four or five miles. But soon it becomes heavy again, so he decides to throw his blanket away or maybe cut it in half. But if the march continues at length, sometimes the entire knapsack is discarded with all its contents, except for a change of clothing, dog tent, and gum blanket. These he makes into a roll and slings over his shoulder. This is called light marching order, and most remain this way as long as hard campaigning endures.

On April 25, 1864 they are reviewed by President Lincoln. On April 28 they march through Centreville and Manassas Junction to Bristoe Station on the Orange and Alexandria Railroad, a distance of 14 miles. Here they stay in camp until May 4, 1864.

The Wilderness

The Regiment crosses the Rapidan River on May 5, 1864. Here about 200 men are sent to the right of the Army and deploy as skirmishers, fighting with the Rebels for most of the day, and losing some men killed and wounded. About 5:00 PM the Regiment goes into line of battle and becomes engaged just as night falls.

Heavy firing occurs all day on May 6, with the Regiment engaged for most of the day under infantry fire, and losing heavily. On May 7 there is little fighting and much moving from position to position. The woods are burning from the effects of the previous day's battle, and many wounded men are burned to death before they can be rescued. The unit did not become actively engaged on the 8th or 9th, and is held in reserve on the 10th, but under heavy artillery fire.

Spottsylvania

On May 12, 1864 they move to the left of Hancock's Corps, where they form into line of battle on top of a hill. In their front is an open field and swamp through which a small creek runs. Beyond this is another hill where the Rebels are strongly entrenched. On the left is a thick wood which extends past the swamp to a line held by the Confederates.

As the fog lifts, a regiment of rebels is discovered occupying a pit formed by the banks of the creek. The left of the Brigade is pushed forward into the woods, cutting off the Rebels route of retreat. The Rebels only route of escape is by the open field in the Union front, which, if attempted, would mean certain destruction. The Rebels make a desperate attack to drive the Union forces out of their position, but it is held using very heavy infantry and artillery fire.

During this attempt the Regiment captures 200 prisoners of Gordon's Division. In the afternoon the Regiment assaults the Rebel line, charging forward to the swamp, but having no support and under a galling fire, moves off to the left and returns to its former position.

The next few days are spent in this position and under fire the entire time, but with no major engagements taking place until May 18, 1864. Early in the morning of the 18th the 2nd Division makes a charge upon the rebel defensive line. The first line is taken without much loss, but the second line is protected with heavy abatis and cannot be taken. On this day they also bury 80 rebels in the swamp where they had fought on May 12. On May 19 the Confederates attempt to break through the right. The firing is very heavy and additional troops are quickly sent to strengthen the Union position, which is held and the rebels repulsed. The unit losses one man killed, 15 wounded, and two missing in action.

The following is from the Miners' Journal:

SPOTTSYLVANIA C.H., MAY 15th, 1864

DEAR SIR: I send you a list of the casualties in the 48th P.V. from the 6th of May to this date. In the Battle of the Wilderness the regiment was hotly engaged on the 6th, and skirmished in the front on the 7th. On the 6th, 350 men including nearly all the veterans, skirmished all day on the right, and the rest of the regiment moved with the main portion of the 9th Corps, and were hotly engaged in the center. The rebel army having fallen back, the 9th Corps was moved to Chancellorsville on the 8th. The 48th was not again engaged until the 12th, when our division advanced towards Spottsylvania on the evening of the 11th, but the battle was not begun until the morning of the 12th. We fought all day, and our regiment having caught three Georgia regiments in a little hollow, with rising ground behind them, which prevented them from retreating, completely annihilated them. We took over two hundred prisoners. One squad of them, which I sent to the rear under Lieut. Bowen, amounted to forty eight. Afterwards all the troops of the division were ordered to charge, and the 48th advanced in excellent style through an open, marshy ground under heavy fire, but the troops on both flanks giving way, the regiment was moved by the left flank into a ravine in the woods and shielded from the destructive fire of the enemy. Our loss has been heavy, but the 48th has behaved well, and in the action of the 12th, owing to our position on the brow of the hill, five rebels were killed, wounded or taken prisoner for every man lost by us. Since the 12th, a few men have been wounded by sharpshooters and we still remain on the front line. We have to mourn the loss of many brave men, and one of the best and bravest officers is Lieutenant Henry Jackson.

Yours, etc.
HENRY PLEASANTS

On May 21, 1864 they again resume the march which continues all day and night, and also the same on the 22nd. On May 23 a hard fight is going on in their front. They march until 11:00 PM and camp on the banks of the North Anna River. On May 24 they cross the river and attack the rebel works, but cannot dislodge them.

At 9:00 PM on May 26 they are withdrawn and march back the same route taken to get to this point. They march all day long and up till 11:00 PM on May 27. On May 28 they conduct a forced march and cross the Pamunkey River. Here they run into some enemy skirmishers, which they drive back to the rebel main line. On the 30th and 31st the Regiment is engaged at Armstrong's farm and lose very heavily.

Bethesda Church

On June 3, 1864 the Battle of Bethesda Church or Totopotomy Creek is fought, with the Regiment playing a very important part. They attack and almost annihilate a rebel battery in their front, killing almost every horse belonging to it, and capturing the guns.

In no other engagement of the 48th did they expend as much ammunition as this one. Their line so close to that of the rebel battery, that the men are subjected to the bursting shells of the Union artillery. So much so, that the Union batteries are compelled to move further to the right, where they now use enfilading fire on the rebel guns. The result being, that by dusk, every rebel gun but one has been destroyed, and to finish the job one of our guns is drawn by hand around the right of the regiment and soon destroys the last remaining rebel artillery piece. Finally at nightfall the battle ceases.

Advancing on June 4, 39 dead horses and the dismounted battery, together with several hundred small arms, are found behind the rebel works, with the dead, dying and wounded laying thick all around. The Confederates had fled in haste during the night, and had tried to remove their cannons by hand. They were under such an intense fire that the Rebels had placed the bodies of their dead on top of their works for more protection.

From June 4 until June 10, 1864 the Regiment is in the vicinity of Cold Harbor and under fire the entire time. One charge is made by the Rebels against the unit, but is easily repulsed. Casualties during the period between May 15 and June 4 were three wounded.

Petersburg

On June 16, 1864, after a month of hard fighting in the Wilderness, Spottsylvania, and Cold Harbor, they cross the James River. They arrive in front of Petersburg, Virginia just in time to see the 7th New York Heavy Artillery Regiment make an unsuccessful infantry assault on the Confederate positions, losing many casualties, and also losing its colors.

About two hours later the 48th is thrown forward in front of the same rebel position to, as they thought, assault the same but instead, they are led past the position. They move down to the bed of a creek until they come to a point on the left, and at an angle to the Rebel line. By this time darkness has fallen, and they find themselves in an old line of rebel works captured a few days earlier. They cannot see the Rebel position in the dark, but they know they are very close.

At daybreak on June 17 the 48th Pennsylvania and the 36th Massachusetts Infantry Regiments cross a swamp in single file, in complete silence, and with a quick movement carry the Confederate position in front of them. It is a complete surprise, and the Rebels are driven back in confusion, with the Union force capturing four pieces of artillery and 600 prisoners.

In the charge on the rebel line, the Regiment captures the entire line to their front. They take more prisoners then there are men in the 48th, and also capture the colors of the 44th Tennessee Regiment, and recover the colors of the 7th New York which had been lost the day before. The victory is a complete success, and just after daylight another advance is made. They capture two brass field pieces along with their gun crews. The Company casualties for the past two days include six wounded.

The unit spends June 19, 1864 strengthening their position, and between then and June 27 are involved in skirmishing. On June 28 they begin something that will be forever recalled in the chronicles of military history. This would be the digging of a tunnel from the Union position to a position underneath the Confederate defensive line, and the resulting battle called the "Battle of the Crater."

There was a broad ravine running from north to south between the opposing lines, and along the bottom was a small brook and what remained of the Norfolk and Petersburg Railroad. On the western crest, which was the side facing the Confederates is a line of Union entrenchments, with the center of this line being held by the 48th Pennsylvania Volunteer Infantry Regiment.

This trench is the high-water mark for the 9th Corps and the extreme limit of advance. A place where tired men having fired all of their ammunition, lay in the dark building breastworks out of earth scooped up with bayonets, tin plates, and bare hands. Since the fight to take this line, it has been made very strong. There now is a deep trench with a high parapet facing the rebels, and out in front a tangle of abatis.

A quarter of a mile to the rear on the eastern side of the crest of the ravine are gun pits, with artillery strategically placed to stop any Rebel attacks that might attempt to storm the infantry position. The slope just behind the trench offers protection from rebel fire, and to make moving to the rear safer is a deep covered passage. This left the trench at almost a right angle, crossed the ravine, and ended behind the artillery positions.

On the Confederate side things are much the same. The trench is deep and strong at a point directly opposite of the 48th, with brass cannons emplaced. Like the Federals, the Confederates have abatis out front, covered ways leading to their rear, and artillery posted to break up any attacks. Five hundred yards behind the Rebel trench the ground rises up to a long, round ridge, and just over this ridge is the Jerusalem Plank Road. This road had once been an undefended avenue leading into Petersburg, but not is heavily guarded.

As far as the men can make them, the opposing lines here are almost attack proof. The soldiers occupying both sides remain on a high state of alert. They had to, because the trenches here are closer to each other then at any other point along the front. Everyone keeps under cover, and anyone exposing himself even for a moment is immediately fired upon, and usually hit. The sharpshooters on both sides are keen, accurate, and the range is short. There are also mortars amongst the gun pits, and these are also very active.

The trenches are deep and although the men take every security precaution, holding this part of the line is very expensive in the number of lives lost. Since many of the men in the Regiment are from coal mining country, and many were coal miners before the war, they know a thing or two about digging in the earth. One day the commander of the Regiment happened to be passing along one of the trenches, and came upon a soldier who was peering through a firing slit at the rebel fortifications. The man stepped down, turned to a fellow soldier, and said, "We could blow that damned fort out of existence if we could run a mine shaft under it."

The commanding officer was Lieutenant Colonel Henry Pleasants, and that was talk he could understand because he was a mining engineer before the war. Before becoming a mining engineer he had done railroad construction work and had experience in tunneling under obstructions. Trained as a civil engineer, he had worked for the Pennsylvania Railroad in the early 1850s, and he had taken part in digging a 4,200 foot tunnel through the Alleghenies. A few years before the war, he quit the railroad for coal mining, and made his home in Schuylkill County.

He was 31 years of age now, slim, neat in appearance, with a dark complexion and bearded, and as he passed along the trench he kept thinking about what that soldier had said. A while later he goes down into a ravine to a bombproof shelter where the officers of the regiment live, and bluntly says to the officers, "That God damned fort is the only thing between us and Petersburg, and I have an idea we can blow it up!"

Soon after this, Pleasants formally passes the suggestion along to his division commander, Brigadier General Robert Potter. General Potter then sends a staff officer to see what this is all about. Pleasants takes the staff officer to a place in the trench where they have a good view of the Rebel fort. As the staff officer peers over the parapet, a Confederate sharpshooter fires, the bullet striking the officer in the face. Pleasants has him carried away and draws a rough sketch of the terrain and sends it to General Potter. A few days later General Potter sends for Pleasants and takes him back to IX Corps Headquarters to see General Burnside.

It is a very hot night, and the two officers find General Burnside sitting in his tent, coat off, and his bald head glistening in the candlelight, with a long cigar sticking out the side of his mouth. Burnside puts the young colonel at ease immediately, and listens intently as the plan is explained, as he mops beads of sweat off his forehead with a big silk bandana.

With modesty Pleasant admits to getting the idea from a chance remark made by one of his enlisted soldiers. He then goes on to explain how they could begin a tunnel on the sheltered side of the hillside, 40 or 50 yards behind their trench, where the Rebels would not be able to see what they are doing. The shaft would slant uphill, which would take care of the drainage problem, and although the tunnel would have to be more than 500 feet long, Pleasants thought he could devise a way to provide adequate ventilation.

General Burnside likes the idea and says he will take up the idea with General Meade. In the meantime he tells Pleasants to begin digging. The next day Pleasants organizes his coal miners into details, leads them to the spot on the protected side of the ravine, and puts them to work. Lacking picks, they begin digging using nothing but bayonets, but in no time at all they are underground.

Lieutenant Colonel Pleasants gets a list from each of his company commanders of all men who were actually coal miners. He then organizes these men into shifts, with Sergeant Harry Reese as the mine boss, exactly as if he were going to mine for coal. He puts them to work around the clock, seeing to it that each man gets a dram of whiskey when he is finished with his shift. Eventually picks and shovels are supplied, and although they are not the kind used in coal mining, there are plenty of blacksmiths in the IX Corps artillery units who reshape the implements. The work progresses faster then anticipated, and in short time timbers are needed to shore up the ceiling and walls.

Now Pleasants finds out that the army is letting him do his job rather than helping. Meade had promised Burnside to furnish a company of engineers and any other assistance needed, but the engineer company never materializes, and no timbers are supplied when requested. Pleasants sends a detail from the regiment down into a ravine behind the lines, and has them tear up a railroad bridge for the timber. He then discovers an abandoned saw mill four or five miles to the rear, and gets Burnside to issue a pass and to provide horses and wagons to haul the timbers. Pleasants also sends two companies back to operate the mill and cut the necessary lumber.

After a week of working at the tunnel the digging comes to halt when they hit a belt of wet clay, which causes the ceiling to sag, snapping the timbers, and nearly closing the tunnel. The men re-timber the shaft and shore up the ceiling with heavier props, and continue with their digging. Next they strike a bed of marl which has a way of turning into rock soon after being exposed to air. The soldiers amuse themselves by carving tobacco pipes out of this stuff in their spare time, but it is nasty stuff to tunnel through, and Pleasants has to increase the angle of the climb to get above it and into softer earth.

The tunnel is five feet high, four feet wide at the bottom, and roughly two and a half feet wide at the top, and is strongly timbered the entire length, including the ceiling, walls, and floor. Cutting, transporting, and getting the timber inside the mine, along with hauling out all the earth and concealing it in a ravine under bushes is very labor intensive. The work keeps requiring more and more men, and soon practically the entire Regiment is involved.

When the shaft has been dug a couple of hundred feet into the hillside, Pleasants feels it is now time to make some exact calculations about the location where the powder magazine should be placed. He requests from the engineers the instruments to make the required triangulations. The engineers laugh off his request, and a plea to Meade's headquarters is somehow lost. At last General Burnside, the only officer willing to be of any assistance, sends a wire to a friend in Washington who sends the necessary instruments.

Pleasants takes the instruments into the front lines to make his calculations; and of course the Rebel snipers are apt to shoot him while doing this. He gets around this by having six soldiers put their caps on ramrods and raising them just above the parapet. While the rebel sharpshooters pepper these caps with great accuracy and frequency, Pleasants drapes some burlap over his head and his instrument, peers over the parapet, and makes the necessary observations and calculations.

Farther and farther into the hillside the tunnel goes, and as predicted, ventilation becomes a problem, but Pleasant comes up with a solution. Close behind the tunnel, at a point just behind the main Union trench, he has a vertical shaft dug. The lower end opens into a little recess in the tunnel wall, and the upper end discharges inconspicuously into a clump of bushes.

The men then build a square tube out of boards that reaches from the mouth of the tunnel all the way to its innermost reach. A door is made by which the outer end of the tunnel can be sealed shut, leaving the open end of the wooden tube protruding out into the air. The rest is simple; close the door and build a fire in the little recess at the bottom of the vertical shaft. The smoke and heated air go up this chimney, and the resulting draft pulls the bad air out of the tunnel, and fresh air is drawn into the tunnel through the wooden tube.

On July 17, 1864, three weeks after the digging started, the inner end of the tunnel is directly beneath the Confederate redoubt. It is 20 feet underground and 510 feet from the entrance and the men in the tunnel can hear the rebel soldiers tramping around overhead. Lieutenant Colonel Pleasants now has the men dig a 75 foot shaft running across the end of the tunnel, so that the tunnel will look like a capital T with a very long shank, with the crossbar of the T running along directly beneath the Confederate defenses.

Pleasants now reports that the mine is ready to be charged with powder. However, operations have to be temporarily suspended because the Rebels have discovered that the Yankees are digging a mine, and are now sinking their own shafts trying to find its location. The Confederates luck is bad and their engineers misjudge the direction of the tunnel, and their probing comes up empty.

While the men stop working, the Rebels in underground listening posts can hear nothing, and in the end all of their efforts fail. Meanwhile, the rebel soldiers are going about their business directly above the dark tunnel, and begin to treat the whole affair as just another camp rumor. Now and then the Rebels even call across to the Union men asking when the big show is going to start.

After this pause, and with the digging and timbering complete, Pleasants has the men lay the powder charges. The men build eight open-topped wooden boxes in the lateral galleries for magazines. The powder is delivered behind the lines in 320 kegs, each keg containing 25 pounds of black powder. The men are busy day and night carrying these into the mine and pouring the charges into the magazines.

All of the magazines are connected by wooden troughs half filled with powder, and the troughs meet at a place where the gallery crosses the inner end of the main shaft. The engineers promised to supply wire and a galvanic battery to touch off the charge, but this was another promise never kept. Pleasants gets a supply of ordinary fuses, has the men splice them together, and strings the fuse back along the tunnel for about 100 feet. As a final step, they solidly pack earth into place, filling the main shaft for 38 feet from the place where it meets the lateral gallery. All that remains now is to light the outer end of the fuse.

Lieutenant Colonel Pleasants never doubts that the mine will blow a huge hole in the Confederate line. But, the only officer of any rank who really believes in it seems to have been General Burnside, and accordingly did his best to make sure the attack that would follow the explosion would be successful.

At 3:30 AM the fuse is lit, but nothing happens. Another 30 minutes go by, and then another 30 minutes on top of that, and still no explosion. Pleasants calls for Sergeant Harry Reese, the mine boss, and tells him to go into the tunnel and see what is wrong. So in goes Reese, on as dangerous and nerve racking assignment as any war could produce. He gropes forward, bent over all along the 400 feet of the dark tunnel, thinking that at any moment the earth may quake and heave and bury him alive. He gets to the fuse and traces it, finding that the spark has died at a splice. He now turns around and starts back out of the tunnel, but is met by Lieutenant Jacob Douty who is coming in at Pleasants direction with the material needed. Lieutenant Douty and Sergeant Reese make a new connection in the fuse. They now light the fuse and come out of the tunnel as fast as they can possibly travel.

At 4:45 AM it explodes. To the men along the front line it seems to occur in slow motion. First a long, deep rumble, then a swaying and swelling of the ground ahead, with the solid earth rising to form a rounded hill, everything seems very slow and gradual. Suddenly the rounded hill breaks apart, and a gush of flame and black smoke shoots upward into the sky.

The air is full of enormous chunks of earth as big as small houses, of cannons and detached artillery wheels, wrecked caissons and fluttering tents, and tumbling human bodies. There is a crash of noise like that of thunder, followed by other lesser explosions. The landscape along the firing line turns to dust and smoke and flying debris, choking and blinding the soldiers, and threatening to engulf Burnside's entire corps.

Different men witnessed it in different ways. A soldier in the 36th Massachusetts Infantry Regiment wrote that, "we witnessed a volcano and experienced an earthquake". Yet another officer standing about one-third of a mile away from the explosion recalled it as "a dull, heavy thud, not at all startling." A soldier in the 48th Pennsylvania remembered it as a magnificent spectacle, and another recalled that an artillery piece was tossed nearly over to the Union line.

The Union artillery crews had been waiting a long time and they had their eyes firmly fixed on the Confederate redoubt. They jerked their lanyards as soon as they saw the ground to begin to rise, so that the crash of their own guns rocked the air before the sound of the explosion even reached them. The concussion from the artillery was equal to the great artillery duel at Gettysburg. An overwhelming cloud of white smoke from the artillery flowed into the ravine and unto the farther crest, mixing with the hanging black dust and smoke from the mine explosion. All along the Union line the air became as dark as midnight, lit by brief stabbing flames as the shells exploded.

The troops which have been waiting to make a charge now see the hillside rising up in their faces. It seems as if this giant mass of earth is going to fall on them, and many turn and run for cover to the rear. It takes five or ten minutes before the officers can reform the men and the order to charge sounded.

The men stumble up the slope through the dust and smoke. They climb to the place where the Rebel redoubt was, and find they are peering down into a huge smoking crater. One hundred and seventy feet of the Confederate line has been obliterated. In its place is a huge abyss, 60 feet across and 30 feet deep. All around the crater, balanced on the rim and over the ground on all sides are big hunks of solid clay, broken timbers, dismounted guns, and wreckage of all kind.

At the bottom of the crater is more of the same, including many human bodies. Some rebels still living are buried up to their waists, while some only have their heads above ground. Other are buried head downwards, their legs protruding into the air. The Union soldiers' pause, stunned by this sight and then slide down into the crater begin to dig out the buried Rebels. One officer gets a squad together and they begin digging out a couple of half buried cannons.

Nothing can be seen very clearly because smoke and dust fill the air. To the rear, the Union artillery keeps up a furious bombardment, and the there is no return fire. The Confederate trenches for 300 yards on either side of the crater are empty, because the soldiers who were stationed there fled when the mine exploded. Here and there a few brave rebels begin to fire into the haze around the crater, but at least 30 minutes pass before their fire has any real effect.

Lieutenant Colonel Pleasants plan could not have possibly been more effective. Right in the center of the unconquerable Confederate defenses it created a gap 500 yards wide and all that had to be done was to march through and take the ridge. But they would have to move quickly, because the gap was not going to stay open for very long. But, at 5:00 AM on July 30, 1864, decisive victory was less then half an undefended mile away. Unfortunately, the one thing which Burnside's corps could not do that morning was to move briskly.

Initially one brigade goes down into the crater, but is more or less acting as a rescue and salvage party, and looking like a group of sight-seers. Most men run up to the rim to have a look, and the officers urge the soldiers to continue the advance. Most of the men slide down into the bottom of the crater, and soon most of Ledlie's division is jammed into the crater, and becomes an aimless mob out of control.

Now not a trace of military organization remains. Officers cannot find their soldiers and soldiers cannot find their officers. Along the farther rim of the crater, some men are trying to prepare a defensive line. The officer who had been digging up the buried cannon has some men pulling and pushing the gun up to the rim where it can be fired. But this proves to be a very difficult job since the final feet of the crater are practically vertical walls. He also has some other men searching for the rebel magazine.

Half-buried rebel soldiers are still being dug up, and some dazed Rebels prisoners are being sent to the rear. Officers are screaming themselves hoarse as they try to get the men to climb out of the crater and continue the attack, but few are paying any attention to them. Meanwhile the Confederates are quickly regaining their senses. On both the right and left flanks, Confederate regiments are forming and firing on the flanks of the attacking Union column. The precious 30 minutes in which the ridge could have been taken effortlessly has slipped away.

Potter's and Wilcox's men move out and into the empty trenches and begin to go forward, but the going is very bad. The ground beyond the trenches is a maze of bombproofs, rifle pits, covered ways, and support trenches. In many places the advance consists of jumping into a hole, scrambling out the other side, jumping into another hole, and then repeating the scramble. The rising pace of Confederate rifle fire is not making the progress any easier either.

Worse still, the Rebel artillery is now coming into action. One quarter mile north of the crater is a Rebel battery, and the gunners train their guns on the Union troops who are trying to capture the trenches. Union artillery pounds this battery mercilessly, but it is well protected, and the Confederate guns remain in action, pouring canister directly into the flank of the Union line of battle. On the other side of the crater the story is the same, with a rebel battery using enfilading fire on the Union lines from the left. This Confederate battery also draws a storm of fire from Union artillery, but there is one gun that cannot be silenced and it keeps firing canister at deadly close range.

West of the crater the Rebels place 16 cannons in line, and the Union gunners sweep the ridge with overwhelming fire. But the rebel guns are in the Jerusalem Plank Road, which is a sunken road and offers natural protection. Ten of the 16 guns are eventually destroyed, but the six that remain can not be driven off. In addition to the cannons the Rebels have mortars tucked away in protected positions beyond the crater, and these now begin to toss shells into the dense jam of Union troops.

Minute by minute the situation for the Union forces grows worse. Potter's men gain some ground on the right side of the crater, but are under tremendous fire and their battle line is slowly pushed back. Mixed elements from half a dozen different commands crawl forward a few dozen yards from the crater in a valiant attempt to reach and silence the guns on the ridge. But the Rebels have a strong second line of defense in operation now, and there just aren't enough men to break it with an attack. On the left side of the crater Wilcox's men can do nothing but stay in the captured trench and keep up an effective rifle fire.

The first attack has failed, and the failure is both unbelievable and lasting. What should have been easily accomplished by 5:00 AM has become a matter of great difficulty by 6:00 AM, and by 7:00 AM is virtually impossible. The fighting now is just one more tedious attempt to capture entrenched positions. Most of the men in the attacking force know this perfectly well now, and they hug the ground.

For all intents and purposes the battle is already lost. All over except for the killing. Hundreds of Union soldiers are crammed inside the crater, and most of those are down at the bottom where they cannot contribute to the fighting. The men up along the rim are standing on a slope so steep that after he fires his rifle he has to turn around, dig in his heels and brace his back against the dirt in order to reload.

Confederate mortars really have the range now and are dropping shells into the crater on the helpless mob that they cannot miss. The men who did escape the crater alive remember later the horrible debris of severed limbs and heads flying through the air after each explosion. The Sun is high in the sky now and beats down upon the men relentlessly with heat. It is terribly magnified in the steaming crater, and thirst seems to be a worse foe then the Rebels.

Somehow, and finally long after Noon it ends. Through it all Pleasants has been standing on the parapet of a battery where he watches the attack. He storms and swears furiously, telling General Burnside's that "he had nothing but damned cowards in his brigade commanders!" One of the soldiers in the 48th Pennsylvania recorded that, "Pleasants was awful mad when he saw how things were going on." A soldier in the 48th wrote to his sister, "I expected to write you of one of the most glorious victories that was ever won by this army, but instead of a victory I have to write about the greatest shame and disgrace that ever happened to us. The people at home may look at it as nothing but a mere defeat, but I look at it as a disgrace to our corps."

Pegram's Farm

On September 30, 1864 the battle of Pegram's Farm takes place. At the opening of the battle the Regiment is held in reserve. As the fight progresses the Brigade line is broken, which almost results in the capture of the entire Regiment. By some skillful maneuvering the Regiment preserves its cohesiveness, even though its lines are broken through three times by frightened troops from other units. The Company loses one man wounded and four missing in action during this engagement.

On October 14, 1864 the entire Division is ordered to witness the execution, by firing squad, of a deserter from the 2nd Maryland Infantry Regiment. The Division forms in an open square, and at 9:00 AM the prisoner is brought out. The condemned soldier is accompanied by a chaplain, and a band playing a funeral march leads the procession. Following the band is a formation of guards, then the prisoner, four men carrying the coffin, and finally another formation of soldiers. This procession marches all around the inside of the square formed by the Division to the open end where a grave has been dug.

Here the band is dismissed and the coffin placed at the open grave. The Provost Marshall now reads the charges, findings, and sentence to the prisoner. The prisoner is left with the Chaplain, who seats him upon the coffin, blindfolds his eyes, says a prayer with the prisoner, and finally shakes his hand before departing. The firing squad of 12 men with 11 rifles loaded with live ammunition, and one with a blank cartridge comes forward. The reason for having one rifle loaded with a blank cartridge was, so that each of the men on the firing squad might be able to comfort himself with the thought that his was the blank. The Officer-In-Charge gives the command to fire and it is over. The entire Division then marches past so that all must see the body.

On October 27, 1864 the unit is involved in a fierce fight at Hatcher's Run, in which the Union forces are repulsed. The troops are then ordered back to Pegram's Farm. November 29, 1864 finds the unit stationed at Fort Sedgwick, which is also called Fort Hell because of the very warm climate.

The fort is a large and strongly built structure, with bombproofs erected to protect the soldiers. These excavations are seven to nine feet deep into the earth, covered with heavy logs, and tree boughs on top of that, and three to seven feet of earth. The Rebels have two forts opposite to the Union fort and these forts are named Mahone and Damnation.

In Fort Damnation the Rebels have two batteries of 10-inch and 12-inch mortars. The forts are only a few hundred yards apart, and the picket lines are a mere 80 yards from each other. An unofficial treaty is made between the pickets on both sides that they will not fire on each other during daylight. The treaty was faithfully kept by both sides, and both Union and Rebel soldiers frequently talked with each other, and even traded goods back and forth.

On a clear day the mortar projectiles could be clearly seen from the moment they left the mortar. If the men could not see it plainly as it rose into the air, the odd wobbling sound it produced made it easy to locate on its path, and the men would speculate to how close it would come to them. A direct hit would go right through a bombproof. The bombproofs were useful at night for sleeping purposes, and during the day to protect the soldiers from the fragments of bursting shells.

On December 19, 1864 the unit is shelled very hard all afternoon. A large shell exploded in one of the Company's bombproofs, wounding quite a number of the men, one of them being George Hartz, who died the following day. On January 2, 1865 they are again shelled heavily, wounding a number of men, and several members of the 96th Pennsylvania Infantry Regiment who are visiting. On March 9, 1865 the unit is relieved of duty at Fort Sedgwick by the 35th Massachusetts Infantry, and goes into camp in the rear of the lines.

On March 31 and April 1, 1865 hard fighting takes place. The unit has no part in the fighting on these two days. On the morning of April 2nd their time has come, and at daylight they advance upon the Rebel Fort Mahone. The Union batteries open fire to cover the advance of the infantry. The Rebel guns vigorously reply, and the bombardment is tremendous. The sight is one rarely seen by the men. From hundreds of cannons, field guns, and mortars came a stream of living fire as the shells screamed through the air, the noise deafening.

The 48th Regiment leads the assault from Fort Sedgwick. Each column is accompanied by pioneers with axes to cut away the abattis. The troops are eager to avenge the repulse at the crater eight months earlier and fight as if possessed by demons. In the center of a terrible storm of grape and canister shot, and rifle fire, they push forward, charging without flinching, and reach the inside of the Confederate line. The Company loses eight men wounded and one missing in action during the assault.

The Rebels begin to flee now and the Union army takes pursuit. On the night of April 4, 1865 they camp at Sutherland, and on the 5th they pass Fords and Wellville and camp near Nottoway Court House.

On April 7 they reach Farmville where they escort Confederate Generals Ewell, Kershaw, Curtis, and a few other notable names of the Confederate army, along with 8,000 captured rebel prisoners. They are escorted to Burkeville Junction, where while the men are guarding the prisoners on the morning of April 10, 1865, hear the joyful news of the surrender of General Lee and the Confederate forces the previous day.

The news creates much enthusiasm among the troops. Large, strong, bearded men embrace, kiss each other on the cheeks, and shout with joy. The bands now join in the celebration and start playing. All suffering and hardship that they endured are forgotten and every heart is overflowing with happiness. Even the Confederate prisoners vent their feelings now, for most of them are also tired of war. On April 12 the Confederate prisoners are paroled at this camp and start their journey home.

On April 21, 1865 the unit marches to City Point. On April 23 they reach Petersburg, Virginia where they remain for the night. Most of the men take advantage of this and pay a visit to the crater made by the explosion on July 30, 1864. They march to City Point and on April 26 take the steamer *Starlight*, and sail up the James River to Alexandria, Virginia. They arrive there on April 28 and go into camp near Fort Lyons. On May 22, 1865 they participate in the Grand Review in Washington. On July 17, 1865 they are mustered out of the United States service, leave Alexandria on the 19th, and arrive in Harrisburg, Pennsylvania on July 20. There they receive their final pay and discharges on July 22, and reach their homes the same day, after nearly four years of service.

CHAPTER 5

THE BLUE MOUNTAIN LEGION
1875 - 1917

After the Civil War the unit seems to have vanished until 1875 when it again reappears. The unit was reorganized on April 13, 1875 in the Pennsylvania National Guard at Hamburg as Company E, 4th Regiment. The Annual Report of the Adjutant General of Pennsylvania for 1875 lists the officers as: Captain Edward F. Smith, First Lieutenant William R. Smith, and Second Lieutenant H.S. Beitenman. According to the *History of Berks County I:252*, "the military company authorized at Hamburg was a continuation of a distinguished company called the Blue Mountain Legion, which had kept up its organization upwards of 50 years, and was originally an artillery company and then changed to infantry."

During the late summer and fall of 1874, it appears that the town was interested in forming a military unit again, and 63 men were signed up. The men gathered in the evening and practiced marching and the manual of arms. They had to use broom sticks and other pieces of wood because they had no rifles. The drills were held on what was then a commons behind the Catholic Church, or sometimes on the streets in the town.

The Pennsylvania Militia was re-designated on April 9, 1870 as the Pennsylvania National Guard. The *Act of April 15, 1873,* provided that in time of peace the National Guard of Pennsylvania should not comprise more than 10,000 officers and enlisted men. In times of war or invasion the Governor was empowered to increase the Guard as the situation might require. The Guard was to conform to the provisions of the laws of the United States, and the system of discipline and training was to conform as closely as possible to that of the Federal Army.

This law raised the standards of the National Guard and greatly improved its organization. The Constitution of 1873 contains the important provision, "The freeman of this Commonwealth shall be armed, organized and disciplined for its defense when and in such manner as may be directed by law. The General Assembly shall provide for maintaining the militia by appropriations from the treasury of the Commonwealth, and may exempt from military service persons having conscientious scruples against bearing arms."

As was stated earlier, the unit was part of the 4th Regiment Pennsylvania Infantry. The 4th Regiment was organized in pursuance to Special Order No. 184, December 6, 1864, from the Philadelphia Fire Zouaves, under the command of Colonel Alfred J. Sellers, and consisted of 19 officers and 236 enlisted men. On August 1, 1873 it was mustered out. On June 30, 1874, the 4th Infantry, as it would be known up until the start of World War I, was reorganized from the following companies:

Company A – First Reading Rifles, Reading
Company B – Allen Zouaves, Allentown
Company C – Reading Zouaves, Reading
Company D – Allen Rifles, Allentown
Company E – Selfridge Guards, Bethany
Company F – Easton Grays, Easton

Company E was mustered out on November 12, 1874 and was reorganized at Hamburg on April 13, 1875. The 4th Regiment was part of the 5th Brigade, 2nd Division.

The unit obtained as their meeting place a small hall in "Pop's Hall." Christian Baum, then Chief Burgess (Mayor) of Hamburg observed that their quarters were too small. He offered to put a hall on the second floor of his blacksmith shop he was building on State Street, where Hecky's is now located. Later the unit had to move and they secured the fourth floor of the Confer building at the corner of Fourth and State Streets.

The company was equipped with State uniforms, and presented an obvious appearance of reliability, strength, and sturdiness. The uniform furnished consisted of a coat and pants, but without shoes. It was impressive and striking, combining neatness, convenience and style compared to the old uniforms.

In 1876 the unit attended its first annual encampment in Fairmount Park, Philadelphia. No State funds were provided at this time to pay for summer training encampments. However, the company commander and some public spirited contributors furnished the necessary money and supplies. The men only received pay from the State for the day of inspection. Sanitation was practically unknown at these encampments and inspecting officers were necessarily lenient. Camp kitchens were at the mercy of the elements. Food was prepared in containers suspended over fires from "spiders", and fresh baked bread was unknown. No beds or floors were provided in the A-Shaped tents used and the men slept on the ground, if its contours and weather conditions allowed any sleep at all.

Railroad Riots of 1877

Railroad riots erupted in the central and eastern parts of Pennsylvania in 1877, with each outbreak having its own peculiar characteristics. The busy and populated valleys of the Schuylkill and Lackawanna rivers offered large opportunities for the strikers and roaming looters. These looters abounded all over the State, and never before had such wide open chances to kill, steal, and destroy. Mining, manufacturing, and railroad activities required thousands upon thousands of workers. These workers of various jobs were scattered in large groups over central and southeastern Pennsylvania.

Recent murders and crimes by the "Mollie Maguires," followed by extensive hangings of convicted murderers, left the survivors and many members and sympathizers of the organization with a very nasty temper. They gladly cast their lot with the other thousands of discontents that were awaiting an opportunity for a general uprising. When news of the riots, raping, burning, and murders reached these groups, they immediately began their own activities.

The Reading riots were launched in a manner that left local and State authorities in no doubt about the situation and intent of the rioters. The strikers and those cooperating with them began with arson and other crimes, when they set fire to and destroyed the bridge over the Schuylkill River on the night of July 22, 1877. This bridge was in use by the Reading and Lebanon Valley Railroads and its destruction cost these companies $150,000. The bridge was burned to prevent the transportation of troops to the larger cities and towns in central Pennsylvania, and created lengthy and expensive detours.

That night and the following day found Reading mobbed by strange and suspicious people, none of whom had been seen in the city before. At the request of the General Manager of the Philadelphia and Reading Railroad companies, Lieutenant Governor Latta ordered the 4th Regiment and other regiments to report to Reading to protect property. Several of the companies arrived in the suburbs of Reading late in the evening, where torn up tracks forced them to leave the trains.

The companies were to report to the Reading depot where they would be quartered, and General Reeder decided to march the men down the railroad tracks instead of using the city streets. These tracks passed through a long, deep cut, the tops of its sides providing perfect cover for the frenzied mob from which they could throw objects and shoot at the soldiers below. The soldiers were unable to climb the sides of this cut, or to even run out of it without being exposed to the shower of missiles that the mob rained down upon them. The mob was composed of men, women and children, and was one of the most cowardly and evil crowds during all the disturbances in Pennsylvania.

When the soldiers reached Penn Street, the mob pelts them with stones and other objects and occasionally fires a pistol or revolver. As the troops near the railroad depot, the mob realizing that the soldiers will take possession of it, become much bolder. They close in on the troops, grabbing at their rifles and striking them with clubs and other various weapons. Shortly, one of the soldiers being attacked fires his weapon into the mob of rioters. This instantly causes other soldiers to do the same, killing ten rioters and wounding many others. The firing disperses the mob which does not regroup, and the soldiers go into their quarters in the station.

The disgrace of the Reading episode came the following day when several companies of the Guard arrived from Conshohocken and Norristown. These units were brought in to relieve the contingent already there. This change the local authorities thought wise, to relieve the situation caused by the shooting the night before. The relief troops detrained about five miles outside Reading and then marched into the city and were quartered in the Reading depot.

These relief troops became very friendly with members of the mob thronging the streets, readily listening to their stories of the night before. The new troops became very resentful of the conduct of their fellow soldiers and began to fraternize with the rioters. Soon they were drinking with the rioters, and as a show of good faith even handed over their guns to the rioters. This desertion and its incidents angered the other soldiers who had not yet left the city. Its vileness and disloyalty so angered them that it was with great difficulty that they were stopped from punishing the deserters. The deserters did not wait for the trains, but left Reading on foot, and without their rifles. Later in the day the arrival of 300 Regular Army soldiers calmed the situation in Reading.

In 1878 the unit was part of the 2nd Brigade under the command of Brigadier General Frank Reeder. The 2nd Brigade included units in the counties of Adams, Berks, Bucks, Chester, Cumberland, Dauphin, Delaware, Franklin, Lancaster, Lehigh, Montgomery, Northampton, and York. It consisted of the 4th Regiment Infantry (6 companies), 6th Regiment Infantry (6 companies), 8th Regiment Infantry (6 companies), 11th Regiment Infantry (7 companies), Washington Troop, and Griffin Battery. Captain Edward F. Smith was the company commander and the unit participated in many parades, inspections, and target practice sessions throughout the year.

On August 27, 1879, the Adjutant General of Pennsylvania prescribed that the Keystone would be the designated badge of the Pennsylvania National Guard. Two other events of interest for the year of 1879 were the unit parading in Harrisburg for the inauguration of Governor Hoyt, and the dishonorable discharge of Corporal John Grim for appearing at the armory drunk and disgracing the uniform.

The company attended the annual encampment at Fairmount Park in Philadelphia, along with the 4th Regiment and other units during August 6 to 12, 1880. The clothing issued to the men included a great coat, blouse, trousers, cap, chevrons, stripes, woolen blanket, rubber blanket, clothing bag, canteen, haversack, tin cup, tin plate, spoon, knife, fork, waist belt, bayonet scabbard, and cartridge box. Some of the civilian occupations of the men belonging to the unit at this time included shoemaker, cigar maker, blacksmith, farmer, molder, spiker, baker, printer, confectioner, butcher, hatter, railroad man, tinsmith, broom maker, drover, boatman, miller, carriage painter, wheelwright, tailor, millwright, silk worker, and jeweler, just to mention a few.

On March 4, 1881, as a unit of the division, they participated in the inaugural parade of President Garfield in Washington, D.C. In order for the men to be allowed to participate in this parade they were required to attend all drills without failure. Each man that went to Washington was paid two dollars and furnished with one pair of white gloves. The annual encampment was held from August 23 to 29, 1881, at Petty's Mill just south of Wilkes-Barre. This encampment was considered a huge success due in large part to the fact that the Legislature passed an Act fixing a per diem pay rate for both officers and enlisted.

May 30, 1882, Decorations Day (Memorial Day), found Company E in full dress uniform and decorating the graves of their fallen comrades. The unit encamped along with the rest of the 4th Regiment, and the entire division, at Lewistown during the period of August 5 to 12, 1882. They also took part in the Bicentennial Celebration in Philadelphia on October 27, 1882, along with other units of the 3rd Brigade.

It is interesting to note that the unit still elected its officers, even at this late date, and they did so once again on August 2, 1883. A change of command took place and Captain Charles F. Seaman was elected as commanding officer. The encampment this year was held on the Packer Farm near Williamsport from August 11 to 18, 1883.

The citizens of Williamsport very generously donated the land, baggage transportation, water, wood, ice, and lumber. The unit along with the rest of the 4th Regiment and the division held their annual encampment at Gettysburg from August 2 to 10, 1884.

The unit paraded along with the rest of the 3rd Brigade in Washington at the inauguration of President Grover Cleveland on March 4, 1885. The summer encampment and inspection was held at Camp Siegfried in Mount Gretna from July 25 to August 1, 1885. The following schedule was followed at the encampment, with roll calls taken at both Reveille and Tattoo:

> Reveille (one gun) – 6:00 AM
> Police Call – 6:30 AM
> Mess Call – 7:00 AM
> Sick Call – 7:30 AM
> Guard Mount – 8:30 AM
> Regimental Drill – 9:00 AM
> Recall Drill – 11:00 AM
> Mess Call, Dinner – 12 Noon
> Brigade Drill – 4:00 PM
> Recall Drill – 6:00 PM
> Dress Parade – 6:30 PM
> Mess Call, Supper – 7:00 PM
> Retreat (one gun) – Sunset
> Tattoo – 9:00 PM
> Taps – 10:00 PM

Company E along with the 4th Regiment encamped at Camp Allen in Allentown from July 10 to 16, 1886. The total expense of holding the encampment amounted to only $887.00, and this included a cost of $200 for the rent of the ground, and $258 for music. The expenses were defrayed with voluntary donations by the citizens of Allentown, the Lehigh Valley, and the Philadelphia and Reading Railroad companies.

As a unit of the 3rd Brigade, the unit paraded at the inauguration of Governor Beaver in January of 1887. The annual encampment was held at Camp Winfield Scott Hancock in Mount Gretna from August 6 to 13, 1887. The unit also participated in ceremonies that were part of the Centennial Celebration of the adoption of the Federal Constitution on September 16, 1887. New uniforms were issued in September of 1887 and the members of the company could purchase the old uniforms, being sold to the highest bidder. Also during 1887 all unit members were notified that they would be fined for not attending drills, and that these fines would be strictly enforced.

The unit attended its annual encampment from July 21 to 28, 1888 at Mount Gretna, as Company E, 4th Regiment, 3rd Brigade, with every man present for duty. In 1888 the unit was furnished with .45 caliber rifles, and also changed the color of their trousers to a darker blue to conform to the Regular Army. In 1889 a regimental encampment was held at Slatington. The unit paraded at the inauguration of President Harrison in Washington, D.C. on Match 4, 1889. They also paraded in New York City on April 30, 1889 celebrating the centennial of the inauguration of George Washington as President. Each soldier was paid two dollars for participating.

During the unit's annual encampment at Camp John F. Hartranft at Mount Gretna from July 19 to 26, 1890, they were inspected by the President of the United States, the Secretary of War, the General commanding the armies of the United States, and other prominent officials. The unit also attended the annual encampment at Mount Gretna in July of 1891.

In compliance with General orders No. 19, Adjutant General's Office, the unit moved to Lewistown in preparation of moving to Homestead on July 12, 1892. These moves were made to assist in suppressing disorder and quelling riots there. They reached Homestead on July 12 and were stationed near the Edgar Thompson Steel Works. The unit remained there until July 28, 1892, when it was relieved and departed for home.

The company commander, Captain Charles F. Seaman was promoted to Major and assigned to Regimental Headquarters in 1893. The unit held its annual encampment in 1893 at Columbia and at Gettysburg in 1894. On October 24, 1894 they paraded in Philadelphia as part of a dedication ceremony of a statue erected in the memory of Major General George B. McClellan. In 1896 the unit attended the annual encampment in Lewistown.

The organization of the Company at this time consisted of one Captain, one First Lieutenant, one Second Lieutenant, one First Sergeant, four Sergeants, eight Corporals, two Musicians, and 35 to 45 Privates. The following letter of interest is from the commander to all unit members:

HEADQUARTERS, COMPANY E, 4TH REGT., N.G.P.

HAMBURG, PA., Oct. 2d, 1896

Dear Sir:

The vacation season for Company E has come to a close. Weekly drills will be resumed next Wednesday evening, Oct. 7, 1896. After our pleasant encampment at Lewistown and a vacation of over two months we should all feel fresh and prepare to resume our drills with interest and renewed vigor during the coming winter.

I desire to impress upon each member of the Company the importance of regular attendance at drills. Heretofore attendance at drills was not included in the ratings of the Company for the year, but by an order recently issued, the percentage of attendance at weekly drills will hereafter be one of the prime factors in making up the ratings of the companies for the year. The importance of regular attendance will therefore readily be seen, and I earnestly trust it may be the ambition of each member of Company E to do his utmost to secure the highest percentage possible. To do this will require earnest work, and above all, regular attendance.

Now, boys, let us put our shoulders to the wheel and make Company E the banner Company, at least of the regiment, if not the State, next year.

I also desire to state that the competitive rifle match for the Gold Medal of the Company will take place on Saturday, October 17th, 1896. This match is open to all members of the Company and those who desire to enter will report at the Armory in full regulation uniform (leggings excepted) at 12:30 P.M. sharp, on above date.

Yours Respectfully,
John F. Ancona
Captain Comd'g

The annual encampment for 1897 was held in July at Mount Gretna. On September 10, 1897, the unit was ordered to Hazleton to quell industrial disturbances that had broken out in the coal fields. Arriving at 5:00 PM on September 11, they were held on a train and moved to Audenreid where they camped. On the night of September 14 they were ordered to Drifton, and encamped on some high ground that afforded them a good view of the immediate area. The duty ended on September 27, 1897 and the unit returned home.

On October 27, 1897, a special meeting was held for the election of a new company commander to succeed Captain John F. Ancona, who resigned for unknown reasons. Major John F. Earnest of Pine Grove conducted the election. Forty three men were paraded in State uniform, and when the vote was counted, John R. Wagner was unanimously elected by the company to be the new captain. Having received the required number of votes, Major Earnest declared John R. Wagner duly elected. Captain Elect Wagner was escorted into the Hall and took the oath of office. The calls for "speech" from Captain Wagner being loud and prolonged, to which he happily responded. He was followed by Major Keller, Major Earnest, Major Potteiger, and Ex-Captain Ancona. Three hearty cheers were given for Captain-Elect Wagner.

Spanish-American War

Under the command of Colonel David Brainard Case, the 4th Regiment mobilized at Mount Gretna during the morning of April 28, 1898, arriving in the midst of a severe snow storm. There were no tents available for the men when they arrived there, and the men suffered considerably until they were given quarters offering shelter.

The War Department intended not to use National Guard troops as organized, but to form new units of volunteers. Through the determined stand made by Governor Hastings and General Stewart, the program to break up the existing units was abandoned. All officers and enlisted men were permitted the option of not entering into Federal service is they so desired, but the large majority volunteered.

The unit went through routine drills and training while at Mount Gretna, and was mustered into Federal service on May 10, 1898 as Company E, 4th Regiment, Pennsylvania Volunteer Infantry. Thirty two men of Company E initially entered Federal service. It was decided to raise the number of men in the Company to 75, which was accomplished by recruiting additional volunteers from the Hamburg area. Later it was decided to raise the number to 106 men.

On May 11, 1898 they receive orders to move to New York City, where a number of ships are waiting to transport them to Key West, Florida. However, as they are about to board the trains it is discovered that due to an error in transportation orders, the regiment would be without rations for the sea trip, and the orders are changed. They remain at Mount Gretna for two more days, and then depart in the evening of May 14 for Chickamauga Park, Georgia.

Upon arrival at Chickamauga, the 4th Regiment is assigned to the 2nd Brigade, along with the 4th Ohio and 3rd Illinois Regiments. These three regiments comprise the 2nd Brigade, 1st Division, I Army Corps and remain at Chickamauga until July of 1898. In June the Company is detailed to recruit additional men in order to bring the company strength to 106 men. They do this by enlisting new recruits from the Hamburg area. The 4th Regiment consisted of the following companies:

Company A – Reading	Company G – Pine Grove
Company B – Allentown	Company H – Lebanon
Company C – Columbia	Company I – Harrisburg
Company D – Allentown	Company K – Columbia
Company E – Hamburg	Company L – Lancaster
Company F – Pottsville	Company M – Pottstown

Orders are received on July 4, 1898 directing the 2nd Brigade to proceed to Charleston, South Carolina. Each man is to take 50 rounds of ammunition and an additional 150 rounds per man to be shipped there. It is believed that their destination for the expedition is Santiago, Cuba to reinforce General Shafter's command, or possibly to Puerto Rico. It was not until July 21 that they learn they will first proceed to Newport News, Virginia, and from there embark for Puerto Rico.

While at Chickamauga Park the unit busily trains the new troops, preparing them for the deployment. The Regiment finally breaks camp at Chickamauga and moves at 9:30 AM, Friday, July 22, 1898, and arrives at Rossville, Georgia at Noon. There they load onto trains at 12:30 AM on July 23, arriving in Newport News at 6:30 AM on July 25, where they establish a temporary camp, named Camp Brooke. The Regiment remains there until July 27, 1898, when they embarked on board the ship *Seneca*.

On July 28, 1898, at 1:45 PM the *Seneca* passes out of the harbor bound for Puerto Rico. It arrives at Guanica, Puerto Rico at 11:30 AM on August 2, 1898 and anchors about five miles off shore. At 2:30 PM the ship weighs anchor and sails for Ponce, Puerto Rico, arriving there at 5:00 PM and remains in the harbor there all night. The next morning orders are received from General Brooke to proceed to Arroyo, Puerto Rico, which is a port about 50 miles to the east, and there to disembark.

The troops disembark while the *St. Louis,* the cruiser *Cincinnati*, and the *Gloucester* bombard the hills behind the town. It is near midnight before the entire regiment is ashore. A temporary camp is set up along the Guayama road, about one mile northeast of Guayama, and on August 4, 1898 a permanent camp is established about one half mile east of Arroyo.

On the Patillo and Guayama roads, and on the road leading from Arroyo north into the mountains, ten companies of the regiment are placed to conduct outpost duty, with five companies rotating the duty every day. It rains on and off practically every day and night, making conditions very unpleasant and dangerous, but the morale of the men is high at all times. The unit is equipped with the Model 1896 .30 caliber rifle at this time.

The forward movement of the Brigade begins on August 6, 1898, with the 4th Ohio and 3rd Illinois advancing on the town of Guayama. The town has a population of about 10,000 people and is considered strategically important since it is situated at the entrance of mountain passes with roads leading to Cayey and San Juan. The 4th Pennsylvania forms the Brigade reserve during this movement and also during the battle that follows, and Guayama is captured without the Regiment being actively engaged.

General Brooke sent for Colonel Case on the night of August 12, 1898 and orders him to take the 4th Regiment and move on the enemy the following day. The Regiment is to attack the enemy's strongly entrenched positions on the mountain north of Guayama, using the road to Cayey for the main attack, as the 4th Ohio conducts a flanking maneuver. Colonel Case is ordered to move two battalions of the 4th Regiment early on the morning of August 13, with two days rations and 100 rounds of ammunition for each man.

One battalion is to move at 4:00 AM to Guayama and halt at the outskirts of the town until further orders are received from the commanding general. The other battalions are to move at 6:00 AM to the same point, where they are to halt and remain in place to cover the town. Another battalion is to remain at Arroyo to protect that town.

On August 13, 1898 the 1st and 2nd Battalions break camp at Arroyo at 4:00 AM. The 1st Battalion and wagon train, under the command of Lieutenant Colonel C.T. O'Neill move at 5:45 AM, advancing to an iron bridge about one mile northwest of Guayama. There they remain as support for the advancing force consisting of the 4th Ohio, 3rd Illinois, four dynamite guns, Battery A of Missouri,

Battery A of Illinois, Battery B of Pennsylvania, and the 27th Indiana Battery. Thirty minutes later the 2nd Battalion, which the Hamburg unit is part of, under the direct command of Colonel Case, moves to the same point, with the 3rd Battalion remaining in Arroyo.

Intelligence is received that the enemy is executing a flanking movement against the 4th Ohio. The 2nd Battalion, 4th Pennsylvania is immediately placed on the high ground commanding the entire country from the Cayey road to the road on which the 4th Ohio is operating. Company F, 4th Pennsylvania, under the command of Captain Dyson, is sent forward in extended order to cover the front. Company B is detached and takes possession of the barracks and public buildings in the town. While the Regiment is engaged in this operation news arrives of a Peace Protocol and General Brooke orders the 1st and 2nd Battalions to withdraw to a point on the Ponce road just south of the edge of town. Here the regiment remains on outpost duty until orders arrive on August 28, 1898 to break camp and proceed to Ponce.

During this time the men are noticeable by the health and cleanliness of their camp, and by their appropriate conduct, with none being arrested for misconduct the entire time. On August 28 the Regiment moves out of the camp in a column consisting of nearly 1,200 men, ambulance wagons, 28 supply wagons, and ten ox carts. On that first afternoon the Regiment marches ten miles, and on the next two days marching about 20 miles each day. On the night of August 30 the Regiment encamps within the limits of the city of Ponce, and the following day marches to Porte de Playa. The loading of the transport *City of Chester* takes all of August 31 and part of the following day to complete. At 2:00 PM on September 1, 1898 the ship weighs anchor and the Regiment is homeward bound, with the exception of the sick that are moved to a hospital in Ponce, Puerto Rico.

The Regiment arrives in New York City on September 6, 1898, where the men learn for the first time that they are to have 60 days furlough before being mustered out of Federal service. On October 27, 1898 the Regiment, over a thousand strong, participates in the

Peace Jubilee in Philadelphia, and is mustered out of Federal service on November 16, 1898.

During August of 1900 the unit attends their annual encampment at Mount Gretna. On September 22, 1900 the 4th regiment is ordered to Shenandoah to assist in suppressing industrial disorders. They go into camp at Columbia Park and immediately start the regular routine of guard duty and drill. On the night of October 15, two battalions of the regiment are ordered to Panther Creek Valley. The order is carried out within 45 minutes of being received, which is quite remarkable considering that most of the men were sleeping at the time the order was given.

Having received intelligence that a large group of striking miners are descending upon Colliery No. 10, Companies A, C, D, F, and G get off the train and form into a line of skirmishers. The striking miners are ordered to withdraw. They ignore this order and the troops move forward with fixed bayonets. Several arrests are made but the troops have very little difficulty in restoring order. The Regiment departs the area, receiving very high praise from the Commanding General, and with the warmest commendation of the law-abiding citizens of the troubled communities.

The unit attends the inauguration of President McKinley in Washington, D.C. on March 4, 1901, and held its annual encampment at Mount Gretna during July of that year. During July of 1902 the unit was at Gettysburg for its annual encampment, and was once again called up for strike duty in September of 1902. More coal strikes erupted in Schuylkill and Carbon Counties, primarily in Nanticoke and Plymouth, and the unit is called out on September 30, 1902. They remain on strike duty until being relieved on October 30, 1902.

Between the years of 1903 and 1915, the unit participates in the annual encampments at Mount Gretna, Gettysburg, and once at Selingsgrove. Other events include participating in the inauguration of President Theodore Roosevelt on March 4, 1905; participating in the dedication of the new State capitol building on October 4, 1906; and taking part in the parade of the Division in Philadelphia on October 5, 1908, in full dress uniform for the first time.

On December 15, 1909, in accordance with General Order No. 42, Adjutant General's Office, the 4th Regiment was detached from the 3rd Brigade, and with the 6th and 8th Regiments, formed a separate brigade. By General Order No. 17, Adjutant General's Office, dated April 21, 1910, this new brigade was designated as the 4th Brigade.

Mexican Border Service

In March of 1916, Mexican General Francisco (Pancho) Villa and a group of his men cross the border into the United States, and raid Columbus, New Mexico. The President of the United States orders a "punitive" expedition into Mexico, and as a result the Pennsylvania National Guard is mobilized. All troops of this expeditionary force are under the command of General John. J. Pershing.

The unit receives orders from Headquarters to assemble at Mount Gretna and to recruit enough men to bring the unit up to a minimum strength of three officers and 65 enlisted men. Lieutenant Casper was detailed by Colonel Shannon as the unit's recruiting officer, and within a few hours six men enlisted with more coming. Major Surgeon George F. Potteiger performs the medical examinations on all the new recruits.

The unit reports to the armory at 8:00 AM on June 22, 1916 for departure to Mount Gretna. Unexpectedly, and while they are marching to the train station, a spontaneous flood of Hamburg citizens gathers to bid farewell to Company E. It must be noted that the local citizens were very supportive and loyal to the Guardsmen and some former members from the Spanish-American War ask if they may enlist again.

It must have been quite an inspirational sight as the long parade of marchers filed down State Street, flanked by hundreds of people, as the unit marched to the Reading Railroad Station in Hamburg. Several Civil War veterans headed the escort, joined by Burgess (Mayor) James F. Prutzman. Everyone was carrying the national flag, and the escort was followed by Burkey's Band, along with 60 members of the Washington Camp No. 78 of the Patriotic Order Sons of America, in full regalia.

Company E has 70 men in full marching order, with the officers being Captain Lewis A. Loy, First Lieutenant Harrison F. Seaman, and Second Lieutenant Raymond E. Casper. The crowd energetically cheers the unit all along the route. Ten cars filled with citizens follows the company, and after the cars is a large group of citizens who follow the soldiers all the way to the train station. At the station, the Patriotic Order Sons of America forms a column and presents arms as the unit passes through.

The unit travels to Mount Gretna via the train, and is mustered into Federal service on July 4, 1916. They are now part of the 3rd Brigade, commanded by Brigadier General Christopher T. O'Neill, and the Pennsylvania National Guard was designated the 7th Division. While at Mount Gretna they receive physical examinations and inoculations, and have the distinguished honor of being the unit in the Regiment with the least number of men rejected for service. At this time the Regiment is under the command of Colonel E.C. Shannon. On July 8, 1916 the unit entrains at Mount Gretna along with many other units and departs for the Mexican border.

The unit arrives in El Paso, Texas on Thursday, July 17, 1916 at 4:30 AM, and has to stay in the railcars until 8:30 AM. When they leave the train, they march under a hot sun and extremely dusty conditions to their camp. Life in the camp proves to be very hot during the day and very cool at night. They drill every morning with afternoons off due to the extreme heat, until such time as the troops are acclimated to the climate.

The camp is named Camp Stewart and is located on a sandy plain which is many miles long, with a branch of the Sierra Madre mountains nearby. The Company has a fine quartet of singers, who sing in German under the direction of Heinrich Gustav Miller. The unit is also noted for having the best cooks in the regiment. The unit remains at Camp Stewart conducting patrols on the border with Mexico, and departs El Paso on January 7, 1917 for home. They are mustered out of Federal service on January 17, 1917.

CHAPTER 6

World War I
1917 - 1919

Soon after the men return home from their expedition on the Mexican border, war is declared on Germany and its allies on April 6, 1917. The unit is called into Federal service on July 15, 1917 and musters in at Hamburg on July 27, 1917. The unit immediately begins preparations for movement, and before long learns that they are going to Camp Hancock, Georgia. They arrive at Camp Hancock on September 12, 1917.

Shortly after their arrival at Camp Hancock the unit learns that it will be reorganized from an infantry company to a machine gun company. They later receive orders assigning them to the 1st Cavalry as Company A (Machine Gun). Later the unit is again reorganized and re-designated per General Order No. 22, 28th Division, dated October 11, 1917, as Company A, 107th Machine Gun Battalion, 28th Division. In December of 1917 the unit is again re-designated, this time as Company A, 108th Machine Gun Battalion, 55th Infantry Brigade, 28th Division. The company is commanded by Captain Ralph C. Crow of LeMoyne, Pennsylvania, and the battalion commanded by Major Robert M. Vail. Machine gun units are a new part of the American army, and the old 4th Infantry Regiment is the nucleus around which these new machine gun battalions are constructed.

During the latter part of 1917 all of the machine gun units of the Division are placed under the command of Colonel Ezra H. Ripple. Under his direction, and with the assistance and instruction of Captain L.H. Pinell of the British Army machine gun corps, an intensive training program is started. The training is greatly hindered due to a lack of materials and equipment. However, they follow the training schedule as closely as possible from November of 1917 to April of 1918, when preparations begin to deploy overseas. Captain Pinell is an excellent instructor and takes great joy in developing the new machine gun units. He creates much interest in the machine gun effort, which in turn increases the unit morale.

Conditions at Camp Hancock are primitive, to say the least. The lack of clothing, blankets and shoes makes life for the soldiers uncomfortable. Failure to supply the equipment which the unit is to fight with makes the training very difficult. Because of a shortage of the real thing, for some time the unit uses wooden guns for training. Many of the buildings are only partially complete, roads are in poor condition, and nothing has been done to put the drill fields in proper shape. Immediately upon arrival the troops begin the work of putting the place in shape. The men endure long periods of training, working long hours and during holidays, but they perform their tasks willingly.

On a positive note, the food is good and plentiful at Camp Hancock. As the cooks gain more experience the meals improve even more. A good Mess Sergeant is a treasure and always receives the highest praise. Since the morale of the men depends greatly upon the quality of the mess, close supervision of food preparation is made at all times. A system of daily inspections by company officers and sanitary officers insures not only the ideal preparation of each meal, but also that sanitary practices are followed.

The troops arrived at Camp Hancock in their summer uniforms. It was well into winter before woolen uniforms are received in sufficient quantity to properly clothe all the men. Fortunately woolen underwear and overcoats are received early enough to avoid any serious discomfort. Firewood is never an issue and each tent procures its own wood from the surrounding pine forests. It is late in the fall before floors for the tents are available, and still later before tent side walls are issued. Sufficient numbers of blankets are not issued until January of 1918, causing much distress for the men.

Equipment for training purposes is never obtained in suitable quantities. Many of the rifles, automatic rifles, and machine guns used in combat are not issued until the unit reached France. The unit has one bayonet for every three men, which means much changing during bayonet drills. For several months the unit has to improvise and use wooden guns for machine gun training. Another problem is the lack of gas masks, with the unit only having one mask for every six men, thus making gas warfare training very slow and difficult to perform.

Training requires a minimum of eight hours per day, and many nights. The training of the machine gun units is the most difficult, since very little use was made of machine guns before this point in time. Also the shortage of real machine guns greatly handicaps the training. The issue rifle is the Model 1917 Rifle. This rifle is awkward and crudely made by today's standards. Their fire is not very accurate, even after intensive marksmanship training, but the men make the best of it and eventually become fairly accurate with the rifle.

Both the training requirements and the standard of discipline are very hard, almost to the point of being extremely harsh. Leave is only granted in the case of a dire emergency at home. Drilling, field training, inspections, and reviews fills six days of each week, and after the troops become fairly hardened, 20 mile hikes over dirt roads become routine. One system used to qualify privates as non-commissioned officers is to test their voices. They must bark out commands through a wood thicket 200 feet deep, and if their words can be heard and understood on the other side, the soldier is on his way to being promoted.

Even though the entire winter at Camp Hancock is spent in strenuous training, the men do find time for various forms of recreation. The camp has many YMCA huts, a theatre, library, and other places for comfort and recreation. Commanding officers encourage athletics, and many football and baseball games are played on the drill fields and in the company streets, with the result being good, healthy fun. The games also help to foster esprit de corps in the company, since the company often competed against another company. The men play with the abandonment of school boys and the results make for clean and open minds.

Augusta, Georgia is the nearest town to the camp, and the citizens are very friendly, opening their homes and churches to the soldiers. Frequent boxing and wrestling bouts are held, and the weekly matches draw large crowds from both the camp and Augusta. Shows are also put on by the soldiers that are always very clean and clever. In many cases the acts take considerable time in preparing, which the men do after training. This entertainment keeps the soldiers happy and increases the morale considerably. Wednesday and Saturday afternoons are half holidays for the enlisted men, and the majority of the men go into town on these days. Unfortunately for the officers, these afternoons are spent attending various schools to make up deficiencies in training and tactics.

The relationship between the soldiers and the city of Augusta is very good. The businesses realize that much is to be gained by properly handling the situation when thousands of soldiers come to town. They take steps to prevent profiteering and regulate the prices of items that the soldiers buy. Regardless of every precaution taken, arguments sometimes occur between the soldiers and the merchants. On one occasion, the Military Police have to intervene to rescue a questionable citizen who sold a quart of plain "tea" to a soldier. The soldier discovered that it was something else before the vendor could make his escape. Civilian and military bands play an important part in keeping up the morale of the soldiers, and community sing-alongs, accompanied by bands do much to make the evenings pleasant.

In camp itself the rigorous training is lightened by much variety. The natural humor of the soldiers always makes them appreciate anything that might make them laugh, regardless of whose expense it might be. The officers foster this spirit as long as it does not interfere with discipline.

An example of this good natured humor was when a high ranking officer, mounted none too securely on his horse, passed through an infantry regiment's area, drawing an uproar of laughter in which the officer also joined. Seems a private who was loitering by the mess shack failed to distinguish the difference between the officer's hat cord and that of a cavalryman's, and mockingly called upon the "Blinkety blank yellow legs to come down offa there and join the infantry." Sometimes the humor of the situation failed to appeal to the principal until afterwards. Such was the case of a new lieutenant, being assigned to the infantry. During a training lecture on the rifle he tore his rifle completely down and then found that he was totally unable to put it back together again.

Chaplains hold regular religious services, which are well attended by the men. The services usually consist of talks on the proper conduct by the soldiers, and many lectures are given by prominent officers. The health record of the camp is remarkable when you consider the number of troops living there. There are constant inspections of kitchens, mess shacks, enlisted quarters, latrines, picket lines, and store houses. The men keep themselves in good condition by frequently bathing, taking care of their teeth, and wearing clean clothes. During the evening an officer would inspect the tents to insure that the soldiers had sufficient ventilation.

All these measures contribute to the fact that very few men report for sick call. However, when anyone comes down with measles, chicken pox, or mumps, he is kept in the barracks so that every other susceptible man contracts the illness and acquires immunity before going overseas. The conduct of the men while in camp is noteworthy. Their behavior while on leave in Augusta is particularly worthy of praise, considering the number of men. Arrests are few, and little trouble is experienced from soldiers being drunk or disorderly.

By the spring of 1918 the thorough training brought the unit to a high standard of readiness, and the men were now chafing over the delay that kept them in America. They were anxious to get across the Atlantic Ocean and do their part in the Great War. In April orders finally arrive and they are ordered to pack in preparation of going to Europe. However, before leaving Camp Hancock the troops strenuously work to learn the new combat tactics that have evolved in the war, assimilating them with the American ideals of fighting.

The performance of the unit in Europe will demonstrate how essential it was to have this tough and thorough training. Time after time, sergeants, corporals, and even privates assume positions of greater responsibility. They perform their jobs so skillfully that they often receive the highest commendations from their superiors, and in many instances are recommended for promotion. The discipline instilled at Camp Hancock never leaves the men, even when under the most trying and difficult circumstances.

On April 21, 1918 the unit entrains for Camp Upton at Yaphank on Long Island, New York. There additional equipment is received and the final physical examinations given to the soldiers. The unit boards the *H.M.S Anchises* at Bush Terminal on May 2, 1918 and sets sail 24 hours later. A great amount of time is used in putting the men aboard the ship. Going aboard, each man is checked against the passenger list. Once aboard the ship they may not leave and go ashore unless they have a special permit. These strict security measures are taken to prevent enemy agents from coming aboard the ships and entering the ranks. The ship, sailing in a convoy of at least 15 other transports is escorted by a cruiser.

The trip across the Atlantic Ocean is uneventful and the unit arrives at Birkenhead, which is near Liverpool, England on May 16, 1918. The troops go ashore on boats and board trains immediately for Shorncliffe Station. Arriving there after midnight and then marching some distance, reaching Folkstone on the Channel, and billeting there in some big and beautiful homes. The soldiers find the homes to be desolate but very comfortable in comparison to the billets that will soon follow.

On the afternoon of May 17, 1918 the troops entrain again, this time proceeding to Dover, via Canterbury. Arriving at Dover they make a hard march up a steep cliff to the South Gate of Arcacliffe Fort. The fort overlooks the port of Dover and commands a superb view of the English Channel. From there the men watch the hundreds of water craft, battleships, destroyers, torpedo boats, transports, ferries, hospital ships, and fishing vessels in the waters below. Here the men spend their last night in England, passing most of the evening lying on the grassy terraces high above the old fort and observing the activities in the Channel. The soldiers watch with great interest the countless signal lights, departing fleets, and airplanes bound for the war across the water. They also observe with great interest the unloading of wounded soldiers from hospital ships to Red Cross trains.

Traveling across England to Dover in the troop trains with British soldiers who carefully supervise every detail, ensuring all movements are promptly carried out. The trip across England is very pleasant. The weather is beautiful and the farms are wonderful appearing to the men. All along the route the troops receive loud cheers from the British people, and notice the American flags abundantly decorating almost everything. The troops particularly notice both here in England and later in France that the cheering crowds largely consist of women, children, old men, and disabled soldiers. Most of the men of military age are at the front fighting or in training.

The following morning the unit embarks along with the rest of the 108th Machine Gun Battalion on cross-channel transports; destination Calais, France. As they cross the Channel aboard the *Dieppe*, a boat fast enough to keep up with the escorting destroyers, the destroyers sink a German submarine. Two hours after leaving England the men arrive in Calais, France and disembark shortly after Noon.

This was May 18, just following Sir Douglas Haig's declaration that the British are "fighting with their backs to the wall." The arrival of the Yanks is very encouraging to the British soldiers at Calais. At first rumors abound that the 28th Division is to go into the Ypres salient in Belgium. For three days the men remain in British Rest Camp No. 6 at Calais, enduring several air raid alerts, and then entraining for Desvres, Pas de Calais. Upon arriving at Desvres the men march from there to Henneveux, not far west of Boulogne sue Mer.

The men arrive in hot woolen uniforms with choker collars, which in the heat adds another thing of discomfort to the Western front. Coming down the gangplank, the men stand tall, appearing all-powerful, thanks partly to the campaign hats they are wearing. Soon they are issued the overseas cap and now look bigger eared than robust, but yet they radiate heartiness and confidence.

There probably was never a prouder, happier, or more talkative army under the American flag. Their favorite expression being "Start arguing, bastards." Amid frequent mix ups, some soldier regularly sounding off with the pet American Expeditionary Force (A.E.F.) phrase "She said there would be days like this." They march over the old roads and sing the bawdiest of songs such as "Lulu," "Frankie and Johnny," and "The Fusiliers." Also of note is the fact that the NCOs had extraordinary authority and prestige, which was firmly upheld by the commissioned officers.

The men were not blind to the hardships or unaware that some things could have been made easier with more thoughtfulness on the part of others. However, above and beyond the turmoil they knew the nation was in danger, that they had been called and that they had to do their duty. With that kind of spirit they went forward, respecting higher authority and orders, and heartened by their faith in America. When the men fought, they whooped it up as if the battlefield were a football arena. Training had not taught them that; they just did what came naturally.

The unit stays in the rest camp at Calais for about three days, and there has their first introduction to "8 Chevaux, 40 Hommes." French military trains at that time were made up of box cars and very poor third class passenger coaches. Some of the box cars had seats and all were covered with straw. The outside of the box cars were plainly marked "8 Chevaux, 40 Hommes" which translated is "8 Horses, 40 Men." The box cars are really more comfortable than the old worn out third class passenger coaches because the men can lie down in them. The passenger coaches are of the compartment type and when you crammed in eight men with all their equipment, little room is available for rest or the taking of food and drink. The French military train is certainly an eye-opener for the men who are accustomed to the more luxurious trains of the U.S. Such things as trains, billets, and rations did a lot to cause the men who had never been outside of the U.S. to gain a real appreciation for our nation.

Rest Camp No. 6 is very unpleasant and difficult. Fortunately the men are kept there just long enough to discard their extra clothing and equipment which had been so carefully issued before leaving the U.S. "Rest Camp" is a misnomer and almost any other name would be more appropriate. There is not enough space upon which to erect the camp and the tents are bunched together very closely along narrow streets. Dirty bell-shaped tents are used and are fortified by being sunk two feet into the sand. Because of the large number of troops in the camp, as many as two squads are quartered in one of these tents. In order to have sufficient room, the men sleep with their heads against the tent sides with their feet all coming together in the center.

While in camp, British gas masks are issued along with British sergeants lecturing the men on the horrors of gas warfare. In the cramped conditions of the camp thousands of troops continually stir up the sand. The sand blows around in huge clouds that settle in the drinking water, on the food, and unto the blankets, to the thorough disgust of everyone. In this camp the men are also introduced to British rations, including tea and jam, and these rations by no means satisfy the appetite of the Americans. Corned beef, salmon, and cornmeal are made into mush. These items along with black coffee, for the most part make up the rations for the men, who taste little else except Welch's Grapeade, French "monkey meat" (a slimy bully beef), and hard biscuits.

In the camp the supply sections work day and night so that each man might have an extra uniform, shoes, underwear, socks, and other assorted items. Unfortunately many of these items are later discarded by the men, along with many treasured personal items. Many expensive and handy items are given to the men that they might enjoy some of the comforts of home. The men are greatly disappointed later when deprived of these things.

After the disposal is complete, each man is left with just an extra set of underwear, two pairs of socks, and some personal hygiene items. Sadly, long underwear arrives in June, with short drawers only being issued to the men in October. They wear hobnailed shoes with British issue socks, and of course the steel helmet. Many of the men carry a spiked ash walking stick which makes marching easier. These they buy themselves.

A few weeks later the officers are ordered to discard their extra equipment. While at Camp Hancock the officers were required to have certain equipment and clothing before being shipped overseas. They had to buy this clothing and equipment themselves at a cost of several hundred dollars, and in many cases this imposed a considerable burden on the younger officers. The required items were things such as white shirts, white collars and cuffs, various types of uniforms and boots, shoes, rubber boots, moccasins, different styles of top coats, cot, mattress, pillows, etc. All this weighs several hundred pounds. But now all extra clothing, bedding, etc., had to be discarded since each officer was limited to 50 pounds. Eventually, many of the officers kept nothing except for the articles they could carry in their packs.

While at Calais the troops experience their first bombing, although not suffering any casualties. The hum of the German airplanes, the playing of search lights, and the barking of anti-aircraft guns are the signals for the men to come out and observe. At this time it is just a picturesque display to the men however, later the men learn the great danger the planes pose and take shelter. From this time until the end of the war the men are never really out of hearing range of heavy artillery, or out of danger from bombing or shellfire.

At Calais the U.S. rifle is exchanged for the British Enfield rifle, and they use the Lewis machinegun. The Lewis machinegun is an American invention that satisfactorily serves the British in all of their campaigns. The failure of the American military to have a machinegun at the start of the war is another example of the United States being unprepared for war. Many of the most successful weapons used during World War I were American inventions. However, at the start of the war our country did not have machineguns, automatic rifles, hand grenades, and even suitable artillery with which our men could train.

At Henneveux, where the unit remains until June 9, 1918, additional training in the use of the British Vickers machinegun is given. At this time the plan is to use the 28th Division as a reinforcing unit for the British near Arras. Later a change in plans at General Headquarters results in the moving of the Division southward to join the French. While the unit is at Henneveux some of the officers and NCOs attend a British machinegun school at Le Wast.

The unit always took advantage, even during fighting when possible, of every opportunity for additional training. By doing this they become one of the best trained organizations of its kind in the Corps, and greatly increase their efficiency during combat operations. Intensive training for the men starts on May 22, 1918, with target practice the top priority. They also receive thorough training on the techniques of using hand grenades, trench raiding, and gas warfare, about which they knew very little.

On June 9, 1918, just as the men become accustomed to the typical French billets in barns and any other buildings that serve as shelter, the march to Maresquel begins. The movement requires three days of hard marching, passing through Desvres, Campagne, and Chapelle-Nouvelle, to Maresquel where HQ Company, and Companies A and B remain for two nights. Companies C and D bivouac at Hesdin and later entrain from there along with units of the 110th Infantry Regiment.

In most of the villages of northern France the men are the first Americans to appear, and the French people try to make things as pleasant as possible for them. Most places the men are quartered in barns and other out buildings, while the officers stay inside the rooms of homes if available. It is assumed that all French water is polluted, and so they chlorinate it heavily which ruins the taste, especially for the coffee. Even the French do not drink the water, and of course, wine is much better anyway. A raid by the men into French orchards or berry patches is forbidden under penalty of court-martial, and the rule is strictly enforced.

The administration of the army was very bad when compared to today's standards. The ration flow is irregular at first, as is the supply of tobacco. Tobacco chewers resort to using Bull Durham tobacco because cut plugs can not be gotten. There are also weeks when no vegetables other than onions are available. The men feel lucky if mail delivery occurs more than once a month, and sometimes months go by without the men receiving pay. There are no soldier shows, no soft drinks, no ice cream, but life was simpler then, and the soldiers hardly miss what they have never known. Most discouraging of all is the effort by the average soldier to learn enough of the French language to get by.

On the night of June 14, 1918 the entire Battalion arrives at Esbly. Traveling in trucks all night they reach Nantouillet, near the large American hospital at Juilly on the following morning. By successive marching the unit proceeds through Thieux. There they are paid in French money. Then they move through Mitry-Mory to Gressy near Claye Souilly. After a week of training with French equipment the unit loads unto French trucks driven by Chinese coolies, and moves to billets near Montmirail, a few miles from Chateau-Thierry.

Several maneuvers are held at Gressy during this period. First Lieutenant Andre Doret of the French Machine Gun Corps is assigned to the Battalion, and serves continuously with the unit throughout all the following engagements. Lieutenant Doret is an outstanding officer and proves very helpful and gallant. After this week of training, the march is again resumed, with the Battalion moving to Ville Moyenne on Sunday, June 30, 1918.

Chateau-Thierry

July 4, 1918 was a day that none of the unit members would soon forget. At 2:30 AM a courier arrived at Battalion Headquarters with orders to rush the companies into position north of Pargny. With suppressed excitement the supply trains and men begin to move. In the chill of the morning, and forgetting their plans for a Fourth of July celebration, the men start for the front carrying only light packs and rations. They trudge towards the front lines in total darkness along the dusty road. Occasionally they move off to the side of the road, allowing truck convoys carrying ammunition and supplies to pass by them.

This is the beginning of the great adventure for which they trained and waited so long, and which many thought at times would never come. In their minds it is the most trying period of the long wait, but they do not receive their baptism of fire this time. The danger on the British front subsides, but the French north of Paris are being pressed hard by the Germans, so the 28th Division begins to move in that direction. Before they start the British Enfield rifles are exchanged for the American 1917 Eddystone rifles, which were turned in a few days ago in Calais. The Lewis machineguns are also returned to the British.

On through Artonges to Pargny the column moves, with Companies C and D leading and taking positions at Ragronet Farm. Companies A and B remain near the village of Pargny as an emergency reaction force. Late in the morning it is apparent that the German attack is not going to occur, so the battalion returns to their billets, but remains alert for any sudden orders.

Back in the billets in Ville Moyenne there is much discussion and real disappointment among the men because they wanted to take positions along the front lines. Late in the afternoon of July 5th they receive orders to move and set out for Pargny, where they go into bivouac. On July 8th the men start work on emplacements in the reserve line, continuing with this work until July 13, 1918.

During the night of July 14, 1918, the artillery firing on both sides increases steadily, and by midnight reaches huge proportions. Platoon size elements of the battalion hold the hills in the vicinity of Conde-en-Brie on the left flank and as far as Montigny on the right, with some detachments flanking both sides of these towns. During the opening of this offensive, the 109th and 110th Infantry Regiments are engaged with the Germans on the banks of the Marne River, with two companies of the 108th Machine Gun Battalion also engaging the Germans. Company A loses one man killed and one man is gassed during this engagement. It doesn't take the men long to become accustomed to the heavy artillery fire. The noise of the German machineguns loses some of its terror.

Until the end of the war, gas warfare continued and grew more complex. All soldiers wore protective masks and anti-gas discipline became commonplace. The first attacks from cylinders changed to gas barrages fired by the artillery. There was also a weapon called a "Projector", which lobbed a large gas filled container into the enemy trenches, where it exploded. It looked like a drop-kicked football in flight. The gases were given unusual names like "Yellow Cross" and "White Cross", according to the markings on the shell. Mustard Gas or "Yellow Cross" is extremely deadly, and no protective mask could protect the soldiers from its effects. It burned through their clothing and into their flesh, destroying their vision, and causing them to choke. Phosgene Gas was twice as effective and twice as deadly as Chlorine Gas.

Champagne-Marne

On July 15, 1918 at Chezy, the 109th Machine Gun Battalion is ordered to protect a ravine running in a northwesterly direction from Dannejue by using enfilading machinegun fire. The 108th Machine Gun Battalion placed additional guns at the disposal of the 109th. During this battle the Germans reached St. Agnan in great strength. The unit experiences severe fighting in the area, and proves to be an invaluable part during the battle. During the battle Major Vail displays his characteristically aggressive machine gun tactics, which became well known in latter campaigns, not only in the 28th Division, but in other divisions also. The farthermost advance of the German advance reaches St. Agnan, but they are completely stopped at that point.

July 16, 17 and 18 are critical days in the second German attempt to take Paris. The days are very nerve racking for the men who remain idle in their gun positions. Sporadic shelling both day and night and bombing by airplanes does nothing to increase the humor of the men, but does add to their fighting spirit. The unit leaves their positions either on July 18 or the following day, and are now held in readiness for any further emergencies. They then move to a position north of the Marne River. Company A loses one man killed and one gassed during the action on July 16, and loses an additional man as missing in action on July 20, 1918.

Aisne-Marne

The traversed trench line with its alternate firing bays and earth bulkheads is purposely designed to prevent enfilading fire and to confine the damage of a shellburst to a small area. Communication trenches, which are used to move troops and supplies to the front, are also dug in a zigzag pattern for the same reasons. The support trenches, 100 or more yards behind the front line, which are used for feeding purposes, are less exaggerated. Every suitable location along the front line is made into a strong point. These are usually a slotted, thick walled bunker or a concrete turret which houses a crew served weapon.

Machineguns are placed to fire diagonally across the front in order to have interlocking fire, which normally breaks up an attack. Where high ground is convenient, command posts are located, normally above ground in defilade on the lower reverse slope. Listening posts are located forward into "no mans land" to warn of night attacks or to ambush small enemy patrols however, the enemy usually has these posts spotted and targets them with fire. Trenches are protected in the front with barbed wire or concertina wire strung in wide aprons. The barbed entanglements are frequently 150 feet or more in depth, with the Engineers emplacing them at night, and the German artillery blasting them apart during the day.

On July 21, 1918 while in positions south of the Marne River, the men are ordered to go out in search parties to cover the ground held by the brigade at the time of the German attack. They seek out the wounded and try to identify any dead soldiers found to reduce the list of missing in action, thereby accounting for as many of these men as possible. The search parties are also trying to find the remnants of four infantry companies (L and M of the 109th Regiment, and B and C of the 110th Regiment). These men for nearly a day held one of the two positions which alone prevent the entire German line from moving in a united advance towards Paris. However, these four companies are nearly wiped out in the process.

Patrols are sent forward by the 109th and 110th Infantry Regiments, the 108th Machine Gun Battalion, and the 1st Battalion of the 103rd Engineers. The units cover the ground in the Bois de Rougis and north as far as Hill 200. They also cover the slopes of the ravine north of the Danneju Ferme with some parties getting as far forward as La Grange aux Bois. Because of hostile machinegun fire and enemy artillery shelling which never ceases, the French Police do not allow the search parties in the northern section of the Bois de Conde or on the slopes south of the Marne.

On July 26, 1918 at Ourcq the Battalion crosses the Marne and takes up positions on the right flank of the Corps. The Corps is preparing for an assault and the Battalion's mission is to guard the bridges in the area of Mezy and Chateau-Thierry. The Battalion is posted in the area of Ferme des Aulnes Bouillants-Grand Ballois-Petit Heurtebise. In the event of a German attack, the 55th Brigade is to move to the high ground which dominates the left bank of the Marne. Here they will be in a good position to defend these heights and the passage leading to the river. Since July 18 the Germans have been retreating, when their drive towards Paris is completely stopped, and a counterattack starts.

On July 27, 1918 at 2:00 AM movement orders are received, and with only a few hours rest the foot sore soldiers are again in motion. While there had been much grumbling during previous marches, on this one the men move forward cheerfully for they are now headed northward in the direction of the enemy. They all hope to repay the Germans for the damage done along the Marne in the unequal fight of a few days before.

The weather now is rainy and the roads are nearly impassable. But regardless of the extreme difficulties, the unit makes an impressive march and reaches its position several hours ahead of schedule. The unit encamps in the Foret de Fere and receives a hot meal, which will be their last hot meal for the next three days. The unit moves through Nesles and Chateau-Thierry, crosses the Marne River near Brasles over pontoon bridges, and arrives at Mont St. Pere, passing through Jaulgonne before reaching Foret de Fere. During this movement enemy planes continually harass the unit and there are many gas attack alarms.

Over 100 men from the 42nd Division are cared for by the unit, and on July 30, 1918 the Division is relieved by the 32nd Division. The unit now moves to Foret de Ris, east of Le Charmel. From July 27 to the 30, the company supports the 110th Infantry Regiment in its several attacks on the Bois-de-Grimpette. They remain in line with elements of the 109th Infantry Regiment which arrive to support the 110th, and repulse enemy counterattacks made against their position.

During the final assault on these woods and the repulsing of the German counterattack made against Cierges, the Battalion supports both the 109th and 110th Infantry Regiments. In this attack the men move with such precision that it looks more like a drill on a parade field than a battle. Our victory is complete and decisive with more than 400 Germans killed and large numbers taken prisoner. The unit has seven men wounded on July 30, and one man gassed on July 31, 1918.

Shortly after midnight on August 1, 1918 a German plane bombs the 55th Brigade area causing many casualties among the infantry and killing one man in the Hamburg unit. The men of the unit react by giving first aid and providing stretcher bearers for all the wounded. At 6:00 PM on August 3, amidst the rain, the unit is again moving forward via the Roncheres-Cierges-Coulonges road to a hillside northwest of Cohan, where they bivouac for the night. The entire division is moving on the same road, and the numerous halts prove very tiresome and upsetting to the men. The road is completely jammed with ambulances, wagons, guns, horses and men. This is by far the worse march the unit experiences.

They pass over the battlefield of the previous week which is an absolute slaughter house. Unburied dead, both American and German, as well as horses and mules, grimly testifies to the horrible fighting around Cierges and Grimpettes Woods. As night falls the rain becomes heavier, and adding to their discomfort a wind starts to blow, chilling the thoroughly soaked men. About 1:30 in the morning of August 4 the movement is complete and the unit is in position. On the following day dugouts are constructed on a hillside near Mont St. Martin just south of Fismes. This valley is later called "Death Valley" because of the terrible fighting and severe losses which are sustained there.

The Germans start shelling the village of Cohan. This adds to the woes of the tired, wet and burdened soldiers. About the time the positioning of the unit is determined the rain starts to fall even harder and continues all night, soaking the clothing and blankets of the men.

The men leave the roads and trails to take up their required positions in the fields. This same area had been fought over during the proceeding days, and their attempt to move cross-country during the darkness is full of hazards. They walk blindly into obstructions of telephone and telegraph wires, and barbed wire. Finally exhausted from the long march, the men drop to the ground and huddle together in the mud and water and wait for daylight.

Because of the rain and mud, the men in charge of the wagons are forced to remain with their horses and mules since they could not be taken from the road. During the march, and in spite of the seriousness of the situation, many things happened to relieve the tension. The men were cautioning each other to march as quietly as possible. No cigarette smoking is permitted and any equipment making the slightest noise is thrown away. It is almost an invisible column as it silently trudges along. Just as the stillness and darkness become almost unbearable the voice of a mule skinner rings out clearly over the fields as he cusses in a truly American manner his "Blankety blank mules." The men now know they are safe because no German would dare remain close to that outfit, and the profanity brings some relief to the men.

Fismes Sector

Between August 3 and August 19 there is constant activity in the area. The fighting in and around Fismes and Fismette rises and falls, with the unit losing four men killed, ten wounded, four gassed, and five men becoming shell shocked. At varying intervals the Battalion is called to assist units of the 56th Brigade and successfully clears the town on each occasion.

At 1:30 in the afternoon of August 19, 1918 the battalion is ordered to the right of the division sector to a position just north of Arcis-le-Ponsart. This movement in broad daylight and under the direct observation of the Germans creates severe losses, with two men of the company becoming shell shocked, and results in considerable criticism. After passing the town the battalion again suffers heavy casualties, and it is not until the following day that the unit takes up a position in a quarry east of Courville.

The unit is placed on the front line again, and in a position of great disadvantage. The ground is low and vulnerable to heavy concentrations of gas. The days are spent by the troops closely observing enemy activity, but in fact they see few Germans. While the fighting at times is discouraging, the information they receive from prisoners shows conclusively that it is much more discouraging to the Germans. The German losses are extremely heavy. Even though the Germans are using large amounts of mustard gas against their opponent, the morale of the men is very high. The machine guns frequently lay down standing barrages while the special gas troops do their work.

Oise-Aisne

From August 19 until September 1, 1918 the unit is under almost constant artillery fire and observation by enemy planes. They suffer one man killed, one wounded, and three shell shocked as they support the 110th Infantry Regiment. The sector is quiet between September 2 and the 4, and on the September 4 the Battalion crosses the Vesle River on improvised foot bridges which have been built by the men of the battalion.

While crossing this river Major Vail goes across on a fallen tree, and with a wire cutter cuts through the German entanglements. Returning to the American side he performs a similar act on the river bank near his own men, whom he then leads across the river. For this act he is later awarded the Distinguished Service Cross. The Battalion superbly performed all its missions and great credit must be given to the Battalion Commander, Major Vail. He was one of the most active men in the Division, courageous to a fault, able to make decisions quickly, and possessing very sound judgment. Loyal to both his superiors and subordinates alike, he commanded the admiration of all with whom he came in contact. He knew the mission of machinegun units, but constantly went beyond what was required to accomplish the desired results.

On September 5, 1918 the unit attains perhaps its highest success. It not only advances ahead of the infantry without any support, but also takes about 24 German prisoners. This attack occurs at 7:00 AM and the unit loses one man wounded and one shell shocked during the action. It must be noted by this time in the war that all of the infantry regiments had been greatly reduced in strength because of the long, hard, and continuous fighting. They do receive replacements, but in many cases they are not sufficiently trained for combat duty. The unit volunteers for this duty. Machinegun units are supposed to have certain infantry support, but this fine unit, without comment, takes its position on the front line. You can further appreciate the importance of their quick action when it is realized that a counterattack by the Germans is expected at any moment.

On September 6, 1918 there is heavy shelling by the Germans along the entire sector, and the unit loses one man killed, one wounded, and one missing in action. During the fighting from September 5 to the 7 the Battalion occupies advanced positions all along the line, maintaining contact with the French Army on the right and the 110th Infantry Regiment on the left. On many occasions the battalion occupies positions far in advance of the infantry. On September 7 the company suffers extensive casualties with two men being killed, two wounded, and 17 gassed.

Positions are now consolidated and during the following night the battalion is relieved by French troops, and then marches south to a location near Arcis-le-Ponsart where they rest for two days. During the movement on September 8, 1918 the unit has one man gassed. After resting for two days the unit marches to Oeuilly where it goes into bivouac for a day. It then loads onto trucks, passing through Chalons sur Marne, Epernay, Vitry-le-Francois and Ser Maiz, and unloads at Contrission the following afternoon. From there they march to Cheminon-le-Ville.

At Cherinon the battalion participates in a formal French wedding. This elaborate ceremony provides some relief for the troops and takes their minds from the harsh realities of the war for a short time. Now one of the most difficult forced marches is done by the unit from Cheminin-le-Ville to the woods near Lisle-en-Barrois; a distance of 21 miles. This march is made in about ten hours. The march is over congested roads and the new shoes worn by most of the men serves to hasten their exhaustion. The march starts on September 16, 1918 and the wagon train and kitchen does not join the column until the September 18.

The beginning of the end finally comes. July had seen the terrible German offensive stopped. August witnessed the hurling back of the powerful German attack, with many of the enemy's best units breaking, and the German defenses weakening. The day has now arrived to strike a decisive blow, and the delivery of that blow is left to the powerful and confident American Army.

Meuse-Argonne

The Meuse-Argonne has been held by the Germans for four years. During several campaigns, none of the Allied army units dared to undertake an attack against this naturally difficult region. The attitude of fear created so much confidence within the ranks of the Germans that it proves to be an additional obstacle and hardship to overcome.

The 28th Division is in the central sector of the great Argonne Forest. The river Aire cuts through a valley, creating a German defensive position so strong that they erect huge storehouses, railroads, and even military schools in the area. The Meuse-Argonne offensive is one of the greatest battles in which American troops have ever fought. It is important because of the large numbers of units involved in the fight, and the tactical skill in which the units were used and the results obtained.

To illustrate the enormity of the Meuse-Argonne offensive, a comparison with Gettysburg is given. General Meade at Gettysburg had roughly 200 artillery pieces and the artillery action during the battle was the most powerful in history until that time. General Pershing in the Meuse-Argonne had more than 2,700 artillery pieces of 3-inch or larger caliber. Gettysburg lasted for three days, while the Meuse-Argonne offensive lasted for 47 days. The Meuse-Argonne can also be compared with the Wilderness Campaign during the

American Civil war, as the terrain of both battles is covered with heavy thickets and dense underbrush. The Wilderness Campaign, known as a long drawn-out battle lasted seven days. The Meuse-Argonne lasted more than six times that long. 100,000 men were engaged during the Wilderness, and twelve times that number in the Meuse-Argonne.

On September 20, 1918 the Battalion moves to the edge of the Argonne Forest near Neuvilly. It remains there until September 25 when orders are received to be ready to participate in the attack, which is to start at 5:30 AM on September 26, 1918. Prior to taking its position in line, the battalion, in platoon formation moves out, encountering much traffic congestion as scores of tanks move up into assault positions. Even though they are under heavy shelling, the unit moves safely through Neuvilly. One mile past the town the unit moves east over a badly congested road, and is held up by the tanks and troops of the 35th Division which had not found its sector.

The unit finally gets into position and is ready to open the barrage at zero hour. The Company is assigned to the 109th Infantry Regiment at this time. Due to German aerial observation nearly all movement is made under the cover of darkness. The roads are limited and also in many cases in bad condition because of the continuous shelling. During the day the troops rest in concealed places, and in order to save time, energy and road space, many units are transported in trucks.

By 1:00 AM the unit is in place. While it is well known to them that the forthcoming battle will be one of the largest battles in the world's history to that point, most of the men sleep soundly upon the ground, waiting for the word to advance. These are the tried and true veterans. The roads and fields are dotted with shell holes, the result of four years of artillery explosions, making advancing extremely difficult. As the troops advance the condition of the roads makes re-supply not only difficult but extremely hazardous. It is also difficult for runners to deliver messages since there are no roads to follow and it is very easy to become lost. The morning of the jump-off is foggy and at times the men can barely see 50 feet in front of them.

Their instructions for the advance are clear. Gaps will be cut in the wire and all available means of overcoming obstacles will be used. Penetration is to be gained by using lanes of least resistance to advance and to attack strong points by flanking them. The attack is to be pushed on with the greatest energy, and defensive positions when occupied are to be strongly organized in depth and the terrain exploited. Moving of the machinegun units proves very difficult during the first day.

Late in the afternoon of September 26, 1918 the Battalion moves to a point about 100 yards south of Varennes and spends the night in what had been German trenches. Early the following morning the company advances independently through the town, which had been a German strongpoint, and later occupies a line of dugouts north of the town. Parts of the battalion assist the infantry attack on Montblainville, with Company A losing two men killed during this action. During this engagement it is necessary because of the congested roads, to fill their ration sacks with loose ammunition for the machineguns, and to sling the bags across the backs of the mules. The mules are taken from the limbers and put into service as pack mules in order to get the ammunition to the gun crews on the front line.

Montblainville is taken at 10:00 AM on September 27, 1918 after two violent German counter attacks are successfully repulsed. The beating back of the German force results in heavy casualties. When the advance line of the infantry enters the town the Germans seem not to realize the force of the attack, and as a result many prisoners are taken. The fighting is so severe that many men are killed or wounded by the Germans, some of which had been passed by and left in dugouts and cellars. Some Americans are shot in the back while passing these points.

The attack strikes the Germans with such force that they are driven out of the village in disorder, rushing to the next hill. The right and left flanks could not move as rapidly however, and in short time the Germans reform. The line north of Montblainville is subjected to enfilading fire from the flanks, and rifle, machinegun, and artillery fire from the front. During the afternoon the attack is renewed with increased fury, and the unit is put into the front line. They use captured German machineguns in large quantities, and save the day by keeping up a continuous fire during the entire afternoon, which proves to be the longest of the campaign.

Between September 28 and the September 30 there is intensive fighting in and north of Montblainville, and the company lost one man killed and four wounded. While in the Apremont sector, the battalion occupies Strong Point No. 1 and 2 along with other positions in and around the town. In the counterattacks made on the town of Apremont on the morning of October 1, 1918, the entire battalion is engaged. The Company loses one man wounded and two gassed.

Thousands of rounds of ammunition are brought forward in anticipation of an assault. Just as the assault is to begin the Germans start an intense artillery barrage, which is followed closely by German infantry advancing in tightly packed formations. A dense fog prevents the early detection of the German advance until they are within close range. The machine gunners had been instructed to hold their fire until the Germans are within close range. Almost simultaneously the machineguns all along the wide front opened fire. Mowing down hundreds of the enemy, breaking up the assault and totally demoralizing at least three German regiments. The German attack lasts about an hour, but in that short time a terrible disaster befalls the German ranks.

The Germans launch their attack on Apremont at 4:45 AM with two regiments in line and one in support. They are aided by machineguns and hand grenades, and drive fiercely and with determination against the American line. The unit is on alert, awaiting their own zero hour, and consequently the Germans are surprised by the resistance the men put up. With the help of the artillery and machineguns, the Division repulses the German attack all along the entire front. The Germans are forced to retire in disorder, leaving their dead piled thick around Apremont and Le Chene Tondu. That the Germans intended to hold this line and, if driven back, to retake it any cost, was shown by orders found on prisoners captured in this fight. The Germans were trying desperately to halt the Argonne advance by any means. The town of Apremont is also shelled by the

Germans on October 4, 1918 with mustard gas. The troops located there suffer considerably.

In spite of the heavy fire they receive, the unit remains in this position all day and the following day, losing one man killed as they fire intermittently into Chatel Chehery and Le Menil Farm. During these few days the unit suffers many casualties, losing four more men as wounded and seven being gassed, with one man killed on October 2, 3 and 4. However, the success of the engagement serves to keep the morale of the men high. On October 5, 1918 the unit crosses the Aire River, losing one killed and one wounded in the process. On October 7 the unit wades across the river carrying all of its equipment and supplies and once again occupies Chatel Chehery. Later in the day the unit advances beyond the town in support of the 109th Infantry Regiment, losing one man killed, and then losing two more men wounded and two gassed on October 8, 1918.

On the morning of October 9, 1918 the Division is relieved by the 82nd Division, with the battalion leaving the line and marching to Neuvilly. A night's ride in busses takes the unit to some barracks. On October 14 the wagon train finally arrives after being on the road for three days. On this date the unit has one man gassed, and the battalion receives large numbers of replacements. The unit's participation in the advance lasted from September 26 until the night of October 8, 1918, with almost continuous fighting. An advance of almost six miles had been made against stubborn and desperate German resistance, and over terrain that afforded the enemy a great defensive advantage.

As a rule, while the unit was in the front line was served with hot food twice a day. When they did not receive food it was not due to a lack of food, but due to the fact that the food details were cut off by the German shelling. There was always plenty of ammunition for the machineguns in spite of the fact that the ammunition expenditure by the machineguns was very high. The wounded were promptly evacuated and cared for. The ambulances came into Apremont and later into Chatel Chehery over the main road, even though it was constantly shelled by the Germans.

Following is a letter of commendation to the 108th Machine Gun Battalion from the Commanding General of the 28th Division:

HEADQUARTERS 28TH DIVISION, U.S. ARMY

FROM: Chief of Staff
TO: 108th MG Bn
SUBJECT: Commendation

The Division Commander desires me to express his appreciation of the good work performed by all the officers and soldiers of the 108th Machine Gun Battalion during the offensive in the valley of Aire and the Argonne Forest.

During the fifteen days of the advance, starting on the 26th of September, this battalion at all times gave valuable assistance and support to the 55th Brigade. The work done during the capture and defense of Apremont and again in the taking of Chatel-Chehery deserves the highest commendation.

By command of Major General Muir:
W.C. Sweeney
Chief of Staff

Steadily and surely, though still fighting desperately, the Germans fall back. The German leadership now begins to see that the end is drawing near. However, they make every effort to lengthen the time when the collapse would come.

At last rumors are heard of an "armistice". From day to day during this period the men discuss the chances of the Germans capitulating and the reality of an end to the war. On November 7, 1918 word comes that parliamentarians will be at hand at some point along the front line to submit a request for an armistice, this being the first official news of a definite event of this kind. The same day a report that the Armistice has actually been signed spreads throughout the unit. However, the end is not yet, though it seems to be very close at hand. Regardless of these events, the Americans continue to relentlessly press forward, crushing the ebbing resistance of the Germans. Meanwhile the "active waiting" continues.

Thiaucourt

Captain Crow assumes command of the battalion because Major Vail is evacuated due to being gassed while at Menil-la-Tour. The Battalion remains at this place until October 17, 1918 when it moves to Noviant and occupies billets there. Until October 29 the unit conducts training, with the newly assigned replacements receiving special training.

During the evening of October 28, 1918 the Battalion moves to the Thiaucourt sector in the old Saint Mihiel salient, and the vicinity of Hattonchatel, Vigneulles and Saint Benoit. These positions are held until November 10 with frequent position changes but little fighting. During the period of November 1 through November 10 the company loses one man killed, one wounded, and three to gas. On November 10 there is heavy artillery fire and the unit is ordered forward to support the 109th and 110th Infantry Regiments in the capture of Haumont.

In anticipation of a general attack on the morning of November 11, 1918, a memorandum is issued on November 10, directing that a strong reconnaissance be made along the enemy front to find weaknesses in the German defenses. At 8:10 on the morning of the 11 word is received of the approaching Armistice. All units are directed to push forward in small groups to consolidate positions. About this time the German artillery cuts loose all along the line with tremendous force. The Division and Corps artillery now fires with every available gun in retaliation with an awesome display of firepower that is kept up until five minutes before the hour of the Armistice.

There is four minutes of silence while the guns are readied. At one minute to 11:00 AM all of the Allied artillery cuts loose with terrific force, firing at maximum rate for 30 seconds. Then all is quiet. A quiet made more striking and fateful by its contrast with the noise just ended. At last the "doughboys" in the lines know that the end has really come. A stunned, awed pause, and then all along the line the men from Pennsylvania shout with joy.

During this last day the battalion suffers many casualties however, the Hamburg unit is spared and suffers none. Though rumors of an armistice had been common, the men had no indication of its nearness. The Company is still supporting the 109th and 110th Infantry Regiments on November 11, 1918, and there is spirited fighting on both sides. It is not until about 9:45 in the morning that word is received that the scheduled attack is not to be made. The Armistice had been signed effective as of 11:00 AM that day. Immediately upon arrival of the eleventh hour all firing ceases and there is general rejoicing in the ranks on both sides of "no mans land."

The end of the fighting finally arrives, with the unit still pushing forward, still driving the enemy back. No advantage won is to be lost in case the Armistice fails, but really in case the Germans play any more of their devilish tricks. Every foot of ground gained is to be kept, and they keep on gaining that morning. Many casualties are taken that morning, but those casualties are insurance against the possibility of more. The orders come quickly. No communications are to be held with the enemy. The ground won is to be held, positions consolidated, and units organized to actively defend against any possibility.

The reaction of the Germans is vastly different. The burden of certain defeat and imminent disorder and catastrophe is now lifted from their minds. Individual comforts crowd out any thought of organized lines and unit morale. Immediately after 11:00 AM, the Germans throw down their weapons and start walking towards the American lines, seeking to trade whatever they could for white bread and tobacco. The Germans do not understand when they are firmly told to get back and to stay away from the Americans. That night, in the care free elation of the relief that is theirs, the Germans set off their signal rockets and other fireworks making for a wonderful display.

Men stood speechless, mouths wide open as if awaiting some terrible denial. Then they broke into tears and laughter that subsided, followed by wild cheering as they shook hands, slapping each other on the back, and standing straight as they walk cautiously into the open. After the firing ceases, some Yanks and Germans do get together in the middle ground.

There is little handshaking or fraternization in the true sense. The Yanks go forward with slung weapons, while most of the Germans leave their weapons in the trenches. There is much talk in an active trading atmosphere, as the Germans are bribed with cigarettes, rations, and soap. The Yanks come away from the trading with belt buckles, Iron Crosses, bayonets, and even a few Luger pistols. In the clearing where shells fell only an hour before they now play games, with alcohol coming along later in sufficient quantities to make it a proper celebration.

The day after the Armistice the battalion moves back to the Hassavant Farm, which had been a German evacuation hospital. It remains there until January 8, 1919 when they march to Saulzures-les-Vannes. Here the unit remains until March 19, 1919 when it entrains for the Le Mans embarkation center.

During the period between October 25, 1918 and December 13, 1918 the Battalion was under the command of Captain Ernest A. Swingle of Company A, because Captain Crow had been ordered back to the United States as an instructor. On April 17, 1919 the Battalion moves from the Le Mans area for St. Nazaire where it remains until April 30. On that day the unit embarks on the *U.S.S. Peerless* bound for the Unites States, arriving in Philadelphia on May 16, 1919. They entrain for Camp Dix, New Jersey the same day. The unit is demobilized on May 18, 1919 at Camp Dix and is mustered out of Federal service on May 28, 1919.

Looking at the achievement record of the unit there are so many noteworthy elements that it is difficult determining the most important. After doing a fair analysis of the unit itself many things stand out. These include the character of the men and their high morale under the most difficult conditions. Their spirit of loyalty which always manifested itself and directed their efforts for the common good of all, the caliber of the officers, and the esteem and respect in which the men held them. From the time in Camp Hancock until the close of hostilities on the Western Front in France the unit enjoyed a high reputation. They always maintained the highest of military standards, and like all good units, refused to allow its success and high standing to run unchecked or affect its distinguished behavior.

Official records prove that the battalion was the only machine gun unit in the entire American Army to ever advance in front of the infantry and capture enemy prisoners. Of that operation someone commented that "it displayed excellent courage but poor tactics." But, the person who said that was most likely unfamiliar with the situation at hand. Not realizing that the men of the 108th were sent forward to hold an unoccupied portion of the line at a time when infantry was not available, and that the infantry later took positions behind the machine gunners who continued to advance. It is possible that prisoners were taken by one machine gun unit of the French Army, but this can not be documented with any certainty. So the 108th can, without conceit, claim to be the only unit of its type in all the armies of the world at that time to take prisoners.

The officers, non-commissioned officers, and the enlisted men worked together as a well trained and led team during the war. They worked in a spirit of harmony and good will, rewarding their efforts with success. Their esprit de corps prevailed under the most adverse circumstances, and criticism and complaints were seldom heard. The greatest comfort to the comrades of a soldier who made the supreme sacrifice is that he fell facing the enemy. The men who died with their faces to the front were soldiers of the highest caliber. They served in a manner that reflects the highest credit upon the American military and their memory will forever be kept alive by those who will never forget the sacrifices they made. They willingly sacrificed all during the springtime of their life, when the joy of living is the greatest and the desire to survive the strongest.

The machine gun units were nicknamed "Suicide Squads" because whenever they went into action, every arm of the enemy went into action against them. They were also quite frequently left behind to cover the withdrawal of other troops, and under these conditions often found it extremely difficult in removing themselves along with their guns.

The Behler-Hein Post No. 637 of the American Legion in Hamburg is named in memory of Mess Sergeant Walter E. Behler and Cook Thomas Hein, who made the supreme sacrifice in "Death Valley" south of the Vesle River. Both were killed by the same German artillery shell. Also, the Wagner-Good Post No. 216 of the Veterans of Foreign Wars in Hamburg is named for Private First Class Clarence J. Wagner and Corporal Charles H. Good who were killed in action in 1918 while serving with the unit.

The following letters are of interest:

FROM: BG Thomas W. Darrah
TO: Commanding General, 28th Div
SUBJECT: Extract from report of Captured American Soldier

In compliance with orders, PVT James R. Mussett, Co E, 137th Inf., who was captured on Sep 29th in the Argonne Forest, has submitted a report detailing his experiences while a prisoner in the hands of the Germans.

He relates being questioned by a German officer, and the following is an extract from this interview:

Q. Who was on your right and left?
A. I don't know, sir.
Q. I will tell you then. The 91st on your right and Pershing's "Iron Men" on your left.
A. I said: "Who is Pershing's Iron Men?" He said: the 28th Div.

The 28th Div made an enviable reputation, and it would appear from the foregoing that this had even reached the enemy.

This may be of value in preparing the history of this Division, and is submitted for you to make such use as you see fit.

(Signed) Thomas W. Darrah

OFFICIAL:
  Richard W. Watson
  Lieutenant Colonel
  Division Adjutant

HEADQUARTERS 28TH DIVISION
AMERICAN EXPEDITIONARY FORCES

France, April 11, 1919

GENERAL ORDERS
No. 13

In compliance with General Orders 41, General Headquarters, American Expeditionary Forces, dated March 4, 1919, the following organizations, by direction of the Commander-in-Chief, are entitled to credit for participation in battle and to be presented with a ribbon with the names of battles printed thereon in lieu of the silver bands.

The silver bands will be presented later to the organizations by the War Department.

109th Inf
110th Inf
111th Inf
112th Inf
107th MG Bn
108th MG Bn
109th MG Bn
107th FA

108th FA
109th FA
103rd Eng
103rd Field Signal Bn

As directed by the Commander-in-Chief, the Division Commander will now decorate the colors or standards of the above mentioned organizations.

By command of Major General

Hay:

DAVID J. DAVIS
Colonel, General Staff
Chief of Staff

January 2, 1923

TO: The Adjutant General of the Army, Washington, D.C.
SUBJECT: Battle Participation of the 28th Division

The Battle Participation Board has searched available existing records bearing upon the service of the 28th Division, and presents herewith its findings:

The elements of the 28th Division arrived in France at the ports and on the dates indicated below:

108th MG Bn . . . . Calais (Pas de Calais) . . . May 18, 1918

The following is the result obtained by the Board: for those units which have previously been given credit, parallel columns are shown in order that the difference between former credits and the present credits may be shown:

108th Machine Gun Battalion

Chateau-Thierry (Champagne) –	Jul 9 – Jul 14 1918
Champagne-Marne -	Jul 15 – Jul 18 1918
Aisne-Marne -	Jul 18 – Aug 6 1918
Fismes Sector (Champagne) -	Aug 7 – Aug 17 1918
Oise-Aisne -	Aug 18 – Sep 7 1918
Meuse-Argonne -	Sep 26 – Oct 9 1918
Thiaucourt (Lorraine) -	Oct 16 – Nov 11 1918

Under the provisions of Section 5, General Orders No. 16, War Department, 1921, as amended by Section 5, General Orders No. 24, War Department, 1922, it is recommended that such of the units of the 28th Division listed below as are entitled to carry colors or standards be authorized to place thereon a streamer in the colors of the Victory Ribbon, bearing the inscription noted, to show battle participation during the World War:

108th MG Bn – CHAMPAGNE, CHAMPAGNE-MARNE, AISNE-MARNE, OISE-AISNE, LORRAINE, MEUSE-ARGONNE

96th Pennsylvania Volunteer Infantry Regiment (1862)

Company D, 103rd QM Regiment (1940)

Full-time staff (1957-1989)

CSM	1SG	CW4	Mr.	MSG	CW4
Michael	Randy	George	Charles	Craig	Daryl
Werley	Kramer	Reitnouer	Eyer	Kleinsmith	Hamm

Convoy to Fort A. P. Hill, Virginia (1982)

Memorial Day Services (1986)

Award Ceremony (1987)

CHAPTER 7

Between the Wars
1920 - 1940

When World War I ended and the men of Company A, 108th Machine Gun Battalion returned to their homes and families, many wondered if their would still be a National Guard. There still would be a National Guard after the "War to end all wars." The National Guard was a mandated by law, and some of the men who served during the war would remain as members of the unit. During this period in time, being a soldier in the National Guard was assumed by many men, and for some was a long standing family tradition. Because of these men the Hamburg unit's long history did not come to an end, but would continue on as it had for many years.

The unit was officially reorganized on September 30, 1921 in the Pennsylvania National Guard as Wagon Company No. 106, an element of the 28th Division. The unit was federally recognized on October 14, 1921, per General Orders No. 29, The Adjutant General of Pennsylvania, dated November 1, 1921.

As the 106th Wagon Company, the unit was part of the 28th Division Quartermaster Train and responsible for furnishing the transportation of personnel and supplies. It consisted of a captain, a first lieutenant, a second lieutenant, and 55 enlisted men. A wagon company was a hard working organization, and normally was on-duty before reveille and usually only completing their duties several hours after retreat. During field training exercises it was not unusual to find the men driving their wagons for 20 continuous hours.

Wagon companies were commonly known to the other branches of the Army as "Mule Skinners." The men didn't resent this name, but rather took it with good character. They knew, as nobody else did what their duties entailed. A great deal within the division depended on the "Mule Skinners" to get personnel and supplies to where they were needed, on time. Often they were called upon to deliver supplies to locations that trucks could not reach. To a great extent the contentment of the division depended upon the efficiency of the wagon companies. Especially since they for all practical purposes fed the division or saw that the food was delivered.

As a wagon company their training was both wide-ranging and interesting. The men trained in the usual soldiering skills such as close order drill, manual of arms, and rifle marksmanship. But in addition to those things, the men also had to be proficient in the operation and maintenance of wagons, care of horses, how to spot a sick horse, remedies in cases of emergency, and how to load, pull, and assemble wagons. The Company Commander, Captain Casper, purchased a life-sized wooden horse. This was used to instruct new soldiers how to harness, saddle, and bridle a horse. When the unit reorganized to a truck company in 1936, the wooden horse was given to the Berks County Historical Society in Reading.

Throughout this period in time the unit held, or participated in special events remembering their fallen comrades, and their lineage. In 1928 First Sergeant Harold W. Dalious was a member of the Escort of Honor that represented the 28th Division Train during the memorial dedication trip to France. He was selected by the company commander for his honorable and faithful service.

As a member of the Honor Battalion sent to France, he participated in the dedication of memorials erected by the Battle Monuments Commission of Pennsylvania. These monuments were erected to honor the Pennsylvania soldiers who lost their lives during World War I. First Sergeant Harold Dalious enlisted in Company E, 4th Pennsylvania Infantry on June 11, 1917 and continuously served with the unit through World War I and for many years thereafter. The year 1928 also marked the last reunion held by the unit which included members from the Civil War. J. Albert Sunday was the last surviving unit member from the Civil War.

The unit excelled in weapons marksmanship competitions during the years between the wars. In January of 1932 they won a

Pistol Cup awarded by the Pottsville Republican newspaper for the best scores in a local pistol league. In 1933 the unit placed 8th in the Militia Bureau Indoor Rifle Match by scoring 2,247 points out of a possible 3,000.

Captain Casper was an excellent marksman and received instruction as a range officer at the National Matches in Camp Perry, Ohio. The unit rifle team was selected to represent the Division and competed in the National Matches at Camp Perry in 1939. Another interesting note is that during this time period, unit soldiers were allowed to take their assigned .30 caliber rifle from the armory and use it for deer hunting.

In 1932 the unit adopted the bugle call as a means of calling the officers and soldiers to drill on Friday evenings. The Bugler sounded drill call promptly at 7:35 PM with assembly at 7:45, and recall was sounded at 9:15 PM. This seems to have been quite a novelty for some time and was adopted by many other units. Private First Class Carl Wilhelm was the bugler and evidently was quite proficient in sounding the calls.

On April 17, 1936 the unit was reorganized as Company D, 103rd Quartermaster Regiment, 28th Division, per General Orders No. 2, The Adjutant General of Pennsylvania, dated April 17, 1936. The unit was now a truck transportation company.

During this time period the unit armory was located on North Third Street in Hamburg. In 1934 funding was approved by the Commonwealth of Pennsylvania to erect a new armory for the Hamburg unit. The construction was delayed for some time due to funding problems however in 1937 $60,000 was finally allotted for a new armory to be built.

In April of 1937 the citizens of Hamburg purchased three acres of land on North Fifth Street for the new armory. The land was purchased from Samuel Myers for $2,000 and donated to Commonwealth, and the property was conveyed (Ord. 193) on October 4, 1937. The State Armory Board inspected the site and gave their final approval of the design in May of 1937. Elmer Adams of Reading was the Architect.

The turning of the first shovel full of earth for the new armory was done by the company commander, Captain Casper, at 2:00 PM on January 12, 1938. After the ceremony, construction of the $72,000 armory got under way. F.C. Kuick of Mahanoy City was the general contractor. In October of 1938 construction was completed and the unit moved into their new armory.

On February 20, 1937 more than 80 men attended a reunion of the former Company E, 4th Regiment. Included were many veterans of the Spanish-American War, Mexican Border service, and World War I. The event was sponsored by the Hamburg Athletic and Military Association, formally known as the Blue Mountain Legion. Member of Company D, 103rd Quartermaster Regiment were present along with guests. Captain Casper served as the master of ceremonies and conducted a brief program.

Captain Casper then read the roster of unit members from 1875, the year the unit was officially organized after the Civil War however no members from that war were present. William M. Smith, John M. Smith, and William Vennerwaldt responded to the roll call of 1885 members. Charles C. Harris, First Sergeant of the company in 1899 read a roster for that year. William F. Seaman, Robert Shollenberger, Samuel Epler, Chester Isett, Clayton Lewars, E. Newton Miller, William Reinhart, Harvey Smith, Abraham Williamson, Edward Lewars, and Levi Williamson responded to that call. Five Spanish-American War veterans were present for the reunion. They were Major George F. Potteiger, Allen Degler, Harvey Smith, William Reinhart, and Samuel Epler. Samuel Epler also served during the Philippine Insurrection and World War I.

As for State Active Duty during this time period, only one instance can be found. The unit was called up in 1936 and sent to Johnstown for flood disaster duty. The time between the wars was spent in rebuilding and retraining in preparation for the next war. Of course the men did not expect nor desire another war, but never the less they were ready when called upon to serve once again.

CHAPTER 8

World War II
1941 - 1945

The peace didn't last and before long the unit was again called to serve the nation. It was inducted into Federal service on January 22, 1941 at Hamburg, per Executive Order No. 8633, dated January 14, 1941. The unit left Hamburg and traveled to Fort Indiantown Gap for further mobilization training and readiness for overseas deployment.

On January 28, 1941 the unit was reorganized and re-designated at the 121st Quartermaster Car Company and relieved from assignment to the 28th Division, per Adjutant General Orders No. 320.2. The main reason the unit was reorganized from a truck company to a car company was because it had one of the safest driving records throughout the entire Army. The Company thus formed was made up of a Headquarters Platoon, 1st Platoon and 2nd Platoon, totaling 78 enlisted men.

The Company was under the command of First Lieutenant Franklin L. Loy, with Second Lieutenant Joseph A. Schwalm assigned as an officer. Immediately upon activation the unit is on alert for overseas duty and the following days are spent by removing all organizational markings and insignias, and packing and loading in preparation for movement. Later the unit moves to Camp Livingston, Louisiana, and on January 31, 1942 they depart that location by train for Fort Dix, New Jersey for embarkation.

Prior to departing Camp Livingston the company is given a farewell parade by the 103rd Quartermaster Battalion. Major General Ord, commanding general of the 28th Division delivers a farewell address to the unit. They arrive at Fort Dix on February 2, 1942.

Almost immediately some of the men are sent to New York City to receive the new authorized vehicles that would be taken overseas. The following two weeks are spent in preparing the vehicles for shipment, and inspections are held to insure that all equipment is in good condition.

At 11:15 PM on February 17, 1942 the company departs Fort Dix by train. They arrive at the New York port of embarkation at 1:00 AM on February 18, with one man being AWOL during the movement. Boarding the ship at 6:00 AM the same day, they set sail from New York at 2:00 AM on February 19. At the time of departure the discipline and morale of the men is excellent. Most of the men are wondering where their destination might be, and what new adventures and experiences are in store for them.

It would not take very long for events to become exciting. Their crossing of the Atlantic is very eventful and exciting because convoy escort vessels sink three German submarines during the voyage. They arrive safely in Belfast, Ireland on March 2, 1942. From there they cross the Irish Sea and land at Stranrahr, Scotland. There they unload, board a train, and arrive in London at 2:00 AM on March 4, 1942.

As soon as they arrive in London, the company is assigned to the London Base Command. Immediate preparations are made to begin motor pool operations. For the first two weeks of their stay in London, the men are kept busy cleaning office buildings, and the drivers are taken on sight seeing tours. The tours are conducted in order to acquaint the men with the city while they wait for their vehicles to arrive.

Upon arrival of the vehicles, the company starts motor pool operations. Their mission is to provide transportation for the European Theater of Operations Headquarters, Allied Force Headquarters, London Base Command, and for other various United States Army units stationed in London. Due to the increased demand for transportation, additional enlisted men are assigned to the company. This brings it up to full authorized strength of two passenger car platoons, and two truck platoons.

Driving on the left side of the road and under blackout conditions are new experiences for the men. However, these only temporarily handicap the men and they soon master these conditions. The typical London fog also causes some concern, but after many hours of driving in foggy conditions, the men become quite confident and proficient. During the middle of April 1942, Lieutenant Loy receives notification of his promotion to captain, which had been in effect since February. The delay in being notified promptly was due to the fact that the U.S. Mail service to the British Isles was still in the elementary and experimental stage. The men only now begin receiving mail from home.

The following months find the company busily engaged in motor pool activities. In July of 1942, London Base Command issues an order requiring the removal of all outer dual wheels on all trucks to conserve rubber and shipping space. Also during July, Second Lieutenant Robert F. Mead is assigned to the Company. In addition to the regular and routine motor pool operations, the next few months find the men working night and day, driving Allied Force Headquarters officers who are busily engaged in preparations for the African Campaign. In November of 1942 Captain Loy is promoted and relieved of his duties as company commander, and Captain Harry D. Fritts takes over as commander. Also during November, Lieutenant Schwalm transfers out of the Company, and Second Lieutenants Carlson and James F. O'Brien are assigned to the Company.

On February 17, 1942 the 3rd and 4th Platoons of the 121st Quartermaster Car Company are activated at Camp Beauregard, Louisiana. They are led by Second Lieutenants George J. Mumma and Charles J. Rosenthal. These two platoons are comprised of men from Companies E and F, and a few from the Service Company, 103rd Quartermaster Regiment. This is the same Regiment that the Hamburg unit was part of as Company D, before being reorganized and reassigned. The two platoons total 56 enlisted men and two officers.

Immediately upon activation the two new platoons move to Camp Livingston and begin basic car company training. The training includes first echelon maintenance, how to report to officers, the necessity of presenting a neat and military appearance at all times, and map reading. They are also given aptitude tests and driver tests for the purpose of issuing Drivers Operators Permits. At the same time, vehicles are drawn from the 103rd Quartermaster Regiment which is being reduced to a battalion because of the tri-angularization of the 28th Division.

On March 17, 1942 the 3rd Platoon consisting of 28 men and led by Second Lieutenant Rosenthal is alerted for movement to Fort Sam Houston, Texas. Immediately upon receiving this alert they complete all routine inspections, and on March 20 depart Camp Livingston. They arrive at Fort Sam Houston on March 21 and are assigned to Headquarters, Third Army for the purpose of gaining hands-on experience.

On May 15, 1942 both the 3rd and 4th Platoons are individually alerted for overseas duty. Again inspections are made, vehicles prepared for overseas shipment, and loaded on flatbed rail cars for transportation to the New York Port of Embarkation. The 3rd Platoon departs Fort Sam Houston on May 25, 1942, and the 4th Platoon departs Camp Beauregard on May 26. The two platoons meet for the first time since separation at Fort Dix, New Jersey on May 28, 1942.

The platoons depart New York on June 4, 1942, with each platoon sailing on a separate ship. They arrive at Gurock, Scotland and unload on June 9, 1942. Upon arrival in England the two platoons separate once again, with the 3rd Platoon assigned to the Headquarters, 8th Air Force Bomber Command, and the 4th Platoon assigned to the 8th Air Force Service Command. The following eight months find both platoons busily engaged in courier service and driving both staff officers and many celebrities. This gives the drivers a lot of opportunity to cover all parts of England and Scotland.

On January 30, 1943 all elements of the 121st Quartermaster Car Company are alerted for movement by water. At this time Captain Fritts is replaced as the company commander by Captain Herschell A. Hinckley, and Lieutenant Carlson is also relieved at this time. Excess personnel in the Headquarters, 1st, and 2nd Platoons stationed in London are reassigned to other units. As usual, the Company conducts routine inspections and the vehicles are prepared for shipment by sea. On February 8, 1943 for the first time since activation, the entire Company meets and consolidates into one unit at Litchfield, England.

For the next two weeks the Company conducts preparatory training, which includes the maintenance and use of vehicles in a tropical climate and sandy conditions. They depart England on February 22, 1943 and arrive in Oran, Algeria on March 4. Records of mileage and maintenance during the unit's stay in England cannot be estimated, because all of the records were left at the respective motor pools. The reason the records remained behind was to assist and expedite the task of provisional car platoons that were formed to replace the 121st Quartermaster Car Company.

Upon arrival at Oran, the unit is assigned motor pool operations for the Headquarters, Mediterranean Base Section. From arrival up to and including May 1, 1944, routine motor pool operations take place with the unit averaging approximately 100,000 miles per month of driving. After the campaign, an average of 65,000 to 75,000 miles per month is maintained. Because of the harsh climatic conditions in North Africa and the existing shortages of vehicle parts and rubber, vehicle maintenance is highly stressed. Records are kept to insure that all vehicles receive inspections promptly at every 1,000 and 6,000 miles. In addition, daily and weekly inspections are conducted.

On February 17, 1994 the Company is reorganized under Table of Organization 10-87, dated December 29, 1943, reducing its authorized enlisted strength to 130. Prior to this the unit was authorized 152 enlisted men. Because of this reorganization, 17 enlisted men are rendered excess and transferred to the 1st Replacement Depot.

Unit casualties in North Africa include Private Henry Smith who is killed as a result of enemy action at Sebila, Tunisia on April 1, 1943; and Private Lawrence H. Miller who is killed in an automobile accident while in the performance of duty on May 29, 1943. In March of 1943, Lieutenants Rosenthal and Mead are rotated back to the United States, and Lieutenant Mumma is transferred to the Center District, Mediterranean Base Section. First Lieutenants Ruggierri, James F. McKenna, and Second Lieutenant Joseph P. Stepien are assigned as replacements.

The fighting in North Africa has been bitter, and as a result, infantry replacements are sought in non-combat units. Many men from the company are sent to replacement depots for infantry training, and later assigned to combat units. It should be noted that many of these men went on to distinguish themselves in action in Sicily and Anzio.

The start of 1944 found the company still in Oran and still providing transportation, though now the fighting was further away in Sicily and then in Italy. The various units that remain in North Africa have to be moved, and the unit is actively engaged in this task under the various headquarters that were established.

During this time trips to Misserghin, Camp Sebkra for training in field conditions is ordered, and the unit rotates men through this training. They also take trips to the sea side resort of Ain el Turck, where they have some rest and relaxation for a few days. This proves a very popular diversion for the men, and provides them with some variety to make up for their otherwise monotonous duty.

During the month of July 1944 the unit continues its usual duties. On July 10, 1944 the unit is alerted for movement by water and immediately begins preparations. On July 20, 1944 the 3rd Platoon, led by First Lieutenant McKenna, with 25 enlisted men, departs the Company for Naples, taking with them 22 vehicles. The reminder of the Company moves to the European Theater of Operations. Also during July, Lieutenant Ruggieri is replaced by First Lieutenant Howard E. Weinheimer.

The next to leave Oran is the 2nd Platoon, led by Lieutenant O'Brien, and consisting of 36 men. This detachment departs Oran for Southern France, which has been taken by the Allies less than a month before in September of 1944. The remainder of the company (Headquarters, 1st and 4th Platoons) are relieved from assignment to Headquarters Mediterranean Base Section on September 10, 1944, and assigned to Headquarters, 7th Army.

They arrive in the Bay of Toulon on September 14, but cannot disembark due to congestion in the area, and remain in the bay for four days. They finally disembark on September 21 and go into camp at Toulon, France. On September 22 the 3rd Platoon begins their move from Naples, Italy. They land at St. Topez, France, unload equipment and vehicles and convoy to Marseille, France. On September 17 the 2nd Platoon joins the 3rd Platoon, and five days later the entire company is once again together in Marseille.

The union is short-lived when on October 1, 1944 the Headquarters, 1st and 4th Platoons depart Marseille for Dijon. The 2nd and 3rd Platoons remain in Marseille and are attached to the Continental Base Section for duty. Captain Hinckley commands the element in Dijon while Lieutenant McKenna is in command of the detachment in Marseille.

The drivers are constantly dispatched on extended trips and are seeing France. Trips to Paris, Besancon, Epinal, and the Riveria are constant, and despite the cold weather that was setting in and the incredible amount of work done by the men, their moral is high.

The year 1945 began slowly for the company. The Company totals 254 men as of February 25, 1945, with some men still being transferred to the infantry. Replacements into the company for the most part are men who had been wounded in combat and placed in limited assignment category. The unit then moves to Nancy, France and establishes motor pool operations there on February 20.

Following is an extract from the Narrative Report of the Headquarters, 1st and 4th Platoons for the month of February 1945, which should give the reader an idea of the prevailing conditions at that time.

"Driving conditions were improved during the month due to the disappearance of snow. Due to the better driving conditions a minimum of four motor vehicle accidents were encountered during the month. Considering the fact that the motor pool totaled 185,000 miles for the month, with a fleet of 210 passenger and cargo vehicles, it is believed the number of accidents should constitute a reasonably low average."

"Personnel of the motor pool consisted of 70 enlisted men from the 121st QM Car Company, 77 enlisted men attached from Hq Co, 21st Port (M), plus approximately 60 civilian drivers, 30 of whom were brought along from the old location. Employment of civilian personnel due to the shortage of military personnel eases slightly the personnel situation but also serves as a handicap insofar as they cannot be used for extended trips and also due to the inability of the officers to speak French, therefore making it difficult for officers to explain their destinations".

"The month of February 1945 was celebrated as anniversary month for the Car Company personnel, the original men completing their 3rd year of overseas duty. In view of this long period of overseas service, the boys patiently look forward to that long promised vision of the Statue of Liberty."

"The construction of a Day Room for the motor pool personnel was begun on the basement floor of the billets. Movies are shown 3 nights weekly temporarily in the mess hall but upon completion, will be shown in the Day Room. The morale of the organization which consists of long time overseas personnel and former combat personnel can be classified as satisfactory. A few of the men have submitted applications for furloughs to England, having established acquaintances while stationed there during 1942."

Shortly after this the unit crosses into Germany over the Rhine River, establishing itself in Seckenheim, which is near Manheim, Germany. Once again, the Narrative Report of the unit can sum up the activities.

"Personnel of the organization are billeted in what is known as the Corona Schufabrik. This same building and surrounding grounds serve as the Motor Pool area. The Maintenance Garage is just across the field used as a parking lot for the vehicles."

"The following statistics for the month are as follows for the first 22 days of the month: Mileage: 90,075; Dispatches: 1,140; Gas Consumed: 11,181 gallons; Accidents: 3."

"This organization lost two vehicles in the past month due to enemy action. One was lost due to a mine and the second one was captured by the enemy, along with the driver. The driver was liberated from captivity after being a prisoner for 7 days."

"(Note: Tec 5 Joseph Theodore was driving a Colonel in the vicinity of Saarbracken when his vehicle was blown up by a mine planted in the road. Theodore remained in the hospital for approximately two months with internal injuries, while the Colonel, who suffered a broken leg, was eventually returned to the US as a result of the accident. The second case occurred when Pfc. Ray E. Greenhalgh was driving for several officers in the forward area, in an attempt to secure a surrender of a German town without needless bloodshed. This action resulted in Pfc. Greenhalgh's being awarded the Bronze Star)."

"The mechanical side of the picture was a bit gloomy, with a shortage in the staff causing the deadline report to increase. A priority schedule was set up, giving GI Staff Cars top billing, however it is particularly difficult to keep this priority especially insofar as civilian cars are concerned, because at this time they are like new toys and everyone from Privates to Colonels are interested in them."

Soon after the end of the war in Europe, trips to increase morale are started and the men take in much of the scenery around Heidelberg and Mannheim. A terrace is erected outside the Schufabrik, with beer being served in large mugs. Since fraternization with the Germans is strictly prohibited at the time, the men stay close to the billets, and only travel into nearby CONAD City to catch the occasional movie, or seeing one in the mess hall of the shoe factory. The first post-war casualty of the company occurs when Private First Class George Antelope is killed while driving for General Wilson. He lost control of his vehicle when a tire blew out and crashed into a tree outside of Hamburg, Germany during the night of May 21, 1945. He is found the next morning, pinned under the wreckage of the vehicle.

Again the unit is on the move, and on July 4, 1945 is on its way to Berlin, Germany. They drive all day, reaching Weisenfels where they are billeted in a large room adjoining a beer hall. Before retiring, the men hold a cheerful beer party. The next day they move to Halle, where they spend most of the day cleaning up and working on the vehicles. American flags are pasted on all the windshields of the vehicles, and on July 6 they reach their destination of Babelsberg, near Potsdam and Berlin, where the forthcoming Big Three conference is to be held.

The Company, along with two other car platoons is selected to do the chauffeuring of various officials that are arriving. The drivers find themselves behind the wheel of shiny limousines, driving for VIPs such as Secretary of State James Byrnes, Admiral Leahy, General Vaughn, and other members of the Combined Chief of Staffs.

At this time the company is assigned to Headquarters, Berlin District. Whenever the men can get time off they go into the capital to explore the ruins of the Chancellery and other famous landmarks. As a result of this, the men are treated to an eventful month at the conference area, especially when it is learned that the Russians are buying watches for what seem to be fantastic prices. President Truman before leaving gave the following commendation to Major General Floyd Parks:

"I have noted with pride and pleasure the excellent service provided us by the officers and men of your command. The junior officers in charge of billets, post exchanges, transportation and other services have been especially thoughtful and helpful, and they have contributed materially to the work of the Conference. I congratulate you on the morale, courtesy and military smartness of the officers and men of your command who have come under my observation."

———

Lieutenant Stepien received a Certificate of Merit for directing the transportation from Ceciliechof Palace, where the meetings of the Big Three (United States, Great Britian, and Russia) were held. Staff Sergeant Candella and Tech-5 Kessce also received these certificates for outstanding work in directing and dispatching vehicles at the Motor Pool.

On August 7, 1945 the unit departs Babelsberg and driving on the autobahns arrives in Helmstadt, Germany. Then it is on to Giessen, Germany where they receive a hot meal and news of the first atomic bomb being dropped on Japan. This news, together with the announcement of Russia's entry into the war against Japan causes the men to feel by the time they reached Marseille, the war would be over.

On August 9, 1945 the unit crosses into France and arrives in Nancy. Then it is on to Dijon where the entire company is once again reunited. Lieutenant McKenna now assumes command of the entire company. Here they are billeted in a tent city, living in two-man wall tents with wooden floors and electric lights. On September 1, 1945 the 1st Platoon departs for Nuremberg, Germany, where they will drive for the War Crimes Commission.

The remainder of the Company now dwindles to 70, then to 60, then to 50, and finally to 20 enlisted men and one officer. All the other men were returned to the United States. Lieutenant O'Brien is the last officer, and the dwindling unit will soon only be a unit on paper. What is left of the 121st Quartermaster Car Company in men and vehicles eventually returns to the United States, thus ending its service in World War II. The Company is officially inactivated in Germany on June 15, 1946.

It is interesting to note that during the unit's operations in both England and North Africa, they transported many important persons. Some of which include President Roosevelt, Winston Churchill, General Marshall, General Eisenhower, General Devers, General Clark, Sir Henry Maitland-Wilson. The list also includes many film stars such as Clark Gable, Kay Francis, Humphrey Bogart, Edward G, Robinson, Al Jolson, and Mitzi Mayfair.

CHAPTER 9

Post World War II – Korean War
1946 - 1952

After the end of World War II and the unit's inactivation in Germany, the men of the 121st Quartermaster Car Company returned home. On Saturday, November 9, 1946, Hamburg held a home coming day officially welcoming the men home. It is an all day celebration. Businesses close for the day and the entire town is decorated with red, white and blue bunting and flags. A memorial service is held at St. John's Lutheran Church followed by a parade featuring the veterans, along with local bands, Scouts, floats, and the ladies auxiliaries of both the American Legion and the VFW. Banquets are held at three local churches, along with two shows at the old armory on North Third Street. Dances at both the new armory and the Legion Hall conclude the night.

On December 10, 1946 the unit is reorganized and federally recognized as Battery D, 337th Anti-Aircraft Artillery Searchlight Battalion. On December 1, 1947 it was again reorganized as Battery D, 337th Anti-Aircraft Artillery Gun Battalion. On March 21, 1949 the unit expanded to form Battery D at Hamburg and Battery C at Kutztown, which hereafter has a separate lineage.

The peace didn't last very long and soon the United States was involved in the Korean Conflict. As usual, the National Guard was called upon once more in defense of the nation and on March 28, 1951 local National Guard units were alerted. The men knew it was only a matter of time before they would be called upon for Federal service. This finally occurred on April 21, 1951, when Captain Norman Smith, Sergeant Floyd Berger, Corporal Alfred Baver,

Corporal Floyd Dunkel, and Private Kenneth Fryer of the unit are placed on active duty.

The men of the advance detail prepare all of the unit's equipment for movement, which is sent to Camp Stewart, Georgia, along with some of the men, arriving there on May 1, 1951. The rest of Battery D is placed on active duty effective May 1, 1951 at Hamburg, per Active Military Service Order No. 13, 2nd Army, dated March 28, 1951. While at the armory, the men are sent to St. Joseph's Hospital in Reading for physical examinations.

At Hamburg the unit prepares for mobilization by conducting training and packing and loading equipment in readiness for movement to Camp Stewart. Most of the unit's larger equipment is shipped to Camp Stewart, Georgia by rail. The Battery commander is Captain Norman Smith, and the unit is part of the 337th Anti-Aircraft Artillery Battalion, and assigned to the 213th Anti-Aircraft Artillery Group. The Battalion Headquarters is located in Reading and under the command of Lieutenant Colonel John W. Dry, with Group Headquarters located in Allentown.

On May 7, 1951 Hamburg holds a farewell parade for the men of Battery "D" and on May 8 the unit departs Hamburg for the railroad station in Reading. In Reading several thousand people line the route as the entire Battalion marches from the armory at Rose and Walnut Streets to the train station. At the train station hundreds of relatives jam the loading platform at the Reading Company Outer Station to say farewell to their husbands, fathers, sons, sweethearts, and friends. The Reading High School Band provides music for the march to the train station.

The unit arrives at Camp Stewart, Georgia at 9:15 PM on May 9, 1951. They are met there by the men of the advance party who earlier prepared the unit area, and took care of the equipment and supplies prior to the arrival of the main body. The unit is billeted in the 9200 Block Area in tents and immediately begins preparations for basic military training. While at Camp Stewart the unit is part of 337th AAA Battalion, 227th AAA Group, 47th AAA Brigade. Eventually the Brigade is split up with some units going to New Jersey, some to Florida, and others to Massachusetts and Maryland.

The unit's major items of equipment consist of radars, M9 Directors, M1A1 90mm guns, and .50 caliber machineguns. The unit is ordered to complete all anti-aircraft artillery training, and to be combat ready by the end of a 28 week training cycle for further assignments. During the first few weeks at Camp Stewart the unit is brought up to wartime strength. The unit is brought up to strength with filler personnel from the 213th Anti-Aircraft Artillery Gun Battalion, 238th Gun Battalion, 82nd Airborne Division, and draftees.

They start formal training on June 4, 1951. The first six weeks are basic individual training consisting of general military subjects, combat skills, and weapons instruction. Five weeks of advanced individual training follow that, and include general subjects, and technical and section training, which is complete on August 25, 1951. During this training they also conduct high altitude firing with the 90mm anti-aircraft guns, with which they become very proficient. Excellent logistics and medical services are provided, however there is a shortage of communications equipment which hinders the training to a degree.

Initially there are some problems encountered that could have been avoided. If the officers and NCOs would have been called to active duty prior to the rest of the unit for the purpose of attending refresher training, it would have made the unit training more effective at the very start. Another problem is that some of the officers, warrant officers, and enlisted men are transferred to other units. This breaks up the integrity of the unit and initially has a negative impact on unit morale. However, by the end of their training they have developed into an effective fighting unit, and are ready for whatever might await them.

On February 10, 1952 the unit departs Camp Stewart for Fort Dix, New Jersey. The convoy takes five days and four nights to reach Fort Dix, and they stay overnight along the route at Fort Jackson, South Carolina, Fort Bragg, North Carolina, Fort Lee, Virginia, and Fort Meade, Maryland where they spend a very cold night. The unit arrives at Fort Fox on February 14, 1952. In March of 1952 they move to Germantown, Pennsylvania for a few days, and then move back to Fort Dix. In April of 1952 they move to Gladwyne, Pennsylvania where they provide anti-aircraft protection for the Philadelphia area. The remainder of the battalion is stationed at other locations surrounding Philadelphia.

In July of 1952 the unit goes to Fort Miles, Delaware for two weeks, where they conduct live firing of the 90mm anti-aircraft guns by firing at targets over the ocean. On December 1, 1952 the unit departs Gladwyne for Fort Indiantown Gap for processing and discharge. The unit is released from active duty on December 12, 1952 and returned to State control. Of the 74 men who mobilized with the unit in Hamburg in May 1951, only 30 were still a part of the Battery at the time the unit was deactivated. The unit never deployed overseas during the Korean War. The first drill upon returning home is held on January 12, 1953.

CHAPTER 10

Protecting the Peace
1953 - 1989

The years since 1953 have seen the unit through many changes in designation, organization, and personnel. This period is also characterized by many instances of the unit being called-up for State Active Duty to assist the citizens of Pennsylvania.

Battery D, 337th Anti-Aircraft Artillery Battalion was released from active military service for the Korean War on December 12, 1952. The unit reverted back to state control and held their first drill on January 12, 1953. The unit has no officers assigned at this time and its strength is only 25 enlisted men. Major John P. Fisher of the 213th Anti-Aircraft Artillery Group in Allentown leads the unit until First Lieutenant Wellington R. Ketner is assigned as Battery commander on April 13, 1953. The unit immediately begins a recruiting drive and by years end increases the unit strength to 4 officers and 49 enlisted men.

During this time a person could enlist in the National Guard without having to attend Basic Combat Training or Advanced Individual Training at an Active Army school. Enlisted men with no prior military service received their Basic Recruit Training with and by the unit during drills at the armory. In 1955 a program is started by the Active Army for non-prior service soldiers, where these soldiers could, if they wished, attend training at an Active Army training center from two to six months in length.

This is the beginning of what in 1963 would become the Reserve Enlisted Program of 1963, known later as REP-63. This program requires all non-prior service recruits to attend an Active Army school for the position in which they enlisted. The minimum amount of time was set at 18 weeks, and could be longer depending on the training required. It is also around this time that the requirement is established that all non-prior service personnel have to enlist for a minimum of six years, which today is now eight years.

Unit strength during these years fluctuates. However, even when the unit is severely under strength, it still completes all assigned missions. Initially during the 1950s and 1960s, the majority of the unit soldiers are from Hamburg or the surrounding area. However, as time goes on the unit starts to see men traveling from some distances to join the unit, especially during the Vietnam War era. Even though the unit struggles to enlist and retain soldiers at times, it does receive three awards for recruiting and retention.

In the early 1950s the National Guard did not hold monthly weekend drills as is done today. The unit conducted drills on weeknights, normally one night per week for a four-hour period. In 1958 the National Guard is authorized to hold "multiple drills" consisting of two four-hour drill periods held on the same day and normally during a weekend. Eventually the number of multiple drills that can be held during a year increases to seven multiple drills per year. In the 1960s the number of drills is changed again to a total of 48 four-hour periods of training per year. Throughout this period the unit attends two-week Annual Training periods on a yearly basis.

Most unit drills are held at the armory, but from time to time the unit does travel to Fort Indiantown Gap for training such as weapons qualification, civil disturbance training, and tactical field training. The unit also travels far and wide to attend Annual Training. The soldiers always looked forward to those times since for many of them it was the only chance they had to see other parts of the country.

––––––––––––

February and March of 1958 brought heavy snowstorms to the Commonwealth. The sudden and severe storms strands scores of motorists in the heavy snow on Route 22 (Interstate 78), and they had to be rescued by the Company. The men rescue motorists stranded in stalled and stuck vehicles on the highway and in private homes along the highway. Using the military vehicles they pick up the stranded travelers and transport them to Hamburg where food and shelter is provided for them at two of the local hotels.

All through the day and night of February 16, 1958 the unit rescues stranded motorists from the highway. In all 48 people are rescued. Two women suffer frostbitten feet. Many motorists are forced to remain in their vehicles for up to 12 hours before the soldiers can get to them. Some people find refuge in farm houses along the highway and remain there until the unit can get to them and transport them to one of the hotels in town. Snow drifts are 15 feet high and snow plows are needed to clear paths for the military vehicles to get through. A local grocery store donates crackers and cookies, which are given to the stranded civilians by the soldiers when rescued. In many cases it is the first bite of food the motorists had in 12 hours.

On February 17 the unit receives a call from the Pennsylvania State Police, asking them to attempt to deliver medicine to a sick woman living about four miles outside of Hamburg. The unit promptly responds to this call for help and delivers the much needed medicine. A total of 20 men are engaged in the operations on February 16 and 17, using ¾ Ton, 2-1/2 Ton, and 5 Ton Trucks to rescue the motorists.

Once again the snow begins to fall and on March 20, 1958 the unit receives a call from the State Police. The first call for help comes at 5:00 PM requesting that stranded motorists on Route 22 between Hamburg and Krumsville be rescued. Upon receiving this call for help the unit contacts Lieutenant Colonel Justin D. Harris, Battalion Commander, requesting permission to deploy men and vehicles. Permission is granted and rescue operations commence immediately.

At 6:30 PM the first truck departs the armory and proceeds to the State Police barracks, where a Trooper is assigned to each of the military vehicles. Within an hour the first truck returns to the armory with 35 civilians rescued from their stuck cars and trucks. Till 3:30 AM on March 21 the unit uses two 2-1.2 Ton trucks to transport the people to town. In all 245 men, women, and children are rescued.

Arrangements are made with the Red Cross to supply cots and blankets, as well as hot coffee. At 4:00 AM the last of the stranded motorists arrives at the armory, with 168 cots being occupied. Only about 20 people had to do without a cot. At 4:30 AM arrangements are made with the Salvation Army who dispatches a mobile canteen to feed breakfast to the stranded civilians at the armory.

Eventually the roads are cleared in sections and the unit transports the motorists back to their vehicles. The operation is complete by 3:30 PM on March 21, 1958 after a total of 250 people are returned to their vehicles. During the morning of March 21 the unit receives an urgent call requesting that a pregnant woman who is in labor be rescued and transported to the hospital. The unit battles through the snow drifts to the woman's home, and then transports her to the main highway, where an ambulance is standing by to take her to the hospital. In all a total of 50 soldiers are activated for this emergency.

The unit also went through multiple reorganizations and re-designations during this time. On June 1, 1959 the unit is re-designated as Battery D, 2nd Gun Battalion, 213th Artillery; on May 1, 1962 it is reorganized as Company D, 3rd Medium Tank Battalion, 103rd Armor; and on March 24, 1964 re-designated as Company A, 3rd Battalion, 103rd Armor.

On June 21, 1972, one of the most severe natural disasters strikes Pennsylvania. This is Tropical Storm Agnes. She hits the Commonwealth with torrential rain, resulting in the unit providing disaster relief for eight days. The rains start on June 21 and the unit is officially placed on State Active Duty on June 23. Actually, the unit had already been conducting evacuation efforts in the Hamburg area on June 22, some 24-hours before receiving the official call.

The first call for help is received by Second Lieutenant Stephen Cashman at 6:45 PM on June 22, 1972. This is from the Civil Defense Headquarters requesting vehicles to aid in evacuating flood victims. A volunteer force consisting of Lieutenant Cashman, Sergeant First Class Floyd Spease, Staff Sergeant Eugene Flammer,

Sergeant Neil Billman, Specialist-5 Robert Shollenberger, Specialist-4 Jeryl Seaman, and Private First Class Edward Fisher and Private First Class Mark Krick is quickly assembled. Immediately they make themselves and the trucks of the Company available to the local Civil Defense authorities.

During the night and the next morning the soldiers, accompanied by State Police, Civil Defense, and Civil Air Patrol personnel, evacuate persons and families throughout the local area, including Kempton, New Tripoli, Krumsville, and Shoemakersville. The evacuees are brought to the Hamburg armory where temporary facilities are set up. The Blue Mountain Academy provides cots, and the Red Cross under the supervision of John Ebling, provides and prepares food at the Hamburg YWCA Camp.

These activities are coordinated with the efforts of the Civil Air Patrol, which establishes a temporary command post at the armory. This is under the command of Captain Lee M. Lindermuth, commanding officer of Hamburg Composite Squadron 303 of the Civil Air Patrol. Captain Lindermuth directs the Civil Air Patrol operations from the armory until a permanent command post is established in Reading the next day.

Rescue efforts continue during the daylight hours of June 22, 1972 as the storm continues and the situation grows more severe. Company A, 3rd Battalion, 103rd Armor commanding officer Captain Richard D. Morgan establishes regular contact with battalion headquarters in York, as well as with other battalion units in Tamaqua and Kutztown in anticipation of the imminent call to State Active Duty. Following activities took place on June 22 and 23, 1972:

June 22, 1972:

6:45 PM: Following personnel are present at the armory: 2LT Stephen Cashman, SFC Floyd Spease, SSG Eugene Flammer, SGT Billman, SP5 Robert Shollenberger, SP4 Jeryl Seaman, PFC Ed Fisher, PFC Mark Krick. LT Cashman receives a call from Civil Defense requesting trucks to aid in the evacuation of flood victims.

7:15 PM: Three trucks are dispatched to Civil Defense HQ at Hamburg State Hospital. LT Cashman reports to Mr. Hinkle there.

9:10 PM: Received a call from Mr. Hinkle requesting evacuated people be moved to armory. Affirmative, we need cots.

9:30 PM: Mr. Harry Fisher and Mr. James Gilmartin came to the armory. They inform us that cots are available from the Blue Mountain Academy. A truck is dispatched to the Academy to pick up cots.

11:10 PM: Two trucks returned to the armory. Contacted Mayor Dalious (Hamburg) and Mr. Hinkle and neither needed trucks at present.

12:00 AM: Received call from Civil Air Patrol, LT Lindermuth, to send a truck to Krumsville to evacuate people. Truck dispatched at 12:05 AM.

June 23, 1972:

12:45 AM: Received call from Civil Air Patrol, LT Lindermuth, to dispatch a truck to Shoemakersville. Truck and jeep dispatched.

1:25 AM: Third truck returned from New Tripoli, Kempton areas. Evacuated three families to other houses in that area. Pennsylvania State Trooper accompanied the vehicle.

1:30 AM: The truck returned from Shoemakersville. No evacuations. Jeep remained in Shoemakersville area because Civil Air Patrol was getting two families with a boat and requested the jeep to drive them to the armory. Called E.S. Savage and requested diesel fuel for our truck.

1:40 AM: Dispatched truck for diesel fuel. Driver signed for fuel and informed Mr. Savage we would get the State credit card to him at the earliest convenient time. Fuel bill was $6.10.

2:30 AM: Received a call from Mr. Hinkle to send Civil Air Patrol men to Second and State Streets to relieve the Fire Police.

2:45 AM: Mr. Hinkle requested a truck be sent to the Kempton area.

2:50 AM: Relieved Sergeant Billman to get some sleep. He will remain on call if we needed him.

3:00 AM: PFC Krick went home because he was expected to work at 0700 hours.

4:00 AM: Sent PFC Fisher and SP4 Seaman home to get some sleep.

5:00 AM: The truck from Krumsville returned. They evacuated one family in the area to a neighbor's house.

5:20 AM: Received a call from Police Chief Frankhouser requesting a vehicle be sent to Shoemakersville to evacuate a woman and her daughter.

5:25 AM: Called Chief Frankhouser (Shoemakersville) and requested a guide to meet the vehicle at light on Route 61. Vehicle dispatched to evacuate Mrs. Elfrida Schlease and her daughter.

6:35 AM: Request from LT Lindermuth, Civil Air Patrol, to send a vehicle to Civil Defense Headquarters and pick up inspection party to examine Kaercher Dam east of Hamburg.

7:30 AM: PFC Krick returned to duty as he was not called out to work.

7:35 AM: Vehicle that went to Kaercher Dam returned. Reported the water is receding.

8:00 AM: Contacted CPT Lindermuth over Civil Air Patrol radio. He informed me that vehicle in Shoemakersville is waiting for a helicopter from Willow Grove to evacuate people from roof tops. PFC Fisher returned to duty.

9:55 AM: SP4 Seaman returned to duty. Truck returned from Shoemakersville. They had rescued 8 people and evacuated them to other homes on high ground. Two people were picked up by Civil Defense and taken to the hospital.

10:00 AM: Sent jeep to Cross Keys area to recon and report if some people could return to their homes.

10:20 AM: Vehicle returned and reported that houses in the Cross Keys area are still intact, but are under water. Mr. and Mrs. Walter Keller are evacuated by helicopter from Shoemakersville and brought to the armory.

11:10 AM: LT Cashman, SGT Flammer, and SP5 Shollenberger are relieved and go home to sleep.

11:20 AM: Chief of Police Gust (Hamburg) brought Mr. and Mrs. Royal Ackerman from Stoystown, Pennsylvania to the armory. Their car is stranded on the Lowland Road west of Hamburg.

11:40 AM: Mr. Harry Fisher appointed as Civil Defense Director for Hamburg. He reported to the armory and said that the vehicle drivers should be released as he did not think they would be needed anymore.

11:45 AM: Sent Sergeant Billman home after he supervised securing the equipment in the garage. Also, relieved SP4 Seaman,

PFC Krick, and PFC Fisher. They finished at 1200 hours and went home.

12:00 PM: Called Captain Morgan to come in and relieve me because we still had 10 civilians in the armory that could not get to their homes.

12:05 PM: Sergeant Billman, SP4 Seaman and PFC Krick came in and stated that one 2-1/2 Ton Truck had a flat tire. They volunteered to change it so that it would be operational if needed.

12:45 PM: SP4 Seaman took a jeep and drove Mr. George Koller to Shoemakersville to feed his livestock.

1:25 PM: Received call from Captain Kohutka asking if he could borrow some trucks from us in the event he had to leave Kutztown to report somewhere else. I informed him to call us if this came about, but at the present time it looked like we would be able to give him some. Captain Kohutka told me that Headquarters, 3/103 Armor in York wants us to call them so they will know our status.

1:40 PM: Called Battalion and gave Major Nagle our status and activities up to this point.

2:15 PM: Captain Morgan and Platoon Sergeant James McDonald arrive to take over and Sergeant First Class Spease goes home.

2:38 PM: Captain Lindermuth (Civil Air Patrol) moves their Command Post from Hamburg Armory to the Reading Airport. Informed the State Police of this movement.

3:20 PM: Recalled Sergeant Billman to duty.

3:30 PM: Contacted Headquarters, 3/103 Armor, in York for status report.

4:00 PM: Contacted Company B, 3/103 Armor in Kutztown, about the vehicle to be used by Company B for movement to committed area.

4:15 PM: Called State Police to get information about the areas flooded in order to inform people still in the armory of the situation in their areas.

5:17 PM: Dispatched vehicle to the YWCA Blue Mountain Camp to pick up food for people in the armory. Twelve rations.

6:45 PM: Received alert from Headquarters, 3/103rd Armor to execute alert list and stand by for flood duty.

6:47 PM: Mr. and Mrs. Walter Koller are picked up at the armory by their son.

7:00 PM: The Knoblock sisters are brought to the armory from Port Clinton. They are sisters, one is Mrs. Eva Siders. Both are in their eighties.

7:05 PM: Hamburg Ambulance arrives to transport the Knoblock sisters to the Pottsville Hospital. Same time a Mr. McLaughlin called inquiring about these ladies.

8:40 PM: Mr. and Mrs. George Koller are moved from the armory to the Hamburg Borough Hall.

9:30 PM: Attempted to call Headquarters, 3/103 Armor but was unsuccessful because the telephone is out of order.

10:10 PM: Contacted Headquarters, 3/103 Armor and reported 27 Enlisted Men and 3 Officers on duty. Battalion ordered ration order to be cut for breakfast and dinner Saturday, June 24. Tried to contact food supplier, however truck with rations had already arrived.

10:29 PM: PFC Bodman assigned to duty at Hamburg Armory by Captain Morgan.

11:08 PM: Captain Aumen called. Following warning Orders issued: Company A to move to Harrisburg to arrive between 11:00 AM and Noon, June 24, 1972. Move on order. Equipment to take is M16 Rifle with bayonet, riot batons, steel helmets, and gas masks.

June 24, 1972:

4:54 AM: Captain Peters called from Battalion requesting strength report. Report as follows: 57 Enlisted Men, 3 Officers. Our vehicles should be back from Harrisburg by 9:00 AM.

6:15 AM: Strength report called to Captain Peters. Strength report as follows: 62 Enlisted Men, 3 Officers.

8:00 AM: Wyomissing Police were contacted about Charles Beshara and told to tell him to report to the armory.

8:03 AM: Warrant Officer Keister called Captain Morgan about strength report. 62 Enlisted Men, 3 Officers.

8:05 AM: Called State Police in Hometown to get in contact with 1LT McAlanis.

7:05 AM: Unit is to leave Hamburg in time to arrive at 18th and Herr Streets (Harrisburg) by 1:00 PM on June 24 on orders from Headquarters, 3/103 Armor. Feed noon meal at 18th and Herr Streets.

10:00 AM: Strength report called to Warrant Officer Keister. 63 Enlisted Men, 4 Officers. Reported all vehicles operational however, vehicles have not returned from Harrisburg.

11:12 AM: Reported to Battalion Headquarters (Warrant Officer Keister and Major Smith) that Company A is leaving for Harrisburg.

This ends the unit operations conducted in and around the Hamburg area.

Troops are now needed in Harrisburg for law enforcement and to provide security for the protection of life and property. The unit assembles at the armory, prepares and loads equipment for the movement, and orders rations. Weapons taken are riot batons, rifles with bayonets, but no ammunition. The unit strength for deployment is 4 officers and 68 enlisted men. By Saturday morning mobilization efforts are complete and Captain Morgan receives orders committing the unit to flood duty in Harrisburg.

The Company arrives in Harrisburg shortly after 1:00 PM Saturday, and establishes its headquarters in the 104th Armored Cavalry Armory located at 18th and Herr Streets. The unit is attached to the 104th Armored Cavalry for operations. Preparations are now undertaken for the deployment of the troops to the flood area to protect evacuated areas of the city from looters. First Lieutenant David Bucks, the company executive officer, briefs the unit when it arrives in Harrisburg.   They are briefed about the mission of establishing stationary guard posts along the edge of the flood waters along Third and Fourth Streets. Their instructions are to not allow anyone to enter the area except for emergency rescue personnel.

By 4:00 PM the entire unit is dispatched to the edge of the flood waters along Third and Fourth Streets, in the vicinity of the Polyclinic Hospital.   The duty consists of stationary guard post and mobile patrols, with the mission of sealing off the area from all but rescue personnel. This mission continues until the company is relieved at 4:00 AM on Sunday morning. At 1:00 PM on Sunday the company is back on duty with approximately one-half of the unit returning to the Third Street area.   The rest of the company is deployed along Thirteenth Street to guard that area, from the State Street Bridge south to Sycamore Street.

At 11:00 PM on Sunday the company is relieved from the duty at Third Street and Thirteenth Street. They move next to one of the hardest hit locations in the Susquehanna Township area along the Susquehanna River just north of the Harrisburg city line. Again their mission is to seal off the area from looters and others who do not reside in the area, or who are not involved in either rescue or clean-up activities. The unit provides general security during the daylight hours and strictly enforces the 7:00 PM to 7:00 AM curfew. The mission is accomplished by heavily saturating the area with roadblocks, mobile patrols in trucks, flood lights, and the use of an M113 Armored Personnel Carrier. The armored personnel carrier is extremely useful in protecting a medical supply warehouse which is surrounded by the flood waters.

By Wednesday afternoon June 28, 1972, the flood waters recede, and the residents of the area begin to return to their homes and start the process of cleaning up. The Company is released from duty in Harrisburg and returns to Hamburg that evening with all soldiers and equipment. The unit remains on State Active Duty and performs equipment maintenance duties until officially released from duty at 2:00 PM on June 29, 1972.

Because of Tropical Storm Agnes, the unit performed half of its Annual Training during the period between June 23 and 29, 1972, by providing emergency flood relief duty in the eastern part of the State. The remainder of their Annual Training was held at Fort Drum, New York from August 26 to September 2, 1972. Because not all of the men had been called up for flood duty, some of them remained at Fort Drum until September 9, and were attached to the 104th Armored Cavalry for training. Some men stayed at Fort Drum an extra week beyond that to receive additional training.

––––––––––

During the first months of 1974 independent truck drivers went on strike protesting the shortage and high cost of fuel, and the reduction of speed limits to 55 mph. On January 29, 1974 the unit receives a telephone call from Headquarters placing them on a modified alert for State Active Duty. However, no personnel are called in at this time.

On February 2, 1974, Staff Sergeant Darryl R. Hamm, Unit Administrator, receives a call from Captain Jerry R. Doolin, commanding officer of the 1068th Military Police Company stationed in Pottsville. Captain Doolin requests permission to use the Hamburg Armory because his unit is being activated for the truckers' strike, with the mission of patrolling Interstate 78. The 1068th Military Police Company occupies the Hamburg Armory until February 6, when a detachment from Company B, 3rd Battalion, 103rd Armor from Kutztown occupied the armory and takes over the patrolling duties.

On February 5, 1974 at 9:00 AM, key unit personnel are placed on alert. All officers, the first sergeant, supply sergeant, and the motor sergeant are immediately called in and placed on State Active Duty. They immediately begin preparations for the entire unit being placed on State Active Duty. At 11:00 AM all unit soldiers are contacted and ordered to assemble at the armory by midnight for State Active Duty. Many of the men report in shortly after being contacted to assist in the preparations for deployment.

Captain Morgan is instructed to coordinate with the State Police substation in the assigned area of operations. At 6:00 PM, Captain Morgan travels to Battalion Headquarters where he is briefed on the unit's mission and assigned area of operations. The unit's mission is to move at 1:00 AM on February 6, 1974 to the National Guard Armory at Everett. Once there, their mission will be to conduct patrols from Exit 11 to Exit 16 on the Pennsylvania Turnpike, and south to the Maryland state line. Other missions are to assist the State Police, conduct security operations, and escort convoys.

By Midnight the entire unit of 4 officers and 75 enlisted men is assembled at the Hamburg Armory. The advance detachment consisting of 2 officers and 35 enlisted men depart the Armory at 30 minutes after Midnight on February 6, and head for Everett. The main body of 2 officers and 41 enlisted men leave one hour later. Twenty-four men from Battalion Headquarters Company are attached to the unit in route to Everett. On the way to Everett the main body halts in Harrisburg to pick up additional vehicles, some of which are

Air National Guard pickup trucks. The Company uses all of its vehicles in order to transport the troops to Everett.

The trip to Everett is a very cold one. The temperature is 4 degrees above zero when the unit departs the armory. None of the unit's vehicles are equipped with heaters, and most of the men have to ride in the rear of the cargo trucks during the long trip. Many of the men sit inside their sleeping bags to stay warm during the trip. The convoy does stop at a few rest stops along the Turnpike. The soldiers welcome these stops because they can go inside for some hot coffee and to warm up. However, these halts are few and short in duration since it is urgent that the unit get to Everett with all haste.

The convoy has to slow down along the way when it encounters freezing rain, making driving conditions extremely hazardous. It is so cold that many of the soldiers lose the feeling in their toes. The vehicle drivers suffer the most, and take off their gloves, laying them on the floor just above the transmission to warm them. It wasn't much heat, but it does provide some relief. It is a very long and cold night for a ride, but eventually the main body arrives at the Everett armory at 7:30 AM on February 6, 1974.

When the advance detachment arrives at Everett it is immediately deployed to protect critical overpasses on the Turnpike. Unfortunately, many of these soldiers are required to stay on the overpasses for many hours, with no way of getting warm and without any food. On the way to Everett the unit passes through Breezewood where there is a large truck stop, which has been the scene of some very violent incidents. As the unit passes through it looks like a war zone to the soldiers. There are hundreds of tractor-trailers parked in the truck stop, some of which are burned, with many others having smashed windshields, slashed tires, and cut hoses. This alarming scene makes the soldiers realize the seriousness of the situation.

When the main body arrives in Everett, it is also immediately dispatched to protect the overpasses. It is now seen that, even with the support of the 24 soldiers from the Headquarters Company, that the unit cannot effectively cover such a large area of operation. Reinforcements are immediately requested. At 1:30 PM on February 6, the company receives 21 men from the Tamaqua unit, Company C,

3rd Battalion, 103rd Armor, who have been airlifted by helicopters to Everett. Some real excitement happens this day when a report is received that some overpasses and bridges in the Bedford area are wired with explosives. However, none of the bridges or overpasses is destroyed, and the first day of strike duty ends.

February 7, 1974 starts with the weather still being extremely frigid, and it starts to snow. The unit now establishes mobile patrols in the area of operations along the Turnpike, and reinforces the State Police patrols. One or two soldiers ride along with a State Trooper, and the soldiers consider this the best duty. It is a real luxury being able to ride in a State Police patrol car equipped with a heater.

However, the majority of the soldiers are guarding the overpasses. The reason these overpasses must be guarded is because the striking independent truck drivers are using them to snipe and throw rocks and other objects from them at the trucks passing below. Many of the non-independent and union truckers are traveling in large convoys, and it is not uncommon to see 20 or 30 trucks traveling together for protection. Many of the trucks have someone riding shotgun, and when they approach an overpass they shine spotlights unto the overpass looking for any sign of trouble.

Fortunate are the soldiers who are stationed on an overpass located near a farm house. Many of these families furnish the soldiers with 55 gallon metal drums and some wood so they can build a fire for warmth. Many even provide the soldiers with hot coffee and in some cases food. Their unselfishness is deeply appreciated by the soldiers and is never forgotten. On February 7 the Company receives a report from the State Police that 91 sticks of dynamite, 20 blasting caps, and 30 feet of wire have been stolen from a construction warehouse just outside of Everett. This report really increases the tension of the soldiers, but fortunately the explosives are never used.

February 8 starts somewhat better because the snow has stopped, but it still is extremely cold. The unit continues its patrols and overpass security. The unit is now also assigned the mission of establishing foot patrols in and around the truck stop in Breezewood. The unit continues with all of their assigned missions on February 9, with the weather remaining clear but very cold.

The Breezewood truck stop mission proves to be a very exciting one for the troops. The soldiers patrol in pairs to prevent any more damage to the trucks parked there. These trucks are parked in such a manner that it is impossible to move them without using a tow truck. The trucks parked along the outer perimeter are disabled so that they cannot be moved under their own power. These have to be towed so that the trucks inside the perimeter can move. The trucks are crowded together so tightly that is almost impossible to walk between them. The mission of patrolling amongst these trucks at night, armed only with a riot baton is a very stressful job.

On February 10, 1974 the unit conducts a convoy escort mission for ten steel transport trucks from Everett to Harrisburg. The remainder of the unit departs Everett on the morning of February 10 for Hamburg. The Company is relieved from State Active Duty as of Midnight on February 10, 1974.

During this operation some problems are encountered. First, the area of operations and assigned missions are too large for the unit to adequately cover with the number of soldiers and equipment available. Second, communications are practically nonexistent and it is nearly impossible to quickly react to a situation if a patrol required assistance.

The morale of the troops is high at the beginning of the duty, but as the unit is extended day by day, the morale slowly deteriorates. The reasons for the deteriorating morale are many. First, the weather is extremely harsh and the cold quickly takes its toll upon the men. Second, the armory at Everett is not ideal for billeting troops, and the latrine facilities are inadequate to handle the number of troops staying there.

But the main reason the morale drops as the days go by, is because the soldiers can not adequately defend themselves while on patrol. The situation is potentially very dangerous for the soldiers, but fortunately no serious incidents occur. The troops are not issued any ammunition, and an empty rifle and a riot baton are not much protection. But it must be said, that even though the morale was low at times, the soldiers continued to carry out all assigned missions and duties in an exceptional manner.

One Annual Training period proved a real challenge to the unit. That was when they traveled to Fort Stewart, Georgia in 1975. The unit was returning to a post where their predecessors had spent many months during the Korean War. The Advance Detachment departs Hamburg on May 26, 1975 with all of the unit's vehicles and equipment. It takes them three days of hard driving before arriving at Fort Stewart, and along the way they stay overnight at York, Pennsylvania, and in North Carolina and South Carolina. The rest of the unit flies via a commercial airline from Harrisburg International Airport to Savannah, Georgia. This is the first time the unit traveled anywhere by air, and it was a real treat for the men.

The unit found Fort Stewart in pretty much the same condition as it was during the Korean War; hot, dirty, and extremely swampy. To most of the men it seems like the only things that grow there are pine trees, snakes, and alligators. As a matter of fact, the snakes are such a menace that the men sleep on top of the tanks or in other vehicles instead of on the ground. This is a much better proposition than taking a chance of sleeping on the ground and waking up with one of these wiggly companions. Some of the soldiers do manage to capture a seven-foot long alligator one day, and thought it would make a wonderful unit mascot. However, the alligator disagreed with them on this matter, and the men politely released it unharmed after a few hours of playful fun.

That Annual Training period at Fort Stewart would be the last one for the Hamburg unit as an armor company. On January 1, 1976 the Company is reorganized into a military police unit, and re-designated as Detachment 1, 723rd Military Police Company. The unit's company headquarters is located in Lehighton, with the Hamburg unit comprising two platoons and some support personnel. Many of the men are not pleased with the reorganization, because it downsizes the unit and will cause the loss of many officers and enlisted men. Some of the officers have to transfer to other units, and many of the enlisted men either transfer or leave the unit when their term of enlistment expires.

June 1, 1976 is a very important date in the history of the Hamburg unit. It is on this date that the first woman is enlisted into the unit. Specialist Marydel J. Pistos is enlisted on that date, and thus adds a new page to the history of the Hamburg unit. Between that time and August 1, 1989, when females are no longer permitted to serve in the Hamburg unit because of the type of unit, many serve honorably and faithfully with the unit.

On July 20, 1977 a torrential storm causes devastating floods in Johnstown and the surrounding area. The number of casualties includes 72 killed and 28 missing. The main cause of the death and destruction is the sudden collapse of the Laurel Run Dam. Over 100 million gallons of water flow from this dam when it bursts and rushes down the valley into Johnstown.

On Friday, July 29, 1977 the unit receives orders from the Adjutant General of Pennsylvania to report to flood stricken Johnstown to perform security and traffic control operations. At 6:00 AM on July 31 the unit assembles at the Hamburg Armory and departs for Johnstown shortly thereafter. From Hamburg the unit travels to Fort Indiantown Gap, where it joins the rest of the 165th Military Police Battalion for breakfast and convoy to the area of operation. The convoy takes the Pennsylvania Turnpike and experiences difficulties getting into Johnstown. Many of the roads leading into the city are washed away by the flood waters and are impassable.

Upon arrival at Johnstown the unit is billeted in the Greater Johnstown Vocational-Technical School. Cots are provided for the troops to sleep on, and the gymnasium is turned into one giant barracks. There is very little electrical service and no water available for drinking or cooking. All potable and drinking water is brought into the area from outside sources. There is no public transportation, no postal service, no local newspapers, and very little telephone service in the area. In fact, the soldiers find very little except for mud, debris, damaged property, lost lives, and with more bodies being found every day.

When the Battalion arrives it relieves the 28th Military Police Company which has been on State Active Duty for the flood since

July 24, 1977.   Soon after arrival the unit begins its missions of protecting life and property.   Their duty consists of manning roadblocks to prevent unauthorized personnel from entering into the inner part of the city, operating traffic control posts to direct traffic in and around the city, providing security at food distribution points, and enforcing a 10:00 PM curfew.   The unit performs many of these missions in conjunction with State and local police.

The soldiers also assist the civilians of the flood ravaged community in any way they can.   The troops willingly and without orders or instructions, help move ruined appliances and furniture from victims' homes to the curb.   They also assist in transporting civilians to the Salvation Army disaster assistance centers, and act as messengers and communicating with electricians, plumbers, firemen, police, and other emergency personnel.   The troops also assist by transporting the sick and injured to hospitals located outside of the flood area.

The unit experiences extreme difficulty in getting around within the city.   Many roads and streets are blocked by debris, and in some cases are washed away completely.   A major hazard to both the troops and their vehicles is from nails, shards of glass, and other sharp objects, which cause many flat tires.   As the mission continues around the clock, the toll of flat tires rises and becomes a serious logistical problem because replacement tires become scarce.

As the days wear on the flood waters slowly recede, and the mud begins to dry causing another problem, dust.   In many ways the dust causes more problems then the mud, and makes duty for the troops miserable.   The heavy equipment being used to clean up the city causes much of the dust, and it is impossible for the soldiers to get away from this constant nuisance.   Since clean up operations continue around the clock, not even nightfall brings relief from the dusty conditions.   Eventually some surgical masks are obtained and this eases some of the discomfort for the troops.

Another and probably as serious nuisance that plagues the soldiers is the terrible stench prevailing throughout most parts of the city.   The nauseating odors are caused directly, and indirectly, by the mud itself, by rotting food, and in some instances by decaying bodies of both humans and animals. The surgical masks can not stop these sickening odors and the soldiers learn to live with the smells. The extremely hot and humid weather does nothing to help matters either.

As the soldiers carry out their duties, they find a city full of people who for the most part have lost all their worldly possessions, and in some cases the lives of relatives and friends. But they also find a city full of people in very high spirits, who are determined to building an even bigger and better Johnstown, and the dedication of these people inspire the troops. The unit is relieved of duty on August 7, 1977 and returns to Hamburg the same day. Eight soldiers remain on State Active Duty at the Hamburg Armory for an extra day to clean, maintain, and store all equipment used during the flood operations.

A severe snow storm hit the Hamburg area on January 19, 1978, followed by an even stronger blizzard on February 6 that crippled the region and stranded hundreds of motorists on Interstate 78. The Pennsylvania State Police contacted the unit during the day on February 6, requesting assistance in rescuing stranded motorists. The unit immediately called the 165th Military Police Battalion Headquarters asking permission to assist, and was shortly thereafter placed on State Active Duty.

This storm is so fierce that most of the unit soldiers can not reach the armory. As a result, only eight soldiers manage to report and assist in the rescue operation. The soldiers making it to the armory are First Lieutenant Stephen Cashman, Platoon Sergeant Floyd Spease, Staff Sergeant Michael Werley, Sergeant Roy Berstler, Sergeant Randy King, Sergeant Craig Kleinsmith, Specialist Vincent Reilly, and Specialist Rodger Sandridge. These men will perform numerous rescue operation duties, with little or no sleep for three days.

Lieutenant Cashman immediately asks the Hamburg Union Fire Company if they will provide some men to assist the unit, which they do at once. The State Police are for the most part unable to assist because they are completely snowed-in at their barracks, and the unit has to transport food to them. Local citizens possessing four-wheel drive vehicles and snowmobiles volunteer to also help with rescue operations throughout the surrounding area.

On the night of February 6, 1978, the unit begins dispatching both military and civilian vehicles from the armory to rescue stranded motorists on Interstate 78. However, most roadways are totally impassable and the unit contacts the Pennsylvania Department of Transportation for assistance. The unit requests that the PENNDOT trucks equipped with snow plows, clear paths in front of the military vehicles. This is done, and without their assistance and heavy equipment any rescue operation would have been nearly impossible.

The snow is too deep for even the largest of military trucks, even when equipped with all wheel drive and tire chains. Snow drifts as high as eight feet totally block many roads throughout the area. The storm has dropped an additional 20 inches of snow on top of the 16 inches from the previous storm, and the strong and sustained winds make conditions even worse. The weather is also bitterly cold with lows down to 8 degrees, with the high barely reaching 30 degrees during the day.

The first detail of four soldiers takes a 2-1/2 Ton Truck and heads for the Interstate. By 9:30 PM they rescue 35 stranded travelers and bring them to the armory for shelter. A second detail is dispatched at 10:00 PM and returns at 11:30 PM with another 60 motorists. About this time the unit receives an urgent phone call from the State Police informing the unit that there is a busload of people stranded on the Interstate near New Smithville. Another detail is immediately dispatched, along with some PENNDOT snow plows to the location. Even with the snow plows leading the way it takes almost 90 minutes for the troops to reach the bus, which is only 15 miles from Hamburg.

When the detail arrives at the bus location, they discover it is a show troupe on their way to do a stage performance in Detroit, Michigan. Among the actors and actresses are Howard Keel and Jane Powell, two famous motion picture stars. The soldiers load the troupe into the back of the military cargo trucks, provide them with some blankets, and again make the long and hazardous journey back to the armory. The following day, Tuesday, February 7, at 10:00 AM, the unit transports the show troupe to the Holiday Inn in Reading. It is urgent that they leave the area since they are scheduled to perform that evening at 8:00 PM in Detroit. However, they never make it there on time.

During the night of February 6 and the early hours of the February 7, the unit contacts the Red Cross and local Civil Defense authorities requesting coffee, food, blankets and cots. Many of the motorists have been stranded in the deep snow for six hours and are in need of hot food and warmth. The Red Cross responds and provides hot coffee, soup, and sandwiches but, the supply is quickly used up as the number of stranded civilians brought into the armory swells to more then 250 people.

Local grocery stores are immediately contacted asking for assistance, and they promptly respond, providing the unit with as much food as they can. Some local citizens volunteer their services and prepare the food for the refugees. The local Civil Defense does not have enough cots, so a call is placed to the Blue Mountain Academy. The Academy immediately makes available enough cots and mattresses for the stranded travelers to sleep on.

Throughout the early hours of February 7, 1978 the unit continues rescue operations. The road conditions remain virtually the same throughout the day, even though the PENNDOT snow removal equipment is working around the clock. As the roads are gradually plowed open on the Interstate, some smaller vehicles can be moved. Many of the tractor-trailers are so buried in the snow that they cannot be moved under their own power.

The unit now contacts the 337th Maintenance Battalion of the Pennsylvania Army National Guard in Reading, and requests a military tow-truck be sent to the Hamburg area to assist in pulling out these trucks, which is done. Many of the truck drivers refuse to leave their rigs for fear that their loads will be stolen or destroyed. So the troops provide these brave drivers with food and hot coffee at their trucks, and the drivers keep their engines running for heat. As time goes on some of these trucks begin to run dangerously low on fuel, and the unit calls a local fuel company for assistance. The fuel company provides a tank truck and driver, loaded with diesel fuel, and with the assistance of a couple of soldiers refuels the trucks on the spot.

By February 8 most of the main roads and the Interstate are cleared of snow and traffic resumes once again. The unit now transports the motorists back to their vehicles so they can once again be on their way. These stranded travelers are from almost every part of the United States. Places such as Maine, North Carolina, Texas, California, Idaho, Missouri, and Michigan. The appreciation expressed by these unfortunate people for the soldiers' assistance is incredible, and makes the soldiers know that their extraordinary efforts and lack of sleep was all worthwhile. The unit also expresses its appreciation to the countless local volunteers who assisted with their own vehicles and the preparation and serving of meals to the stranded motorists. The unit is relieved of duty on February 8, 1978.

In 1987 the unit conducts probably its most interesting, complex, and challenging Annual Training period. It travels to the Federal Republic of Germany for "Operation Certain Strike", a REFORGER (Return of Forces to Germany) exercise. The unit had not been to Germany since the end of World War II, and now it would be returning, but this time as an ally and not an enemy.

The unit spends the better part of 1987 preparing for this exercise. Detailed preparations are necessary in the areas of equipment and personnel readiness. All the soldiers receive mandatory inoculations, panographic x-rays of teeth, and numerous briefings to prepare them for the trip. Equipment is readied, entailing everything from thorough maintenance checks and inspections of all vehicles and equipment, to reducing the vehicles to their smallest configuration for shipment.

At times it seems that the work and preparations will never end, and some tasks require extraordinary effort to accomplish. But by August of 1987 everything is ready and the soldiers are anxious to leave. The first soldier to depart for Germany is Staff Sergeant Donald E. Frantz, on August 26, 1987. He is the unit's advance detachment, and will meet the unit's equipment when it arrives in port in Europe.

The unit equipment is carefully packed and sealed in boxes at the armory and then loaded into the unit's trucks. Before any equipment is packed or loaded it receives a Customs inspection. The vehicles are then loaded on flatbed tractor-trailers at the Lehighton Armory and transported to the port in Baltimore, Maryland by the 121st Transportation Company of the Pennsylvania Army National Guard. A few soldiers from the unit also travel to Baltimore. There they assist in off-loading the vehicles from the trucks and on-loading them unto the ship that will take them to the port of Rotterdam in the Netherlands. From the Netherlands, the vehicles are transported by rail to Bremerhaven, Germany, and then finally to Bergen-Hohne where the unit picks them up.

The soldiers fly from McGuire Air Force Base, New Jersey to Hannover and Frankfurt in Germany. The unit deploys in three increments of 35 soldiers each, with a one or two week overlap. The first increment experiences some difficulties in departing due to a mechanical problem with the airplane, thus delaying their departure for one day. This increment stops to refuel in Iceland on the way to Germany and in Newfoundland on the return trip. The next two increments didn't experience any problems in flight. When the soldiers arrive in Germany they are bused from the airports to either Trauen, or Munster, as is the case with the third increment.

Almost immediately the unit goes to work performing their mission of providing military police support in their area of operation. This Annual Training was not really a training period, but was an actual mission in support of the III U.S. Army Corps. The unit performs circulation control, law and order, physical security, as well as providing access control for the Trauen Lager. The mission proves to be the most difficult the unit encountered since being mobilized for the Korean War. Continuous operations are conducted 24-hours a day for the entire seven weeks that the unit is in Germany, and most of the time the unit is over-committed.

The unit works side-by-side with Active Army military police units stationed in Germany, and with the German Feldjagers (military police), as well as with the Germany civilian police. The caliber and professionalism of the unit soldiers is extremely high and inspires the other military police units, Feldjagers, and civilian police alike. Morale is high for the entire seven weeks, even though more than half of the soldiers suffer from head colds.

During this mission, the unit proves beyond doubt that in the event of a war in Europe, that they can be depended upon to carry their share of the load and accomplish any and all missions assigned to them. REFORGER-87 is one of the best Annual Training periods that the unit attended, since it so thoroughly tested their readiness. Once again, when they were called to serve, they did so in an extraordinary manner.

Between 1953 and 1989 the Hamburg unit was reorganized numerous times. As a matter of fact, more times then in all of its previous history. Even though at times the soldiers did not like the changes, they always made the transition with very few, if any problems. They proved that regardless of the type of unit, it is the soldiers within the organization that make it a good unit.

Also during this era the full-time manning of the unit steadily increased and changed. For many years there was one full-time Administrative Supply Technician who took care of the daily business of the unit. In December 1980 a second full-time soldier was added as the Unit Training NCO. In 1983 a Supply Sergeant and an Assistant Training NCO were added to the full-time manning of the unit. In 1984 a Unit Armorer was added, bringing the total of full-time soldiers to five. Still later in 1987, a full-time Unit Production Recruiter was assigned to the unit. As the unit's mission and priority increased, these full-time soldiers were needed to help in keeping the unit in a high state of readiness in the event of a mobilization.

Throughout this period the unit participated in a countless number of events. The unit could always be counted upon to provide their services for Hamburg's Memorial Day activities to pay tribute to their fallen comrades. They also provided firing squads for other places such as Bernville, Shartlesville, and at Belleman's Church outside of Centerport. As a military police unit they were often called upon to participate in a multitude of events and ceremonies. The unit soldiers always carried out these duties in a most professional manner, and received the praise and gratitude of those they served. Following is a partial listing of some of the events in which the unit participated.

Duryea Hill Climb in Reading; Mount Gretna Art Show; King Frost Parade in Hamburg; Good Samaritan Hospital Street Fair in Lebanon; military displays and exhibitions at Fort Indiantown Gap; dedication of the National Cemetery at Fort Indiantown Gap; Berks County Easter Seal Society campaigns; Ballad of Valley Forge; Battle of Brandywine Re-enactment; Pennsylvania Army National Guard Officer Candidate School graduation ceremonies; Military Academy at West Point football games; World War II monument dedication for the American Legion Headquarters in Wormleysburg; Veterans Memorial dedication in Centerport; Prisoner of War Recognition Ceremony at Fort Indiantown Gap; State Funeral for the Unknown Soldier of the Vietnam War in Washington, D.C.; Escort duty for soldiers of the British Territorial Army; Camp Cadet in Manatawny; both retirement and swearing-in ceremonies for the Adjutant General of Pennsylvania; Korean War and Vietnam War Veterans Monument dedication in Hamburg; Bicentennial of the Constitution ceremonies in Philadelphia; Berks County Vietnam Veterans Parade and Monument dedication in Reading; Veterans Monument dedication in Mohrsville; 125th Anniversary of the Battle of Gettysburg; and countless firing squad details.

The period between 1953 and 1989 was very active for the unit. It was called upon on many occasions to serve and assist the citizens of Pennsylvania. The unit went through much reorganization and other changes in this turbulent time for both the nation and the armed forces. However, this is not the last chapter for the proud and dedicated military organization, which has through the decades faithfully served its community, State, and nation. The Hamburg unit of Pennsylvania Army National Guard will, I am certain, be writing many new chapters to this book in the years to come. I have no doubt that its soldiers will continue to perform any and all assigned duties and missions in a professional, military manner, and will most definitely continue to "Protect the Peace."

Lineage

1755-1763:
Company (Provincial), 2nd Battalion, Pennsylvania Regiment.

1775-1776:
Company, 4th Battalion, Pennsylvania Regiment.

1777-1779:
Windsor Company 6 and Windsor Company 8, 3rd Battalion, Pennsylvania Regiment.

1780-1782:
Company, 4th Battalion, Pennsylvania Regiment.

1783-1789:
Windsor Company 3 and Windsor Company 5, 2nd Battalion, Berks County Brigade.

1790-1800:
Company, 3rd Regiment, Berks County Brigade.

1807:
Part of the 6th Division.

1812-1813:
Companies (2), 1st Regiment, 2nd Brigade, Pennsylvania Militia.

1814:
Company, 2nd Brigade, 6th Division.

1838:
Hamburg Light Dragoons.

May 30, 1840:
Hamburg Artillerists, Hamburg Volunteer Battalion, 2nd Brigade, 6th Division. Authority: *Order Book A, Issue of Ordnance & Quartermaster Stores, PA Militia.*

1842-1847:
Hamburg Artillerists, and Hamburg Light Dragoons, Hamburg Volunteer Battalion, Berks County Brigade.

1848-1855:
Hamburg Artillerists, Hamburg Volunteer Battalion, 1st Brigade, 5th Division.

1856-1860:
Hamburg Artillerists, and Windsor Cavalry, 2nd Battalion, 1st Brigade, 5th Division Pennsylvania Volunteers.

1861-1864: Company G, 96th Pennsylvania Volunteer Infantry.
1861-1865: Company D, 48th Pennsylvania Volunteer Infantry.
- NOTE: Hamburg unit was split into these two units during the Civil War.

April 13, 1875 - October10, 1917:
Company E (Blue Mountain Legion), 4th Pennsylvania Volunteer Infantry Regiment. Authority: *Annual Report, Adjutant General, Pennsylvania, 1875.*

October 11, 1917 - December 5, 1917:
Company A, 107th Machine Gun Battalion, 28th Division. Authority: *General Orders 22, 28th Division, 11 Oct 17.*

Appendix A

December 6, 1917- October 13, 1921:
Company A, 108th Machine Gun Battalion, 28th Division.

October 14, 1921- April 16, 1936:
Wagon Company No. 106, 28th Infantry Division. Authority: *General Orders 29, Adjutant General, Pennsylvania, 1 Nov 21; General Orders, Adjutant General, Pennsylvania, 1 Oct 28.*

April 17, 1936 - January 1942:
Company D (Truck), 103rd Quartermaster Regiment, 28th Infantry Division. Authority: *General Orders 2, Adjutant General, Pennsylvania, 17 Apr 36.*

January 1942 - December 9, 1946:
121st Quartermaster (Car) Company. Authority: *AG 320.2 (1-28-42) MR-M-C, 28 Jan 42; AG 320.2 (2-4-42) MR-M-C, 7 Feb 42.*

December 10, 1946 - September 31, 1953:
Battery D, 337th Anti-Aircraft Artillery Searchlight Battalion. Authority: *Letter, WDSS, C/National Guard Bureau, 21 May 46, WDSNG 325.4 (AAA) Pa-27 (8 Jan 47), 15 Jan 47; National Guard Bureau FR reports.*

October 1, 1953 - May 31, 1959:
Battery D, 337th Anti-Aircraft Artillery Battalion. Authority: *WDSNG 325.455 (Pa), 16 Dec 47.*

June 1, 1959 - April 30, 1962:
Battery D, 2nd Gun Battalion, 213th Artillery. Authority: *NG-AROTO 325.4-Penna, Reorganization Auth 67-59, 20 May 59.*

May 1, 1962 - March 23, 1964:
Company D, 3rd Medium Tank Battalion, 103rd Armor. Authority: *NG-AROTO 325.4 Pennsylvania (Reorganization Auth 43-62) 11 Apr 62.*

March 24, 1964 - December 31, 1975:
Company A, 3rd Battalion, 103rd Armor. Authority: *NG-AROTO 1002-01-Pennsylvania (Reorganization Auth 53-64) 27 Feb 64.*

January 1, 1976 - February 28, 1979:
Detachment 1, 723rd Military Police Company, 165th Military Police Battalion. Authority: *NGB-ARO-O 207-02-PA (Reorganization Auth 10-65) 23 Dec 75.*

March 1, 1979 - December 31, 1982:
Detachment 1, 1068th Military Police Company, 165th Military Police Battalion. Authority: *NGB-ARO-O (Reorganization Auth 31-79) 27 Feb 79.*

January 1, 1983 - July 31, 1989:
1068th Military Police Company (minus detachment in Pottsville), 165th Military police Battalion. Authority: *NGB-ARO-O (Org Auth 2-83) 17 Dec 82.*

August 1, 1989:
Detachment 1, Battery A, 1st Battalion, 213th Air Defense Artillery, 28th Infantry Division (Mechanized).

Campaign Participation

FRENCH AND INDIAN WAR
North America: 1755-1763

REVOLUTIONARY WAR
Long Island: August 27, 1776

CIVIL WAR

Co. G, 96th PA Volunteer Inf:
Peninsula
Antietam
Fredericksburg
Chancellorsville
Gettysburg
Wilderness
Spottsylvania
Cold Harbor
Petersburg
Shenandoah Valley

Co. D, 48th PA Volunteer Inf:
North Carolina - 1862
Second Bull Run
Antietam
Fredericksburg
Knoxville
Wilderness
Spottsylvania
Cold Harbor
Petersburg
Appomattox

Spanish-American War
Puerto Rico

BLUE MOUNTAIN LEGION

<u>World War I</u>
Champagne-Marne
Aisne-Marne
Oise-Aisne
Meuse-Argonne
Champagne 1918
Lorraine 1918

<u>World War II</u>
Southern France
Rhineland
Central Europe

Commanding Officers

CPT Jacob Morgan	1755-1758
CPT Weatherholt	1758
CPT Kern	1763
CPT George May	1775-1776
CPT Jacob Shadle	1777-1778
(6th Company, 3rd Battalion)	
CPT Ferdinand Ritter	1777-1780
(8th Company, 3rd Battalion)	
CPT Godfrey Seidle	1783
(Windsor Company No. 3)	
CPT Jacob Schappell	1783
(Windsor Company No. 5)	
CPT George Ritter	1814-1815
CPT John F. Reeser	1840-1844
MAJ John Alfred Beitenman	1842-1861
(Hamburg Volunteer Battalion)	
CPT Arthur S. Fesig	1842
(Hamburg Light Dragoons)	
CPT William Miller	1842-1861
(Hamburg Light Dragoons/Windsor Cavalry)	
CPT George Heinly	1842-1856
(Berks County Rifle Rangers)	
LT Frederick E. Beitenman	1845-1848
(Hamburg Artillery)	
CPT John A. Beitenman	1848-1858
(Hamburg Artillery)	
CPT William Shomo	1848-1858
(Windsor Cavalry)	

CPT Jonathan S. Herbein	1856
(Pleasant Valley Artillery)	
CPT Benneville Derr	1859-1861
(Hamburg Artillery)	
CPT James M. Douden	1861-1862
(Co. G, 96th PA Volunteer Infantry)	
CPT Jacob Haas	1862-1864
(Co. G, 96th PA Volunteer Infantry)	
CPT Daniel Nagle	1861
(Co. D, 48th PA Volunteer Infantry)	
CPT William W. Potts	1861-1863
(Co. D, 48th PA Volunteer Infantry)	
CPT Peter Fisher	1863-1864
(Co. D, 48th PA Volunteer Infantry)	
CPT John F. Werner	1864-1865
(Co. D, 48th PA Volunteer Infantry)	
CPT Edward F. Smith	1875-1883
CPT Charles F. Seaman	1883-1893
CPT John F. Ancona	1893-1897
CPT John R. Wagner	1897-1898
CPT William Kummerer	1898-1899
CPT Charles E. Seaman	1899-1902
CPT Monroe M. Dreibelbis	1902-1907
CPT Wilson E. Lewars	1907-1911
CPT Mundon L. Machemer	1911-1912
CPT Lewis A. Loy	1912-1917
CPT Ralph C. Crow	1917-1918
CPT Ernest A. Swingle	1918
CPT Harrison N. Seaman	1921-1923
CPT Harold F. Reinhard	1923-1927
CPT Raymond E. Casper	1927-1942
CPT Franklin L. Loy	1942
CPT Harry D. Fritts	1942-1943
CPT Herschell A. Hinckley	1943-1945
1LT Gerald Tonglet	1945
1LT James F. McKenna	1945-1946

Appendix C

CPT Norman Smith	1951-1952
CPT Wellington R. Ketner	1953-1962
1LT Alfred W. Pettit	1962-1963
CPT Edward J. Kelley	1963-1966
CPT Randolph W. Bartholomew	1966-1969
CPT Richard D. Morgan	1969-1975
CPT David W. Bucks	1975
1LT Stephen J. Cashman	1976-1978
1LT Daryl F. Moyer	1978-1979
2LT Dennis J. McGlone	1979-1980
1LT Clifford P. Cardine	1980-1981
1LT Thomas P. Murray	1981-1982
CPT Barrie R. Carr	1983-1986
CPT Martin W. Breidenthall	1986-1989
1LT Patrick N. Hinds	1989

Rosters

Revolutionary War

Pay Roll of Captain Ferdinand Ritter's Company, 6th Battalion, Berks County Militia, commanded by Colonel Joseph Hiester, in the service of the United States from August 10, 1780 to September 9, 1780.

CPT Ritter, Ferdinand
1LT Smith, Andrew
ENS Dietrich, Leonard
SGT Bousher, Peter
SGT Connor, Jacob
SGT Minig, Christian
CPL Conrad, Joseph
CPL Dumm, Peter
CPL Richard, Peter
MUSC Burtchel, John
MUSC Wills, Philip
PVT Albrecht, Adam
PVT Albright, Henry
PVT Bantzy, Christian
PVT Berry, John
PVT Billner, Dewald
PVT Boutcher, Tobias
PVT Brown, Peter
PVT Daubens, Philip
PVT Dengler, Jacob
PVT Donard, Jacob
PVT Drees, Michael

PVT Kauffman, Philip
PVT Kelchner, Jacob
PVT Kisling, John
PVT Kisling, Martin
PVT Laub, Matthias
PVT Lerch, Christian
PVT Lutz, Peter
PVT Miller, Dewalt
PVT New, Jacob
PVT Nonemacker, Jacob
PVT Plott, John
PVT Rangler, John
PVT Schwenk, Nicholas
PVT Shoman, John
PVT Shomo, Joseph
PVT Shreffler, Henry
PVT Shreffler, Stoffel
PVT Smith, Philip
PVT Snyder, Henry
PVT Snyder, Michael
PVT Stear, John
PVT Straser, John

BLUE MOUNTAIN LEGION

PVT Fige, George
PVT Fisher, Christian
PVT Fiss, Peter
PVT Fritz, Melchior
PVT Gerhard, Jacob
PVT Glick, Frederick
PVT Hesier, Godleib
PVT Johnson, Thomas
PVT Kamp, Daniel

PVT Straser, Nicholas
PVT Swabel, Christian
PVT Umbehaker, John
PVT Wagner, John
PVT Wagner, Stoffel
PVT Walls, Frederick
PVT Weber, Christian
PVT Winter, Christian
PVT Zeichman, George

Pay Roll of Captain Daniel Will's Company of Berks County Militia, Windsor Township, over the Blue Mountains, from May to July 1781.

CPT Will, Daniel
QM May, William
SGT Berger, Christian
SGT Lanzer, Abram
SGT Lowinberg, Frederick
SGT Mingle, Frederick
PVT Barret, Zachariah
PVT Billig, Anthony
PVT Bust, Abraham
PVT Coleman, Christian
PVT Derring, Gottfried
PVT Donnath, Martin
PVT Eberhard, John
PVT Gerhard, John
PVT Girling, George
PVT Gruner, Michael
PVT Hartman, Adam
PVT Herring, George
PVT Hewer, Adam
PVT Hollenback, George
PVT Huiser, Godlieb

PVT Keller, George
PVT Kenfirle, Jacob
PVT Kirchner, John
PVT Klockner, John
PVT Kloes, George
PVT Maurer, John
PVT Petru, David
PVT Reegleman, Conrad
PVT Roush, John
PVT Shaffer, Philip
PVT Sharp, John
PVT Shirley, Ludwig
PVT Showing, Adam
PVT Smith, Abraham
PVT Steiner, Christian
PVT Stuerwald, Carl
PVT Stump, John
PVT Thomas, Frederick
PVT Thompson, Alexander
PVT Walter, John
PVT Zittelmeyer, Adam

Appendix D

War of 1812

Following is an extract of the *Muster Rolls of the Pennsylvania Volunteers, War of 1812-1814, Pennsylvania Archives, Second Series, Volume XII.* Two companies were from the Hamburg area.

Muster Roll of Captain George Ritter's Company, in the 1st Regiment, 2nd Brigade of Pennsylvania Militia, under command of Lieutenant Colonel Jeremiah Schappel, at York, Pennsylvania, September 5, 1814. In service from August 28, 1814 to March 5, 1815:

CPT Ritter, George
1LT Berdow, John
2LT Moyers, Isaac
ENS Slotman, Daniel
SGT Beninger, Philip
SGT Breidigam, Abram
SGT Clauser, William
SGT Fox, John
SGT Heaffer, Henry
CPL Acker, Daniel
CPL Berdow, Abraham
CPL Berninger, Jacob
CPL Heaffer, Mathias
CPL Lorah, Michael
CPL Moyer, Jacob
MUSC Bingenman, Yost
MUSC Slotman, John
PVT Adams, John
PVT Andy, Jacob
PVT Andy, Jacob B
PVT Andy, John B
PVT Gerver, Henry
PVT Gilbert, Samuel
PVT Gregory, Peter
PVT Gregory, Samuel

PVT Andy, Mathias
PVT Barker, John
PVT Barkop, John
PVT Beaver, Devald
PVT Beaver, John
PVT Behm, John
PVT Bierman, John
PVT Borger, Henry
PVT Bouman, Jacob
PVT Boyer, John
PVT Brown, Jacob
PVT Clark, David
PVT Daupet, Peter
PVT Dillinger, Daniel
PVT Edinger, Christopher
PVT Ely, Daniel
PVT Emrich, John
PVT Feagley, Henry
PVT Flicker, Jacob
PVT Folick, Henry
PVT Fox, Engel
PVT Miller, John
PVT Moon, Daniel
PVT Moyer, Abraham
PVT Ohrantz, John

PVT Gruber, Michael
PVT Haas, Adam
PVT Haas, George
PVT Haist, George
PVT Heanin, Henry
PVT Herbst, Samuel
PVT Herp, Jacob
PVT Himelreich, Jacob
PVT Himelreich, John
PVT Hoffman, Jacob
PVT Hoppes, Jacob
PVT Keller, George
PVT Kistler, Conrad
PVT Kline, George
PVT Lees, Peter
PVT Lehman, Christian
PVT Ludwig, George

PVT Olinger, David
PVT Paulus, John
PVT Peterson, Severon
PVT Preis, George
PVT Ruppert, Abraham
PVT Ruppert, Herman
PVT Rush, John
PVT Sheiry, John
PVT Shiery, Nicholous
PVT Smith, William
PVT Specht, Peter
PVT Sprigelmoyer, Henry
PVT Steller, Henry
PVT Weller, George
PVT Weastler, John
PVT Windbigler, Philip
PVT Yost, George

Muster Roll of Captain Henry Willoz's Company, in the 1st Regiment, 2nd Brigade, Pennsylvania Militia, under command of Lieutenant Colonel Jeremiah Schappel, at York, Pennsylvania. In service from August 28, 1814 to (not mentioned), from Berks County.

CPT Willoz, Henry
1LT Harman, William
ENS Herberling, John
SGT Cunnius, John
SGT Evans, Samuel
SGT Houder, Solomon
SGT Miller, Daniel
SGT Moyer, Jonathan
CPL Benton, Samuel
CPL Hacket, Daniel
CPL Hoyer, Daniel
CPL Kremer, John
CPL Wingert, Jacob

PVT Boyer, Samuel
PVT Briton, Joseph
PVT Bushe, Joseph
PVT Clouser, George
PVT Coffee, James
PVT Eberly, Samuel
PVT Eck, John
PVT Feather, Daniel
PVT Featherolf, Benjamin
PVT Foust, John
PVT Hamerstine, Nicholas
PVT Haub, Daniel
PVT Heister, Isaac

MUSC Rader, Casper
MUSC Rader, Conrad
PVT Ahman, Frederick
PVT Bast, Dewalt
PVT Hosler, George
PVT Krich, Francis
PVT Lash, Samuel
PVT Learch, John
PVT Louch, Michael
PVT Lupt, John
PVT Maidenport, Nicholas
PVT Malone, George
PVT McCoy, William
PVT McCurdy, James
PVT McMickins, Andrew
PVT Messersmith, Jacob
PVT Miller, Jacob
PVT Miller, Peter
PVT Neadrow, Jacob
PVT Nuss, Michael
PVT Philips, James R
PVT Raber, Benjamin
PVT Raber, George
PVT Reifsnyder, Jacob
PVT Reifsnyder, John
PVT Rhine, Bernard
PVT Rockefeller, Peter

PVT Heister, John
PVT Heister, William
PVT Heller, Isaac
PVT Heller, Jacob
PVT Rollman, John
PVT Rothermal, John
PVT Ruth, Daniel
PVT Ruth, Philip
PVT Ruth, William
PVT Sassaman, Henry
PVT Seiler, Godfrey
PVT Shell, Jacob
PVT Shell, William
PVT Shlegel, Samuel
PVT Smeek, Daniel
PVT Snyder, Henry
PVT Snyder, Isaac
PVT Snyder, Samuel
PVT Spoon, Henry
PVT Star, George
PVT Strunk, John
PVT Wagner, George
PVT Wagner, Isaac
PVT Wanner, Jacob
PVT White, Henry
PVT Wolfinger, Philip
PVT Zweidzig, Jacob

Civil War

Company D, 48th Pennsylvania Volunteer Infantry Regiment:

Ames, Walter P – CPL, Hamburg, Mustered in September 23, 1861, WIA at Antietam, MD September 17, 1862, MIA at Cold Harbor, VA June 6, 1864.

Arndt, Charles – PVT, Mustered in September 23, 1861, Discharged on Surgeon's certificate February 12, 1865.

Artz, George – PVT, Mustered in September 23, 1861, WIA at Antietam, MD September 17, 1862, Mustered out July 17, 1865.

Atchison, William – PVT, Mustered in January 24, 1865, Substitute, Transferred to Department of North West February 10, 1865.

Bailey, Loyal – PVT, Mustered in January 26, 1865, Substitute, Mustered out July 17, 1865.

Bailey, Mattis – PVT, Mustered in September 23, 1861, MIA at Bull Run, VA August 29, 1862, not on muster out roll.

Bambrick, John – PVT, Mustered in September 23, 1861, not on muster out roll.

Bambrick, William – SGT, Mustered in September 23, 1861, KIA at Fredericksburg, VA December 13, 1862, Buried in Military Asylum Cemetery, Washington D.C.

Baum, Charles W – PVT, Hamburg, Mustered in February 26, 1864, Mustered out July 17, 1865.

Baum, James L – CPL, Hamburg, Mustered in February 24, 1864, promoted to Corporal May 22, 1865, Mustered out July 17, 1865.

Baum, Orlando – PVT, Hamburg, Mustered in February 26, 1864, Mustered out July 17, 1865.

Bean, Albert – PVT, Hamburg, Mustered in February 6, 1865, Mustered out July 17, 1865.

Beisel, George S – PVT, Mustered in February 22, 1864, Transferred to Veterans Reserve Corps April 1, 1865.

Bird, Emanuel – PVT, Mustered in January 26, 1865; Substitute, Mustered out July 17, 1865.

Boggs, Alexander – PVT, Mustered in January 17, 1865, Drafted, Deserted May 26, 1865.

Bower, Jonathan – PVT, Hamburg, mustered in March 1, 1864, mustered out July 17, 1865.

Bowman, George – SGT, Hamburg, mustered in September 23, 1861, Discharged on Surgeon's Certificate April 13, 1865.

Boyer, John B – PVT, mustered in February 22, 1864, deserted, returned, mustered out July 17, 1865.

Appendix D

Bradley, James – PVT, Mustered in February 28, 1865, Mustered out July 17, 1865.

Brannan, James Jr. – PVT - Mustered in September 23, 1861, Transferred to Battery E, 5th US Artillery October 24, 1862.

Brannan, James Sr. – PVT, Mustered in September 23, 1861, not on muster out roll.

Brobst, Charles – MUSICIAN, Mustered in September 23, 1861, Mustered out July 17, 1865.

Brown, John – PVT, Mustered in February 20, 1864, Deserted February 25, 1864.

Buddinger, Joseph – PVT, Mustered in March 12, 1864, WIA June 17, 1864, Mustered out July 17, 1865.

Bukman, Philip – CPL, Mustered in September 23, 1861, Died February 9, 1865 at Baltimore, MD.

Burkhalter, H.C. – 2LT, Hamburg, Mustered in September 23, 1861, Promoted to Second Lieutenant May 22, 1865, WIA at Fredericksburg, VA December 13, 1862, Mustered out July 17, 1865.

Casper, Jacob L – PVT, Hamburg, Mustered in February 27, 1864, Discharged on Surgeon's certificate June 27, 1865.

Clark, George – PVT, Mustered in January 26, 1865, Substitute, Mustered out July 17, 1865.

Cook, George – PVT, Mustered in January 23, 1865, Substitute, mustered out July 17, 1865.

Cooligan, Patrick – CPL, Mustered in February 15, 1864, Mustered out July 17, 1865.

Cooper, George W.H. – PVT, Mustered in March 8, 1864, Mustered out July 17, 1865.

Cullen, James – PVT, Mustered in January 31, 1865, not on muster out roll.

Dalious, James J – PVT, Hamburg, Mustered in March 1, 1864, Mustered out June 7, 1865, General Order.

Dentzer, Henry – PVT, Mustered in February 23, 1864, Mustered out July 17, 1865.

Derr, Eli – PVT, Mustered in September 23, 1861, not on muster out roll.

Derr, Jacob – PVT, Mustered in September 23, 1861, Discharged on Surgeon's certificate February 7, 1865.

Derr, John H. – CPL, Mustered in September 23, 1861, WIA December 13, 1862 at Fredericksburg, VA, Died of wounds January 2, 1863, Buried in Military asylum cemetery.

Derr, John W. – PVT, Mustered in September 23, 1861, WIA at Bull Run, VA August 29, 1862, Mustered out July 17, 1865.

Derr, Levi – CPL, Mustered in January 1, 1864, Mustered out July 17, 1865.

Dietrich, Charles – PVT, Mustered in February 22, 1864, Mustered out July 17, 1865.

Dietrich, Daniel – PVT, Mustered in February 22, 1864, Mustered out June 15, 1865, General Order.

Dietrich, John – PVT, Mustered in February 22, 1864, Died at Mt. Carmel, PA March 26, 1864.

Dietrich, Jonathan – CPL, Mustered in September 23, 1861, WIA June 17, 1864, Mustered out July 17, 1865.

Dietrich, Lewis – PVT, Mustered in February 22, 1864, WIA at Petersburg, VA June 17, 1864, absent in hospital at muster out.

Dolan, John – PVT, Mustered in March 12, 1864, Transferred to Company C, date unknown.

Doner, Christian – PVT, Mustered in September 23, 1861, not on muster out roll.

Donohue, John N – PVT, Mustered in January 23, 1865, Substitute, Discharged on Surgeon's certificate June 27, 1865.

Dorward, Franklin – SGT, Hamburg, Mustered in September 23, 1861, WIA at Bull Run, VA August 29, 1862, Promoted to Sergeant May 22, 1865, Mustered out July 17, 1865.

Dorward, Henry – PVT, Hamburg, Mustered in February 4, 1864, KIA at Petersburg, VA July 5, 1864.

Ebert, Edward J – PVT, Mustered in March 10, 1864, Deserted, Returned, Mustered out July 17, 1865.

Eppley, Samuel – PVT, Mustered in March 12, 1864, Mustered out July 17, 1865.

Evans, James – CPL, Mustered in September 23, 1861, WIA at Anietam, MD September 17, 1862, not on muster out roll.

Appendix D

Eyster, Solomon – PVT, Mustered in September 23, 1861, Died at Philadelphia, PA August 15, 1864.

Fisher, Albert E – PVT, Mustered in January 26, 1865, Substitute, Deserted, Returned, Mustered out July 17, 1865.

Fisher, Peter – CPT, Mustered in September 23, 1861, Promoted to First Lieutenant December 10, 1862, Promoted to Captain September 1, 1863, Dismissed July 21, 1864.

Fox, Alexander H – 2LT, Mustered in September 23, 1861, Promoted to Second Lieutenant November 30, 1861, Died December 25, 1861.

Frankenburg, F – PVT, Mustered in January 16, 1865, Drafted, Deserted May 26, 1865.

Gahagen, R – PVT, Mustered in January 25, 1865, Substitute, WIA at Black & White's Station, VA April 6, 1865, discharged June 16, 1865 General Order.

Geist, Henry – PVT, Mustered in March 13, 1865, Mustered out July 17, 1865.

Goodfleck, William – PVT, Hamburg, Mustered in February 13, 1865, Mustered out July 17, 1865.

Gottschall, Henry – PVT, Mustered in September 23, 1861, Discharged October 9, 1862.

Graeff, Frank B – PVT, Mustered in March 1, 1864, Mustered out July 17, 1865.

Graeff, Henry C – 1SG, Mustered in September 23, 1861, Captured September 30, 1864, Died at Pottsville March 29, 1865.

Grim, Horatio – PVT, Hamburg, Mustered in September 23, 1861, Mustered out July 17, 1865.

Haley, John – PVT, Mustered in January 23, 1865, Substitute, Mustered out July 17, 1865.

Hartman, John – PVT, Mustered in January 26, 1865, Substitute, Deserted date unknown.

Hartz, George – PVT, Mustered in April 30, 1862, WIA at Petersburg, VA, Died December 20, 1864 of wounds.

Hartz, Peter – PVT, Mustered in September 23, 1861, Discharged October 26, 1862, War Department orders.

Heebner, J.W. – PVT, Mustered in September 23, 1861, Sick in hospital October 27, 1862, Died April 22, 1864, buried at Alexandria, VA.

Heinan, Mattis – PVT, Mustered in September 23, 1861, Mustered out July 17, 1865.

Heisler, Henry C – MUSICIAN, Mustered in September 23, 1861, not on muster out roll.

Helms, James K – 1LT, Mustered in September 23, 1861, Promoted to First Lieutenant September 1, 1863, WIA at Petersburg, VA in June 1864, Discharged on Surgeon certificate October 19, 1864.

Hesser, Charles F – PVT, Mustered in February 25, 1864, Died July 26, 1865 at Washington, D.C.

Hoch, Franklin – SGT, Mustered in September 23, 1861, WIA at Antietam, MD September 17, 1862, Promoted to Sergeant May 1, 1865, Mustered out July 17, 1865.

Hoover, John – PVT, Mustered in February 20, 1864, Deserted March 16, 1864.

Houck, William – PVT, Mustered in September 23, 1861, Discharged October 26, 1862 order War Department.

Jacoby, George – PVT, Hamburg, Mustered in March 1, 1865, Mustered out July 17, 1865.

James, George W – PVT, Mustered in September 23, 1861, Transferred to Company E, date unknown.

Jeffries, Alva – PVT, Mustered in September 23, 1861, KIA at Antietam September 17, 1862.

Johnson, Stacey – CPL, Mustered in August 9, 1862, Deserted March 14, 1864.

Jones, Thomas – PVT, Mustered in February 19, 1864, MIA at Cold Harbor, VA June 6, 1864.

Kahler, Elias – PVT, Mustered in March 13, 1865, Mustered out July 17, 1865.

Kahler, John – PVT, Mustered in February 22, 1864, Mustered out July 17, 1865.

Kantner, Phillip – PVT, Mustered in September 23, 1861, WIA at Bull Run, VA August 29, 1862, not on muster out roll.

Kaufman, Jonathan – PVT, Mustered in February 22, 1864, KIA at the Wilderness May 6, 1864.

Kessler, John – PVT, Mustered in September 23, 1861, absent in hospital at Philadelphia, PA November 16, 1862.

Kessler, Nathan – PVT, Mustered in March 12, 1864, Mustered out July 17, 1865.

Kessler, Samuel – CPL, Mustered in February 22, 1864, promoted to Corporal May 1, 1865, Mustered out July 17, 1865.

Kinney, Thomas – PVT, Mustered in September 23, 1861, KIA at Fredericksburg, VA December 13, 1862.

Kister, Daniel – PVT, Mustered in March 6, 1865, mustered out July 17, 1865.

Klauser, Jacob – PVT, Mustered in February 22, 1864, Mustered out July 17, 1865.

Kleckner, Charles – 1LT, Mustered in September 23, 1861, Promoted to First Lieutenant January 1, 1862, Promoted to Colonel of the 172nd PVI Regiment in December 62.

Kline, Benjamin – PVT, Mustered in September 23, 1861, not on muster out roll.

Kline, Charles – PVT, Mustered in September 23, 1861, Mustered out July 17, 1865.

Kline, George M – PVT, Mustered in September 23, 1861, Sick in hospital October 8, 1862, Discharged February 2, 1863.

Kline, Isaiah – PVT, Mustered in September 23, 1861, MIA at Bull Run, VA August 29, 1862, absent sick at muster out.

Kline, Jared – PVT, Mustered in September 23, 1861, Transferred to Battery E, 5th US Artillery October 29, 1862.

Klinger, Zames – PVT, Mustered in March 2, 1864, Mustered out July 17, 1865.

Klock, Andrew – PVT, Mustered in September 23, 1861, Died of disease June 30, 1862.

Knarr, Daniel – PVT, Mustered in February 23, 1864, Mustered out July 17, 1865.

Knittle, Andrew – PVT, Mustered in February 22, 1864, Mustered out July 17, 1865.

Knoll, George W – PVT, Mustered in January 27, 1865, Mustered out July 17, 1865.

Koble, Elias – PVT, Mustered in September 23, 1861, Discharged October 26, 1862, order of War Department to join artillery.

Koons, Jacob – PVT, Mustered in September 23, 1861, Not on muster out roll.

Koons, Joseph – PVT, Mustered in September 23, 1861, WIA at Bull Run, VA August 29, 1862, not on muster out roll.

Kreiger, Daniel T – PVT, Mustered in September 23, 1861, not on muster out roll.

Kreiger, Francis J – PVT, Mustered in February 22, 1864, Mustered out July 17, 1865.

Kreiger, Peter C – PVT, Mustered in September 23, 1861, WIA at Bull Run, VA August 29, 1862, Transferred to Veterans Reserve Corps date unknown.

Lenhart, Edward – CPL, Mustered in September 23, 1861, Discharged December 18, 1861 on Surgeon's certificate.

Letrich, Philip – PVT, Mustered in July 2, 1863, Mustered out July 17, 1865.

Lindenmuth, C.M – PVT, Hamburg, Mustered in September 23, 1861.

Lindenmuth, Joseph – PVT, Hamburg, Mustered in March 15, 1864, Discharged on Surgeon's certificate April 3, 1865.

Manghane, Charles – PVT, Mustered in September 23, 1861, not on muster out roll.

Martz, George – PVT, Mustered in September 23, 1861, Discharged September 20, 1864 on General Order.

Maury, David – PVT, Mustered in February 29, 1864, Mustered out July 17, 1865.

McBride, Richard B – PVT, Mustered in March 6, 1865, Discharged June 14, 1865 on General Order.

McGuire, Edward – PVT, Mustered in January 30, 1865, Mustered out July 17, 1865.

McLane, John – PVT, Mustered in January 28, 1865, Substitute, absent on furlough at muster out.

Meinder, Jeremiah – PVT, Hamburg, Mustered in September 23, 1861.

Merwine, Daniel – PVT, Mustered in March 9, 1864, Mustered out July 17, 1865.

Miller, Charles – PVT, Mustered in September 23, 1861, KIA at Bull Run, VA August 29, 1862.

Miller, Frederick – PVT, Mustered in February 2, 1865, Absent without leave at muster out.

Miller, Gustavas A – PVT, Hamburg, Mustered in February 19, 1864, Discharged on Surgeon's certificate November 18, 1864.

Minder, Jeremiah – MUSICIAN, Hamburg, mustered in February 19, 1865, mustered out July 17, 1865.

Miller, Jonas – PVT, Mustered in February 23, 1864, Discharged on Surgeon's certificate March 16, 1865.

Miner, Philip – PVT, Mustered in January 23, 1865, Substitute, mustered out July 17, 1865.

Montgomery, Levi – PVT, Mustered in January 27, 1865, Mustered out July 17, 1865.

Morgan, Elias – PVT, Mustered in March 9, 1865, Mustered out July 17, 1865.

Morgan, James D – PVT, Mustered in September 23, 1861, not on muster out roll.

Moyer, Henry D – CPL, Hamburg, Mustered in February 20, 1864, promoted to Corporal April 1, 1865, Mustered out July 17, 1865.

Moyer, William F – PVT, Mustered in February 29, 1864, Mustered out July 17, 1865.

Moyer, Zachariah T – CPL, Mustered in March 2, 1864, promoted to Corporal June 16, 1865, Mustered out July 17, 1865.

Nagle, Abraham – PVT, Mustered in September 23, 1861, Discharged on General Order December 5, 1862.

Nagle, Daniel – CPT, Mustered in September 23, 1861, Promoted to Major November 30, 1861.

Nailich, Tilghman – PVT, Mustered in January 26, 1865, Mustered out July 17, 1865.

Niland, Thomas A – PVT, Mustered in January 21, 1865, Substitute, Mustered out July 17, 1865.

Nolan, James – PVT, Mustered in April 23, 1864, not on muster out roll.

Nolan, John – PVT, Muster in date unknown, Deserted March 14, 1864, Returned , Sentenced by General Court Martial to Rip-Raps for three years.

Novinger, A.R. – 1SG, Mustered in April 30, 1862, Promoted to First Sergeant May 22, 1865, Mustered out July 17, 1865.

Nunemacher, John – PVT, Mustered in September 23, 1861, Discharged for disability May 27, 1862.

O'Kane, Daniel – PVT, Mustered in April 7, 1864, KIA at Petersburg, VA June 21, 1864.

O'Karn, Jonathan – PVT, Mustered in February 23, 1864, Mustered out July 17, 1865.

Otto, Bodo – SGT, Mustered in September 23, 1861, Promoted to Sergeant April 1, 1865, MIA at Bull Run, VA August 29, 1862, Mustered out July 17, 1865.

Owens, Henry P – 2LT, Mustered in September 23, 1861, Promoted to Second Lieutenant February 5, 1862, WIA at Bull Run, VA August 29, 1862, Resigned November 27, 1862.

Phillips, Chester – PVT, Mustered in January 26, 1865, Substitute, Mustered out July 17, 1865.

Potts, William W – CPT, Mustered in September 23, 1861, Promoted to Captain November 30, 1861, Discharged January 8, 1863.

Raber, Jonas Z – PVT, Hamburg, Mustered in March 9, 1864, Died at Washington D.C. July 1, 1864.

Ramer, George – CPL, Mustered in September 23, 1861, WIA August 29, 1862 at Bull Run, VA, died of wounds September 1, 1862.

Reeser, Samuel – PVT, Hamburg, Mustered in February 23, 1864, Mustered out July 17, 1865.

Reichard, Edward – CPL, Mustered in September 23, 1861, Sick in hospital November 16, 1862, not on muster out roll.

Risborn, James – PVT, Mustered in January 17, 1865, Drafted, Mustered out July 17, 1865.

Ritter, Simon – PVT, Hamburg, Mustered in February 6, 1865, Mustered out July 17, 1865.

Ritter, Simon – PVT, Mustered in March 2, 1864, Discharged on Order of the Secretary of War July 22, 1864.

Rothenberger, H – 1LT, Hamburg, Mustered in September 23, 1861, Promoted to First Lieutenant June 16, 1864, Mustered out July 17, 1865.

Ryan, William – PVT, Mustered in September 16, 1861, Mustered out September 30, 1864, end of term.

Schmidt, Jacob E – PVT, Mustered in March 6, 1865, WIA at Petersburg, VA April 2, 1865, absent at muster out.

Seaman, Addision S – PVT, Hamburg, Mustered in September 23, 1861, Died July 16, 1862 of disease.

Shaffer, Mattis – PVT, Mustered in September 23, 1861, Died August 4, 1862 aboard the *US Steamer Cossack*.

Shertle, George – PVT, Mustered in September 23, 1861, Died March 21, 1863, Buried in Military Asylum Cemetery in Washington, DC.

Shollenberger, Charles – PVT, Hamburg, Mustered in February 6, 1865, Mustered out July 17, 1865.

Shrishorn, Leonard – CPL, Mustered in September 23, 1861, MIA August 29, 1862, not on muster out roll.

Shriver, Frank B – PVT, Mustered in February 22, 1864, mustered out July 17, 1865.

Smith, David – SGT, Mustered in September 23, 1861, Sick in hospital August 23, 1862, Promoted to Sergeant June 16, 1865, Mustered out July 17, 1865.

Smith, William H – PVT, Mustered in September 23, 1861, Died April 6, 1864, buried in US general hospital cemetery in Annapolis, MD.

Spear, Andrew – PVT, Mustered in September 23, 1861, died April 15, 1862 of disease.

Stelwagon, George W – PVT, Mustered in September 23, 1861, WIA at Antietam September 17, 1862, not on muster out roll.

Stichter, Alfred J – PVT, Hamburg, Mustered in March 2, 1864, Mustered out July 17, 1865.

Stichter, Henry E – 1LT, Hamburg, Mustered in September 23, 1861, Mustered out October 6, 1863.

Stichter, Samuel – PVT, Hamburg, Mustered in September 23, 1861, not on muster out roll.

Straub, Emanuel – PVT, Mustered in March 27, 1865, Mustered out July 17, 1865.

Strausser, Perry L – PVT, Hamburg, Mustered in February 3, 1864, Deserted June 10, 1865.

Sullivan, John – PVT, Mustered in September 16, 1861, WIA at Bull Run, VA August 29, 1862, Died of wounds October 8, 1862.

Timmons, William – SGT, Mustered in September 16, 1861, WIA at Bull Run, VA August 29, 1862, Mustered out September 30, 1864.

Tobertge, Augustus – PVT, Mustered in September 23, 1861, Sick in hospital August 12, 1862, not on muster out roll.

Troup, John – PVT, Mustered in February 25, 1865, Substitute, Mustered out July 17, 1865.

Trump, Peter – PVT, Hamburg, Mustered in March 1, 1865, mustered out July 17, 1865.

Ungstadt, Solomon – PVT, Mustered in September 23, 1862, Sick in hospital at muster out.

Vancannon, Israel – CPL, Mustered in September 23, 1861, MIA at Bull Run, VA August 29, 1862, not on muster out roll.

Wagner, Aaron B – PVT, Mustered in March 3, 1864, Died April 5, 1865, Buried in National Military Cemetery, Arlington, VA.

Walbridge, Amos F – PVT, Mustered in March 30, 1864, absent sick at muster out.

Weikel, John D – PVT, Mustered in March 9, 1864, Mustered out July 17, 1865.

Weikel, William – PVT, Mustered in February 22, 1864, Mustered out July 17, 1865.

Weldy, Daniel – PVT, Hamburg, Mustered in September 23, 1861, Mustered out July 17, 1865.

Wenrich, Samuel – PVT, Mustered in February 29, 1864, Mustered out July 17, 1865.

Werner, John F – CPT, Mustered in September 23, 1861, Promoted to Second Lieutenant September 12, 1864, Promoted to Captain November 28, 1864, Mustered out July 17, 1865.

Whalen, Thomas – PVT, Mustered in September 23, 1861, Not on muster out roll.

Wildt, Christian – PVT, Mustered in September 23, 1861, discharged June 28, 1862 for disability.

Williams, David – PVT, Mustered in February 22, 1864, Mustered out July 17, 1865.

Williams, Henry – PVT, Hamburg, Mustered in January 25, 1865, Substitute, Mustered out July 17, 1865.

Williams, William H – PVT, Hamburg, Mustered in February 6, 1864, POW from August 19, 1864 to February 28, 1865, Discharged on General Order June 21, 1865.

Williamson, Henry – PVT, Mustered in September 23, 1861, KIA at Fredericksburg, VA December 13, 1862.

Willis, Thomas D – PVT, Mustered in January 31, 1865, Mustered out July 17, 1865.

Winkleman, Charles – PVT, Mustered in January 24, 1865, Substitute, Discharged on General Order May 30, 1865.

Wischke, Thomas – PVT, Mustered in January 20, 1865, Substitute, WIA at Petersburg, VA April 2, 1865, Discharged on General Order June 16, 1865.

Wolff, Daniel – PVT, Mustered in September 23, 1861, Mustered out July 17, 1865.

Wolfgang, George W – PVT, Mustered in March 27, 1865, Mustered out July 17, 1865.

Yarnall, Solomon – PVT, Mustered in September 16, 1861, Mustered out September 30, 1864, end of term.

Yerger, Charles – PVT, Mustered in January 26, 1865, Mustered out July 17, 1865.

Ziegler, Joseph – PVT, Mustered in February 19, 1864, Mustered out July 17, 1865.

Zimmerman, Elias – PVT, Mustered in February 22, 1864, Died August 5, 1864, Buried at Alexandria, VA.

Company G, 96th Pennsylvania Volunteer Infantry Regiment: (Hamburg Light Infantry)

Allbecker, Burkhard – PVT, Mustered in August 10, 1862, Discharged on Surgeons Certificate December 29, 1862.

Alvord, David – CPL, Lykens, Mustered in September 30, 1861, Muster Roll of December 12, 1861, Promoted to Corporal (date unknown), Discharged on Surgeons Certificate July 25, 1862.

Alvord, Jacob – SGT, Lykens, Mustered in September 30, 1861, Muster Roll of December 12, 1861, WIA at Spottsylvania May 10, 1864, Transferred to Co. G, 95th PVI October 18, 1864.

Bade, Julian - PVT

Balliet, Joseph – PVT, Mustered in October 10, 1861, WIA at Spottsylvania May 10, 1864, Transferred to Co. G, 95th PVI October 18, 1864.

Batdorf, Philip – PVT, Mustered in February 22, 1864, WIA at Spottsylvania May 10, 1864, Died of wounds June 8, 1864 in Washington, buried in National Cemetery in Arlington.

Bear, George C – PVT, Mustered in March 8, 1864, WIA at Spottsylvania, Transferred to Co. G, 95th PVI October 18, 1864. (member of the Hamburg unit after the war).

Bear, Jonathan C – SGT, Hamburg, Mustered in October 16, 1861, Promoted to Sergeant, Transferred to Co. G, 95th PVI October 18, 1864.

Beard, Charles – PVT, Hamburg, Mustered in April 4, 1864, Transferred to Co. G, 95th PVI October 18, 1864.

Beard, Gideon – PVT, Hamburg, Mustered in October 3, 1861, Transferred to Co. G, 95th PVI October 18, 1864.

Beard, John – PVT, Hamburg, Mustered in October 3, 1861, WIA at Spottsylvania on May 10, 1864, Transferred to Co. G, 95th PVI October 18, 1864.

Beaver, Reuben – PVT, Mustered in March 8, 1864, Died June 9, 1864 (reason unknown).

Berker, William – PVT, Hamburg, Mustered in October 14, 1861, Muster Roll of December 12, 1861, Discharged on Surgeons Certificate March 29, 1862.

Betz, Daniel – PVT, Hamburg, Mustered in October 21, 1861, Discharged on Surgeons Certificate December 29, 1862, Reenlisted on March 2, 1864, KIA at Spottsylvania on May 10, 1864.

Appendix D

Betz, Isaac – PVT, Hamburg, Mustered in March 5, 1864, Transferred to Co. G, 95th PVI October 18, 1864.

Betz, James – PVT, Hamburg, Mustered in October 7, 1861, KIA at Spottsylvania on May 10, 1864.

Betz, William – PVT, Hamburg, Mustered in March 5, 1864, Transferred to Co. G, 95th PVI October 18, 1864.

Billig, Lafayette C – SGT, Hamburg, Mustered in October 7, 1862, WIA at 2nd Battle of Fredericksburg, Promoted to Sergeant, Transferred to Co. G, 95th PVI October 18, 1864.

Bissel, Benneville H – PVT, Mustered in September 17, 1862, Transferred to Co. G, 95th PVI October 18, 1864.

Blank, Edward - PVT

Borkelbach, John - PVT

Brobst, Simon – PVT, Hamburg, Mustered in October 3, 1861, Muster Roll of December 12, 1861, Died August 24, 1862 at Philiadelphia (cause unknown).

Bryan, Washington – PVT, Lykens, Mustered in September 30, 1861, Muster Roll of December 12, 1861, Mustered out with Company October 21, 1864.

Buehler, Jacob K – SGT, Orwigsburg, Mustered in October 23, 1861, Muster Roll of December 12, 1861, Discharged on Surgeons Certificate March 22, 1862.

Buck, William H – SGT, Windsor Township, Mustered in October 14, 1861, Muster Roll of December 12, 1861, Promoted to Sergeant, Transferred to Co. G, 95th PVI October 18, 1864.

Burd, Joel – PVT, Lykens, Mustered in October 10, 1861, Muster Roll of December 12, 1861, Deserted February 27, 1863, Returned November 7, 1863, Transferred to Co. G, 95th PVI October 18, 1864.

Chamounski, Enoch – PVT, Lykens, Mustered in September 30, 1861, Muster Roll of December 12, 1861, Deserted December 28, 1861.

Coley, Samuel - PVT

Cook, Henry Charles – PVT, Hamburg, Mustered in November 4, 1861, Died at Pottsville on January 17, 1864 (cause unknown).

Depka, Frederick – PVT, Lykens, Mustered in October 10, 1861, Muster Roll of December 12, 1861, Discharged on Surgeons Certificate July 25, 1862.

Douden, Franklin N – 1SG, Lykens, Mustered in September 23, 1861, Muster Roll of December 12, 1861, WIA at 2nd Battle of Fredericksburg, Deserted July 2, 1863.

Douden, James N – CPT, Lykens, Mustered in September 23, 1861, Muster Roll of December 12, 1861, Resigned March 1, 1862.

Dreibelbeis, Abraham – PVT, Lykens, Mustered in September 23, 1861, Muster Roll of December 12, 1861, Transferred to Co. G, 95th PVI October 18, 1864.

Dryfuss, Mark – PVT, Pottsville, Mustered in October 23, 1861, Muster Roll of December 12, 1861, Died December 23, 1861 in Washington (cause unknown), Buried in Military Asylum Cemetery.

Ferree, James M – SGT, Lykens, Mustered in September 30, 1861, Muster Roll of December 12, 1861, KIA at Spottsylvania on May 10, 1864, Buried in Wilderness Burial Grounds.

Ferree, Uriah D – PVT, Lykens, Mustered in September 30, 1861, Muster Roll of December 12, 1861, Transferred to Co. G, 95th PVI October 18, 1864.

Fesig, Arthur S – 1LT, Hamburg, Mustered in September 23, 1861, Promoted to First Lieutenant March 5, 1862, Discharged October 15, 1864. (member of Hamburg unit after the war).

Fesig, William H – SGT, Hamburg, Mustered in October 3, 1861, Transferred to Veteran Reserve Corps October 1, 1863. (member of Hamburg unit after the war).

Fey, Lewis I – PVT, Orwigsburg, Mustered in October 14, 1861, Muster Roll of December 12, 1861, Deserted (date unknown).

Fritz, Lewis – PVT, Windsor Township, Mustered in October 16, 1861, Muster Roll of December 12, 1861, WIA at 2nd Battle of Fredericksburg, WIA at Spottsylvania on May 12, 1864, Transferred to Co. G, 96th PVI October 18, 1864.

Geiger, John – PVT, Hamburg, Mustered in October 7, 1861, Muster Roll of December 12, 1861, Deserted January 18, 1863.

Gery, Evan M – CPL, Allentown, Mustered in October 22, 1861, Captured at the Wilderness on May 7, 1864, Promoted to Corporal, Transferred to Co. G, 95th PVI October 18, 1864.

Glass, John – PVT, Pottsville, Mustered in November 1, 1861, Muster Roll of December 12, 1861, Deserted and returned, Transferred to Co. G, 95th PVI October 18, 1864.

Goodfellow, John – CPL, Minersville, Mustered in September 23, 1861, Muster Roll of December 12, 1861, Promoted to Corporal, Discharged on Surgeons Certificate June 1863.

Gratz, John C – CPL, Lykens, Mustered in September 23, 1861, Muster Roll of December 12, 1861, Died January 26, 1862 (cause unknown).

Greaff, Isaac – PVT, Kutztown, Mustered in October 14, 1861, Muster Roll of December 12, 1861, Discharged on Surgeons Certificate March 1, 1862.

Grim, John L – PVT, Port Clinton, Mustered in October 5, 1861, Muster Roll of December 12, 1861, Discharged on Surgeons Certificate March 25, 1863. (member of Hamburg unit after the war).

Haas, Jacob W – CPT, Pottsville, Mustered in September 23, 1861, Muster Roll of December 12, 1861, Promoted to Captain March 5, 1862, Mustered out with the Company on October 21, 1864.

Haines, Thomas – PVT, Hamburg, Mustered in October 3, 1861, Muster Roll of December 12, 1861, KIA at Cramptons Gap on September 14, 1862.

Hardinger, Elias – PVT, Mustered in March 13, 1864, Transferred to Co. G, 95th PVI October 18, 1864.

Harrison, Frank - PVT

Haus, Alfred D – CPL, Hamburg, Mustered in October 3, 1861, Muster Roll of December 12, 1861, Discharged on Surgeons Certificate August 18, 1862.

Hawk, Jeremiah – PVT, Lykens, Mustered in September 23, 1861, Muster Roll of December 12, 1861, Transferred to Co. G, 95th PVI October 18, 1864.

Heebner, George – PVT, Pottsville, Mustered in October 10, 1861, Muster Roll of December 12, 1861, Deserted and returned, dishonorably discharged (date unknown).

Herb, Nathan – WAGONER, Mustered in September 30, 1861, Muster Roll of December 12, 1861, mustered out with the Company on October 21, 1864.

Herber, Jonathan – PVT, Hamburg, Mustered in October 7, 1861, Muster Roll of December 12, 1861, Discharged on Surgeons Certificate January 24, 1862.

Hill, James – PVT, Hamburg, Mustered in October 15, 1861, Died of wounds on July 24, 1864 at Davids Island, NY, Buried in Cypress Hill Cemetery, Long Island, NY.

Hill, Samuel S – PVT, Mustered in February 4, 1864, Transferred to Co. G, 95th PVI October 18, 1864.

Hoffman, Daniel C – MUSICIAN, Lykens, Mustered in September 23, 1861, Muster Roll of December 12, 1861, Transferred to Veteran Reserve Corps September 12, 1863.

Kaercher, James – PVT, Lykens, Mustered in September 23, 1861, Muster Roll of December 12, 1861, WIA at Cramptons Gap on September 14, 1862, Died of wounds February 8, 1863, Buried in National Cemetery at Antietam, Section 26, Lot E, Grave 486.

Kallegher, John - PVT

Keener, Eli – PVT, Mustered in October 14, 1861, Deserted and returned, Transferred to Co. G, 95th PVI October 18, 1864.

Keiser, Henry – SGT, Lykens, Mustered in September 23, 1861, Muster Roll of December 12, 1861, Promoted to Sergeant May 11, 1864, Transferred to Co. G, 95th PVI October 18, 1864.

Killian, Mark – PVT, Hamburg, Mustered in October 3, 1861, WIA, Discharged on Surgeons Certificate January 29, 1862.

Kistling, Christian –PVT, Lykens, Mustered in September 30, 1861, Muster Roll of December 12, 1861, Deserted and returned on November 15, 1863, Transferred to Co. G, 95th PVI October 18, 1864.

Kuntzleman, Amos – CPL, Lykens, Mustered in September 23, 1861, Muster Roll of December 12, 1861, Discharged on Surgeons Certificate (date unknown).

Luke, John – PVT, Mustered in March 14, 1864, WIA at Spottsylvania, Transferred to Co. G, 95th PVI October 18, 1864.

Lynn, Felix – PVT, Mustered in August 14, 1862, Discharged on Surgeons Certificate March 26, 1863.

Machamer, David – PVT, Lykens, Mustered in September 23, 1861, WIA at Spottsylvania May 10, 1864, Captured May 10, 1864, Discharged December 3, 1864 on Surgeons Certificate.

McCarty, John – PVT, Lykens, Mustered in October 10, 1861, Muster Roll of December 12, 1861, Transferred to Co. F, 96th PVI February 15, 1864.

McCormick, John - PVT

Miller, James Jerome – CPL, Hamburg, Mustered in November 4, 1861, Promoted to Corporal, WIA at Spottsylvania May 12, 1864, Transferred to the Veteran Reserve Corps October 17, 1864.

Miller, William – PVT, Upper Bern Township, Mustered in October 14, 1861, Muster Roll of December 12, 1861, Discharged upon expiration term of service October 14, 1864. (member of the Hamburg unit prior to the war).

Moyer, Edwin – CPL, Lykens, Mustered in September 23, 1861, Muster Roll of December 12, 1861, WIA at 2nd Battle of Fredericksburg, Promoted to Corporal, KIA at Spottsylvania on May 10, 1864.

Murray, John – PVT, Mustered in March 22, 1864, not on the rolls at mustering out.

Nester, George – PVT, Albany Township, Mustered in October 14, 1861, Muster Roll of December 12, 1861, Discharged on Surgeons Certificate December 22, 1862.

Nester, Samuel – PVT, Albany Township, Mustered in October 3, 1861, Muster Roll of December 12, 1861, Discharged on Surgeons Certificate November 28, 1862.

Nice, Jacob – PVT, Minersville, Mustered in November 4, 1861, Muster Roll of December 12, 1861, Transferred to Co. G, 95th PVI October 18, 1864.

Perkey, John – PVT, Mustered in September 12, 1862, WIA at 2nd Battle of Fredericksburg, MIA at Spottsylvania May 10, 1864.

Pugh, Edward – PVT, Lykens, Mustered in September 23, 1861, Muster Roll of December 12, 1861, WIA at Spottsylvania, Transferred to Co. G, 95th PVI October 18, 1864.

Rans, John D – PVT, Hamburg, Muster Roll of December 12, 1861.

Rentz, John D – PVT, Mustered in October 5, 1861, WIA at 2nd Battle of Fredericksburg, Transferred to Co. G, 95th PVI October 18, 1864.

Reynolds, William - PVT

Romberger, Henry – PVT, Mustered in September 23, 1861, WIA at Spottsylvania on May 10, 1864, Transferred to Co. G, 95th PVI October 18, 184.

Romberger, Jonathan – PVT, Lykens, Mustered in September 30, 1861, Muster Roll of December 12, 1861, Transferred to Co. G, 95th PVI October 18, 1864.

Romich, Lewis C – CPL, Hamburg, Mustered in October 22, 1861, Promoted to Corporal, Transferred to Co. G, 95th PVI October 18, 1864.

Rothenberger, Charles – PVT, Hamburg, Mustered in October 23, 1861, Transferred to Veteran Reserve Corps September 23, 1863.

Sauerbrey, E. E – 2LT, Mustered in September 23, 1861, Promoted from Sergeant of Co. A, 96th PVI to Second Lieutenant on March 5, 1862, Discharged April 1, 1863 for wounds received at Gaines Mill on June 27, 1862.

Schollenberger, Abraham – PVT, Hamburg, Mustered in October 23, 1861, Transferred to Co. G, 95th PVI October 18, 1864.

Schollenberger, John – PVT, Hamburg, Mustered in October 23, 1861, WIA at 2nd Battle of Fredericksburg, WIA at Spottsylvania on May 10, 1864, Transferred to Co. G, 95th PVI October 18, 1864.

Schmick, Elias – PVT, Windsor Township, Mustered in October 3, 181, Muster Roll of December 12, 1861, Transferred to Co. G, 95th PVI October 18, 1864.

Seidell, Daniel H – PVT, Hamburg, Mustered in November 4, 1861, Muster Roll of December 12, 1861, Discharged on Surgeons Certificate January 8, 1862.

Sell, Fred - PVT

Senger, Peter – PVT, Schuylkill Haven, Mustered in October 18, 1861, Muster Roll of December 12, 1861, Discharged on Surgeons Certificate July 25, 1862.

Sargant, McCoy – PVT, Lykens, Mustered in September 23, 1861, Muster Roll of December 12, 1861, WIA at Antietam September 17, 1862, Died of wounds September 27, 1862.

Slick, Philip – PVT, Hamburg, Mustered in October 7, 1861, Muster Roll of December 12, 1861, Dropped from Rolls October 17, 1862.

Stahl, Daniel – PVT, Lykens, Mustered in September 23, 1861, Muster Roll of December 12, 1861, WIA at Spottsylvania May 10, 1864, Transferred to Co. G, 95th PVI October 18, 1864.

Stahl, Elias – PVT, Lykens, Mustered in October 10, 1861, Muster Roll of December 12, 1861, Transferred to Co. G, 95th PVI October 18, 1864.

Stambach, Edgar – PVT, Hamburg, Mustered in October 23, 1861, Transferred to Co. G, 95th PVI October 18, 1864.

Strasser, Abraham – PVT, Windsor Township, Mustered in November 5, 1861, Muster Roll of December 12, 1861, Discharged on Surgeons Certificate December 15, 1862.

Strasser, Elias – PVT, Windsor Township, Mustered in October 14, 1861, WIA, Died May 9, 1862.

Strasser, Israel – PVT, Windsor Township, Mustered in October 22, 1861, WIA at Spottsylvania May 10, 1864, Transferred to Co. G, 95th PVI October 18, 1864.

Strasser, Joshua – PVT, Windsor Township, Mustered in October 14, 1861, Discharged on Surgeons Certificate December 15, 1862.

Strasser, Simon – PVT, Windsor Township, Mustered in October 14, 1861, WIA, Discharged on Surgeons Certificate January 29, 1862.

Strasser, William – PVT, Windsor Township, Mustered in October 22, 1861, WIA, Discharged on Surgeons Certificate November 28, 1862.

Sunday, Albert J – PVT, Hamburg, Mustered in October 23, 1861, POW from November 19, 1863 to October 1, 1864, Discharged expiration term of service.

Taylor, Charles W – PVT, Lykens, Mustered in October 29, 1861, Muster Roll of December 12, 1861, Discharged on Surgeons Certificate November 28, 1862.

Thompson, William W – PVT, Lykens, Mustered in September 23, 1861, Muster Roll of December 12, 1861, Died December 18, 1862 at Frederick, Maryland, Buried in National Cemetery, Antietam, Section 26, Lot E, Grave 480.

Treon, Frank – PVT, Mustered in September 30, 1861, KIA at Antietam September 14, 1862.

Wagner, Benjamin B – SGT, Hamburg, Mustered in October 3, 1861, KIA at Spottsylvania May 12, 1864. (member of Hamburg unit prior to the war).

Wagner, Frank – PVT, WIA at Spottsylvania May 10, 1864.

Way, Joseph – PVT, Lykens, Mustered in September 23, 1861, Muster Roll of December 12, 1861, Deserted January 26, 1863.

Weaver, Robert D – PVT, Lykens, Mustered in September 20, 1861, Muster Roll of December 12, 1861, Discharged on Surgeons Certificate 1862.

Weigner, Henry – PVT, Mustered in October 1, 1861, WIA and captured at Spottsylvania on May 10, 1864.

Whitebread, Mark – PVT, Mustered in October 1, 1861, Transferred to Co. G, 95th PVI October 18, 1864.

Williams, David – PVT, Hamburg, Mustered in September 23, 1861, Transferred to Co. G, 95th PVI October 18, 1864.

Williams, John – 1SG, Hamburg, Mustered in October 3, 1861, WIA at Spottsylvania, Promoted November 18, 1863, Transferred to Co. G, 95th PVI October 18, 1864.

Williams, P.T. - PVT

Williams, Samuel – PVT, Hamburg, Mustered in October 29, 1861, Died of wounds at Harrisburg on December 17, 1862.

Woodford, Charles – PVT, Mustered in March 14, 1864, Deserted July 16, 1864.

Workman, Frank – PVT, Mustered in February 22, 1864, KIA at Spottsylvania May 10, 1864, Buried in Wilderness Burial Grounds.

Workman, Joseph – CPL, Lykens, Mustered in September 23, 1861, Muster Roll of December 12, 1861, Captured and died of wounds June 9, 1864 received at Spottsylvania on May 10, 1864.

Workman, Joshua – CPL, Lykens, Mustered in September 23, 1861, Muster Roll of December 12, 1861, Promoted to Corporal, KIA at Spottsylvania May 10, 1864.

Workman, Levi – PVT, Mustered in November 8, 1862, Discharged on Surgeons Certificate March 8, 1863.

Zulick, James M – MUSICIAN, Orwigsburg, Mustered in October 14, 1861, Muster Roll of December 12, 1861, Transferred to Co. B, 96th PVI on February 15, 1864.

1878 – 1899

Company E, 4th Regiment, National Guard of Pennsylvania:

(The following men served in the unit sometime between 1878 and 1899)

Adams, Elwood M	Aulenbach, John P
Baker, James M	Barnn, Charles S
Barnn, Christian A	Bear, Calvin D
Bear, Leroy	Becker, Howard D
Behler, Richard J	Berger, Samuel A
Bernhart, Frederick B	Boltz, Landis R
Bordy, Oscar J	Bower, Frank L
Boxmeyer, Henry	Brause, John H
Buck, Harry M	Burkey, Charles D
Confer, Frederic	Dalious, Thomas J
Degler, Allen D	Degler, George H
Degler, Henry J	Degler, William A
Diener, Harry J	Dietrich, Alfred M
Dietrich, William J	Doering, John L
Dreibelbis, Calvin J	Eckroth, George M
Epler, Samuel P	Epler, Solomon
Fichthorn, Charles F	Fiddler, William
Finkbiner, J. Harry	Folk, Frank R

Folk, George M
Folk, John P
Frauenfelder, Adam E
Goodman, Howard L
Greenawald, Daniel A
Hagen, Joseph B
Haines, Louis D
Heckman, John A
Henn, Charles W
Homan, William S
Isett, Chester M
Keifer, Harry
Kline, Charles C
Koller, Charles J
Krick, George
Kummerer, William
Leibensperger, Charles P
Leibensperger, John E
Leiby, James G
Lesher, George A
Levan, Howard H
Levan, John M
Lewars, Clayton H
Lewars, George A
Lewars, Wilson H
Long, Henry J
Loy, Lewis A
Machemer, Llewellyn
Machemer, William H
Martin, Joseph H
Maurer, Charles J
Mengle, Edward
Miller, Ellis N
Miller, Lewis Allen
Miller, Oscar A
Mogel, Levi F

Folk, Joel W
Fox, Thomas
Gehris, Benjamin F
Graeff, Jacob L
Grim, Henry W
Hahn, Harry H
Harris, Charles C
Heckman, Wilson
Henne, Joseph S
Hunsberger, Oswin F
Kalbach, William J
Ketterer, William
Kline, Morris M
Krick, Daniel J
Kroeson, Selah F A
Leibelsberger, Milton
Leibensperger, James L
Leiby, George F
Leiby, William A
Lesher, Wilson J
Levan, Isaac N
Lewars, Charles W
Lewars, Edward J
Lewars, William
Lins, Ellsworth
Loy, Charles H
Libby, Benjamin F
Machemer, Mandon L
Machemer, Wilson
Maurer, Charles B
Mayberry, William
Merkel, Charles B
Miller, John L
Miller, Mahlon S
Miller, William E
Moll, Frank B

Appendix D

Moyer, Charles T
Nies, William B
Potteiger, Charles H
Reinhart, William J
Reiter, David G
Rhoads, George R
Ritzman, Jacob H
Romich, Thomas J
Sands, Aaron J
Savage, James M K
Scholl, Edward H
Schollenberger, Marquis H
Schwander, Henry H
Seaman, Charles F
Seaman, Claudius M
Seering, Theodore
Seidel, Pharon A
Shollenberger, A. Harry
Shollenberger, Irvin K
Shucker, Jeremiah
Shuman, Frederick A
Snyder, James H
Sousley, Stephen
Spayd, Franklin A
Steely, Orlando R
Sterner, John
Sullivan, Timothy J
Sunday, Harry
Tobias, Milton H
Wack, Frank H
Weaver, John
Williams, George N
Williams, Jacob N
Williams, Thomas
Williamson, Abraham
Williamson, Harry P

Moyer, W S G
Paul, Harry J
Reinhart, Harry
Reinsel, Newton
Rentz, Irvin C
Ritter, Albert J
Romich, Harry A
Rothermel, Samuel L
Saul, Calvin E
Schmick, Henry J
Schollenberger, Frederick D
Schollenberger, Robert D
Scott, William A
Seaman, Charles M
Seaman, William
Seidel, Edward W
Shartle, Alvin J
Shollenberger, Howard T
Shollenberger, Samuel D
Shucker, Obediah
Smith, Harvey D
Snyder, Oliver
Spatz, James L
Stansfield, James A
Sterner, Frank
Strasser, Solon E
Sunday, Curtis F
Swab, Samuel C
Trump, William L
Wagner, Anson F
Wilhelm, Marshall C
Williams, Irvin L
Williams, John H
Williams, Titus
Williamson, Eugene
Wilson, Charles P

Witman, Oliver H   Yeager, William H

Zwoyer, Harry V

Spanish-American War

Company E, 4th Regiment Pennsylvania Volunteer Infantry:

Armstrong, Lewis E – PVT, Mahanoy City, Enrolled May 7, 1898, Mustered in May 10, 1898, died at Mahanoy City on September 28, 1898 from illness contracted in Puerto Rico.

Aulenbach, Charles R – PVT, Reading, Enrolled May 7, 1898, Mustered in May 10, 1898, Mustered out with Company on November 16, 1898.

Bagenstose, Charles M – PVT, Shoemakersville, Enrolled May 7, 1898, Mustered in May 10, 1898, Mustered out with Company on November 16, 1898.

Bard, Frank C – PVT, Reading, Enrolled May 7, 1898, Mustered in May 9, 1898, Mustered out with Company on November 16, 1898.

Border, George – PVT, Auburn, Enrolled June 15, 1898, Mustered in June 15, 1898, Mustered out with Company on November 16, 1898.

Borrell, Samuel – PVT, Reading, Enrolled June 15, 1898, Mustered in June 15, 1898, Mustered out with Company on November 16, 1898.

Boxmeyer, Henry – MUSICIAN, Pottsville, (NGP), Enrolled April 28, 1898, Mustered in May 10, 1898, Mustered out with Company on November 16, 1898.

Briner, Clause – PVT, Reading, Enrolled June 15, 1898, mustered in June 15, 1898, mustered out with Company on November 16, 1898.

Buck, Harry M – PVT, Hamburg, Enrolled May 7, 1898, Mustered in May 10, 1898, Promoted to Corporal July 1, 1898, Mustered out with Company on November 16, 1898.

Chesterfield, William F – PVT, Bordeaux, WY, Enrolled May 7, 1898, Mustered in May 10, 1898, died at St. Peters Hospital, Brooklyn, NY on August 29, 1898 from illness contracted in Puerto Rico.

Degler, Allen D – CPL, Hamburg, (NGP), Enrolled April 28, 1898, Mustered in May 10, 1898, Mustered out with Company on November 16, 1898.

Dehart, Charles – PVT, Reading, Enrolled June 15, 1898, Mustered in June 15, 1898, Mustered out with Company on November 16, 1898.

Deiter, Warren F – PVT, Auburn, Enrolled May 7, 1898, Mustered in May 10, 1898, Mustered out with Company on November 16, 1898.

DeLong, George – PVT, Reading, Enrolled May 7, 1898, Mustered in May 10, 1898, Mustered out with Company on November 16, 1898.

DeWalt, Henry A – PVT, Auburn, Enrolled May 7, 1898, Mustered in May 10, 1898, Mustered out with Company on November 16, 1898.

Dietrich, Alfred M – PVT, Hamburg, (NGP), Enrolled April 28, 1898, Mustered in May 10, 1898, Mustered out with Company on November 16, 1898.

Eaches, William H Jr. – PVT, Reading, Enrolled May 7, 1898, Mustered in May 10, 1898, Mustered out with Company on November 16, 1898.

Ebling, Frederick A – PVT, Auburn, May 7, 1898, mustered in May 10, 1898, Mustered out with Company on November 16, 1898.

Eckert, George – PVT, Cressona, Enrolled June 15, 1898, mustered in June 15, 1898, Mustered out with Company on November 16, 1898.

Epler, Samuel P – PVT, Hamburg, (NGP), Enrolled April 28, 1898, Mustered in May 10, 1898, Mustered out with Company on November 16, 1898.

Ettinger, William H – PVT, Hamburg, Enrolled June 15, 1898, mustered in June 15, 1898, Mustered out with Company on November 16, 1898.

BLUE MOUNTAIN LEGION

Fichthorn, Charles F – CPL, Hamburg, (NGP), Enrolled April 28, 1898, Mustered in May 10, 1898, Promoted to Corporal July 1, 1898, Mustered out with Company on November 16, 1898.

Fidler, William H.S. – SGT, Hamburg, (NGP), Enrolled April 28, 1898, Mustered in May 10, 1898, Mustered out with Company on November 16, 1898.

Fitch, John – PVT, Auburn, Enrolled June 15, 1898, mustered in June 15, 1898, Mustered out with Company on November 16, 1898.

Folk, Frank R – CPL, Hamburg, (NGP), Enrolled April 28, 1898, Mustered in May 10, 1898, mustered out with Company on November 16, 1898.

Folk, George M – CPL, Hamburg, (NGP), Enrolled April 28, 1898, Mustered in May 10, 1898, Promoted to Corporal July 1, 1898, mustered out with Company on November 16, 1898.

Foster, Charles – PVT, Reading, Enrolled June 15, 1898, mustered in June 15, 1898, Mustered out with Company on November 16, 1898.

Gantz, Edward – PVT, Reading, Enrolled June 15, 1898, mustered in June 15, 1898, Mustered out with Company on November 16, 1898.

Geiger, Howard W – PVT, Kutztown, Enrolled May 7, 1898, Mustered in May 10, 1898, Mustered out with Company on November 16, 1898.

Grim, Henry W – PVT, Hamburg, (NGP), Enrolled April 28, 1898, Mustered in May 10, 1898, Mustered out with Company on November 16, 1898.

Harris, George C – SGT, Hamburg, (NGP), Enrolled April 28, 1898, Mustered in May 10, 1898, Mustered out with Company on November 16, 1898.

Hassler, Lewis – PVT, Reading, Enrolled June 15, 1898, mustered in June 15, 1898, mustered out with Company on November 16, 1898.

Heckman, Adam – PVT, Hamburg, Enrolled June 15, 1898, Mustered in June 15, 1898, Mustered out with Company on November 16, 1898.

Appendix D

Heckman, John A – PVT, Hamburg, (NGP), Enrolled April 28, 1898, Mustered in May 10, 1898, Mustered out with Company on November 16, 1898.

Hedley, James G – PVT, Reading, Enrolled May 7, 1898, Mustered in May 10, 1898, Mustered out with Company on November 16, 1898.

Heffner, Robert E – PVT, Dow, Enrolled May 7, 1898, Mustered in May 10, 1898, Mustered out with Company on November 16, 1898.

Heinzman, Henry A – PVT, Reading, Enrolled June 15, 1898, mustered in June 15, 1898, Mustered out with Company on November 16, 1898.

High, Raymond S – PVT, Shoemakersville, Enrolled May 7, 1898, Mustered in May 10, 1898, mustered out with Company on November 16, 1898.

Horton, Charles S – PVT, Reading, Enrolled May 7, 1898, Mustered in May 10, 1898, Mustered out with Company on November 16, 1898.

Hunsberger, Harry – PVT, Pennsburg, Enrolled May 7, 1898, Mustered in May 10, 1898, Mustered out with Company on November 16, 1898.

Jones, John – PVT, Shenandoah, Enrolled June 15, 1898, mustered in June 15, 1898, Mustered out with Company on November 16, 1898.

Kellar, Haywood – PVT, Reading, Enrolled June 15, 1898, mustered in June 15, 1898, Mustered out with Company on November 16, 1898.

Keller, Jacob H – CPL, Reading, Enrolled May 7, 1898, Mustered in May 10, 1898, Promoted to Corporal July 1, 1898, Mustered out with Company on November 16, 1898.

Kohler, Edward – PVT, Reading, Enrolled June 15, 1898, Mustered in June 15, 1898, died in Division Hospital at Guayama, Puerto Rico on August 28, 1898.

Kummerer, William – CPT, Hamburg, (NGP), Enrolled April 28, 1898, Mustered in May 10, 1898, Mustered out with Company on November 16, 1898.

Leibensperger, John E – PVT, Reading, (NGP), Enrolled April 28, 1898, Mustered in May 10, 1898, Mustered out with Company on November 16, 1898.

Leibensperger, Milton – PVT, Shoemakersville, Enrolled May 7, 1898, Mustered in May 10, 1898, Mustered out with Company on November 16, 1898.

Leiby, George F – CPL, Reading, (NGP), Enrolled April 28, 1898, Mustered in May 10, 1898, Mustered out with Company on November 16, 1898.

Leiby, William A – PVT, Hamburg, (NGP), Enrolled April 28, 1898, Mustered in May 10, 1898, Mustered out with Company on November 16, 1898.

Lenhart, Oscar R – PVT, Reading, Enrolled June 15, 1898, mustered in June 15, 1898, Mustered out with Company on November 16, 1898.

Lesher, George A – 1LT, Hamburg, (NGP), Enrolled April 28, 1898, Mustered in May 10, 1898, Mustered out with Company on November 16, 1898.

Lesher, Wilson I – SGT, Hamburg, (NGP), Enrolled April 28, 1898, Mustered in May 10, 1898, Mustered out with Company on November 16, 1898.

Levan, John M – PVT, Hamburg, (NGP), Enrolled April 28, 1898, Mustered in May 10, 1898, Mustered out with Company on November 16, 1898.

Lewars, Wilson H – QM-SGT, Hamburg, (NGP), Enrolled April 28, 1898, Mustered in May 10, 1898, Mustered out with Company on November 16, 1898.

Machemer, Llewellyn – PVT, Hamburg, (NGP), Enrolled April 28, 1898, Mustered in May 10, 1898, Mustered out with Company on November 16, 1898.

Medlar, Valentine W – PVT, Mahanoy City, Enrolled May 7, 1898, Mustered in May 10, 1898, mustered out with Company on November 16, 1898.

Meshey, Amos – PVT, Hamburg, Enrolled June 15, 1898, mustered in June 15, 1898, Mustered out with Company on November 16, 1898.

Miller, Harry Y – PVT, Reading, Enrolled May 7, 1898, Mustered in May 10, 1898, Mustered out with Company on November 16, 1898.

Miller, John I – PVT, Hamburg, Enrolled June 15, 1898, mustered in June 15, 1898, Mustered out with Company on November 16, 1898.

Miller, Louis A – SGT, Reading, (NGP), Enrolled April 28, 1898, Mustered in May 10, 1898, Mustered out with Company on November 16, 1898.

Miller, William E – PVT, Hamburg, (NGP), Enrolled April 28, 1898, Mustered in May 10, 1898, Mustered out with Company on November 16, 1898.

Minner, Jacob H – PVT, Reading, Enrolled May 7, 1898, Mustered in May 10, 1898, Mustered out with Company on November 16, 1898.

Moyer, Charles D – PVT, Landingville, Enrolled June 15, 1898, mustered in June 15, 1898, Mustered out with Company on November 16, 1898.

Naftzinger, Frank – PVT, Reading, Enrolled June 15, 1898, Mustered in June 15, 1898, died at Division Hospital at Guayama, Puerto Rico on September 4, 1898.

Nein, Harry D – PVT, Reading, Enrolled May 7, 1898, Mustered in May 10, 1898, transferred to Hospital Corps, 1st Army Corps June 13, 1898 per General Order No. 58.

Paul, Harry J – PVT, Shartlesville, (NGP), Enrolled April 28, 1898, Mustered in May 10, 1898, Mustered out with Company on November 16, 1898.

Pennell, William – PVT, Gibraltar, Enrolled June 15, 1898, mustered in June 15, 1898, Mustered out with Company on November 16, 1898.

Potteiger, Charles H – CPL, Hamburg, (NGP), Enrolled April 28, 1898, Mustered in May 10, 1898, Mustered out with Company on November 16, 1898.

Potteiger, George F – 1LT, Assistant Surgeon, Hamburg, Enrolled May 5, 1898, Mustered in May 12, 1898, Acting Surgeon from June 3 to 17, 1898, on duty as examining Surgeon from November 7 to 12, 1898 for Mustering out of the 5th Pennsylvania Volunteer Infantry, Mustered out with Regiment on November 16, 1898.

Potteiger, John B – MAJ, Surgeon, Hamburg, (NGP), Enrolled April 28, 1898, Mustered in May 5, 1898, resigned May 12, 1898 because of physical disability.

Potts, Edward S – PVT, Pottsville, Enrolled May 9, 1898, Mustered in May 10, 1898, Mustered out with Company on November 16, 1898.

Quinter, George – PVT, Reading, Enrolled June 15, 1898, mustered in June 15, 1898, mustered out with Company on November 16, 1898.

Reed, William H.J. – PVT, Albany, Enrolled June 15, 1898, mustered in June 15, 1898, Mustered out with Company on November 16, 1898.

Reeser, Charles W – PVT, Reading, Enrolled May 7, 1898, Mustered in May 10, 1898, Mustered out with Company on November 16, 1898.

Reimert, Moses A – PVT, Kutztown, Enrolled June 15, 1898, mustered in June 15, 1898, Mustered out with Company on November 16, 1898.

Reinhart, William J – PVT, Hamburg, Enrolled May 7, 1898, Mustered in May 10, 1898, Mustered out with Company on November 16, 1898.

Reiter, David G – PVT, Shoemakersville, Enrolled May 7, 1898, Mustered in May 10, 1898, mustered out with Company on November 16, 1898.

Rentschler, Howard M – PVT, Centerport, Enrolled May 7, 1898, Mustered in May 10, 1898, Mustered out with Company on November 16, 1898.

Rhoads, George R – PVT, Hamburg, (NGP), Enrolled April 28, 1898, Mustered in May 10, 1898, Mustered out with Company on November 16, 1898.

Ringler, Charles – PVT, Reading, Enrolled June 15, 1898, mustered in June 15, 1898, mustered out with Company on November 16, 1898.

Ritzman, Jacob H – CPL, Shartlesville, (NGP), Enrolled April 28, 1898, Mustered in May 10, 1898, Promoted to Corporal July 1, 1898, Mustered out with Company on November 16, 1898.

Rothermel, Samuel L – PVT, Mohrsville, Enrolled June 15, 1898, Mustered in June 15, 1898, Mustered out with Company on November 16, 1898.

Sassaman, Levi B – PVT, Kutztown, Enrolled May 7, 1898, Mustered in May 10, 1898, Mustered out with Company on November 16, 1898.

Scheidt, William L – PVT, Kutztown, Enrolled May 7, 1898, Mustered in May 10, 1898, Mustered out with Company on November 16, 1898.

Schmehl, John S – PVT, Kutztown, Enrolled May 7, 1898, Mustered in May 10, 1898, Mustered out with Company on November 16, 1898.

Scull, Frank – PVT, Reading, Enrolled June 15, 1898, mustered in June 15, 1898, mustered out with Company on November 16, 1898.

Seaman, Claudius M – 1SG, Hamburg, (NGP), Enrolled April 28, 1898, Mustered in May 10, 1898, Mustered out with Company on November 16, 1898.

Seaman, William – 2LT, Hamburg, (NGP), Enrolled April 28, 1898, Mustered in May 10, 1898, Mustered out with Company on November 16, 1898.

Smith, Charles G – PVT, Reading, Enrolled May 7, 1898, Mustered in May 10, 1898, Mustered out with Company on November 16, 1898.

Smith, George N – PVT, Kutztown, Enrolled May 7, 1898, Mustered in May 10, 1898, Mustered out with Company on November 16, 1898.

Smith, Harvey S – PVT, Hamburg, Enrolled May 7, 1898, Mustered in May 10, 1898, Mustered out with Company on November 16, 1898.

Snyder, Augustus M – PVT, Reading, Enrolled June 15, 1898, Mustered in June 15, 1898, Mustered out with Company on November 16, 1898.

Stein, Steffner – PVT, Reading, Enrolled June 15, 1898, mustered in June 15, 1898, Mustered out with Company on November 16, 1898.

Sterner, Frank – CPL, Hamburg, (NGP), Enrolled April 28, 1898, mustered in May 10, 1898, Mustered out with Company on November 16, 1898.

Sterner, John – PVT, Hamburg, (NGP), Enrolled April 28, 1898, mustered in May 10, 1898, Mustered out with Company on November 16, 1898.

Stichter, Samuel – PVT, Reading, Enrolled June 15, 1898, mustered in June 15, 1898, Mustered out with Company on November 16, 1898.

Strasser, Solon E – PVT, Hamburg, Enrolled May 7, 1898, Mustered in May 10, 1898, mustered out with Company on November 16, 1898.

Stuber, Louis P – PVT, Reading, Enrolled May 7, 1898, Mustered in May 10, 1898, Mustered out with Company on November 16, 1898.

Sullivan, Timothy J – MUSICIAN, Pottsville, (NGP), Enrolled April 28, 1898, Mustered in May 10, 1898, Mustered out with Company on November 16, 1898.

Tice, Ray L – PVT, Allentown, Enrolled May 7, 1898, Mustered in May 10, 1898, Mustered out with Company on November 16, 1898.

Trump, William I – PVT, Hamburg, (NGP), Enrolled April 28, 1898, Mustered in May 10, 1898, mustered out with Company on November 16, 1898.

Wagenhurst, William – PVT, Kutztown, Enrolled May 7, 1898, Mustered in May 10, 1898, Mustered out with Company on November 16, 1898.

Weidenheimer, John H – PVT, Reading, Enrolled May 7, 1898, Mustered in May 10, 1898, Mustered out with Company on November 16, 1898.

Wenrich, Harvey K – PVT, Allentown, Enrolled May 7, 1898, Mustered in May 10, 1898, Mustered out with Company on November 16, 1898.

Whiston, Thomas – PVT, Reading, Enrolled June 15, 1898, mustered in June 15, 1898, Mustered out with Company on November 16, 1898.

Wilhelm, C. Marshall – CPL, Hamburg, (NGP), Enrolled April 28, 1898, Mustered in May 10, 1898, Promoted to Corporal July 1, 1898, Mustered out with Company on November 16, 1898.

Williams, Titus E – PVT, Reading, Enrolled June 15, 1898, mustered in June 15, 1898, Mustered out with Company on November 16, 1898.

Wilson, Charles P – PVT, Reading, (NGP), Enrolled April 28, 1898, Mustered in May 10, 1898, Mustered out with Company on November 16, 1898.

Wisotzki, Guy C – PVT, Gettysburg, Enrolled May 7, 1898, Mustered in May 10, 1898, Mustered out with Company on November 16, 1898.

Wummer, Milton N – PVT, Shoemakersville, Enrolled May 7, 1898, Mustered in May 10, 1898, Mustered out with Company on November 16, 1898.

Yenser, Edwin – PVT, Kutztown, Enrolled May 7, 1898, Mustered in May 10, 1898, Mustered out with Company on November 16, 1898.

Company E, 4th Regiment Pennsylvania Volunteer Infantry:

1916

CPT Loy, Lewis A
1LT Seaman, Harrison F
2LT Casper, Raymond E
1SG Schollenberger, Robert D
SGT Bagenstose, William H
SGT Loy, Ivan Daniel
SGT Borrell, Arthur P

PVT Henne, Edwin S
PVT Hess, Jeremiah
PVT James, Edward N
PVT Kessler, Charles H
PVT Kessler, Ralph R
PVT Loose, John
PVT Loose, Paul

BLUE MOUNTAIN LEGION

SGT Essig, Harry J
SGT Showers, Percy
CPL Hassenauer, Franklin J
CPL Machemer, James B
CPL Peters, Elmer L
CPL Williamson, Franklin
CPL Zettlemoyer, Robert E. W
ARTIFICER Williamson, Charles
COOK Balthaser, William J
COOK Dalious, Charles
MUSICIAN Correll, Harvey
MUSICIAN Rau, Elwood G
PVT Arndt, Custis V
PVT Bagenstose, John C
PVT Bailey, Raymond J
PVT Bechtel, Lewis
PVT Behler, Lewis C
PVT Bennicoff, Henry
PVT Bieber, Bruce
PVT Brown, John F
PVT Correll, Charles
PVT Dunkleberger, Leroy
PVT Epler, Harry S
PVT Fidler, Charles A
PVT Fisher, Samuel P
PVT Geissler, Elmer J
PVT Greenawalt, Norman S
PVT Hassenauer, Charles J
PVT Heckman, Morris

PVT Machemer, Ralph
PVT Miller, Charles H
PVT Miller, Irvin F
PVT Miller, Robert R
PVT Moll, James F
PVT Motes, George M
PVT Motes, Peter J
PVT Moyer, Warren D
PVT Muller, Andrew P
PVT O'Neil, Scott J
PVT Paulie, John C
PVT Pehlman, Raymond C
PVT Phillipson, Harry E
PVT Rau, Paul H
PVT Saul, John W
PVT Schaffer, Norman A
PVT Seaman, Thomas E
PVT Shank, John T
PVT Shoener, Walter S
PVT Siegfried, William H
PVT Strasser, John W
PVT Van Reed, Fred
PVT Wagner, Charles B
PVT Wehr, Leroy M
PVT Wengert, Edgar
PVT Wessner, Fred M
PVT Williamson, John S
PVT Winters, Miles H

1917

Balthaser, William J
Bartolet, James E
Behler, William
Bell, Thomas J

Mest, Rufus D
Miller, Clark E
Miller, Henry G
Miller, Irwin F

Appendix D

Bolton, John T
Bolton, Samuel B
Bowman, Warren E
Boyle, Michael E
Condon, John B
Dalious, Harold W
Davis, John H
Davis, Thomas J
Dissinger, Irwin
Dissinger, Raymond
Doyle, Harry C
Eldridge, William H
Fidler, Charles A
Fisher, Claud
Fisher, Harry S
Fisher, Larry
Fisher, Samuel P
Fitch, William J
Foorman, John H
Frederick, Lester W
Gehart, Jerry
Good, Charles H
Good, Raymond L
Graeff, Howard
Graeff, William J
Hall, John
Heckman, Edward
Heckman, John M
Hein, Thomas
Hershberger, Herman
Herring, Foster
Hoch, John H
Holahan, David L
Horn, Walter J
Isett, William M
James, Edward N

Moll, James F
Moyer, Daniel H
Moyer, Joseph M
Moyer, Warren D
Moyer, William C
Nice, Frank H
Pehlman, Raymond C
Ramich, Johnson
Rau, Elwood G
Rau, Paul H
Reber, Robert C
Reed, Harrison L
Reed, Norman A
Reeser, Robert W
Reifsnyder, Charles J
Reimert, Joseph A
Reinhard, Harold
Rhoads, Robert E
Roeder, Edward
Rutter, William L
Shank, John T
Shoener, Ralph
Shrader, Harry A
Smith, Clyde L
Sousley, Earl E
Staller Jr., Jeremiah W
Staller, William
Strausser, Alfred J
Sturm, Harry S
Sunday, Frank C
Swalm, Mark M
Sweigert, John E
Trainer, Peter
Wagner, Clarence J
Wehr, Leroy M
Wehr, Leroy M

Kauffman, James
Kelchner, Jefferson W
Kissinger, William H
Knarr, Clarence L
Koch, Charles
Leeser, William
Long, Paul
Long, Ray C
Long, William R
Loose, Paul N
Martin, Emery S
Mathias, Bower
Mathias, Edward D
McKenna, Henry
Mengel, Clarence L

Weidner, Floyd E
Wengert, Darius D
Wengert, Walter
Werner, Harry J
Wike, William B
Williams, Frank
Wolfe, Clarence J
Yeager, Clayton A
Yeager, John H
Young, Walter
Zellers, Howard

World War I

Company A, 108th Machine Gun Battalion

Albrecht, Verne B – SGT, 1257053, Fairfield, IL.
Allen, Morris – PVT, 373605, Amsterdam, NY.
Armao, Tom R – PVT, 3251451, New York, NY.
Bailey, Raymond J – PVT, 1257066, Hamburg, PA.
Baker, Lynn H – PVT, 1257409, Sidney, NY, WIA August 15, 1918.
Baldino, Joseph – PVT, 3384171, New York, NY.
Balk, Harry – PVT, 1780021, Baltimore, MD.
Ball, Jerry – PVT, 2054181, Ada, MI.
Barnes, Roy A – PVT, 2870447, Kedron, AR.
Barnes, Wayne D – PVT, 373737, Regis Falls, NY.
Barese, Carmelo – PVT, 3322125, New York, NY.
Barry, George – PVT, 374011, New York, NY.
Beard, John C – PVT, 2223210, Wagoner, OK, Gassed July 16, 1918.
Beers, Thaddeus – PVT, 626757, Huntingdon, PA.
Behe, Percy H – PVT, 373962, Lockport, NY, Gassed October 1, 1918.

Behler, Walter – Mess SGT, 1257028, Hamburg, PA, KIA August 12, 1918.

Bell, Thomas J – CPL, 1257042, Williamstown, PA.

Bentner, Herman J – PVT, 1374015, Tonawanda, NY, Gassed September 7, 1918.

Biles, Archie B – PVT, 2223145, Alpena Pass, AR, WIA July 30, 1918.

Biven, Richard F – PVT, 2223208, San Antonio, TX, Gassed October 8, 1918.

Bledsoe, Hecklen – PVT, 165647, Dooley, VA, WIA November 5, 1918.

Bolton, John G – PFC, 1257067, Schuylkill Haven, PA, KIA July 15, 1918.

Bolton, Samuel B – PVT, 1257072, Schuylkill Haven, PA, Gassed September 7, 1918.

Bone, Theodore – PVT, 2264896, Sidney, AR.

Bossler, Paul E – PVT, 1257111, Blandon, PA.

Bowman, Warren E – Cook, 1257060, Philadelphia, PA.

Box, Raymond J – SGT, 1257065, Waymart, PA.

Boyle, Clarence J – PVT, 1257065, Oswego, NY, Shell shocked August 12, 1918.

Branton, James A – PVT, 3637871, Pittsburgh, PA.

Breen, Bernard R – SGT, 1257038, KIA September 27, 1918.

Brombacher, Arthur J – Mechanic, 1257112, Scranton, PA.

Burkhart, John – PVT, 2223207, Frisco, OK, Gassed October 4, 1918.

Burr, William C – PVT, 1257048.

Campbell, Joseph – PVT, 3735575, Utica, NY, Gassed October 4, 1918.

Carlton, Lafayette W – PVT, 1257117, Scranton, PA, Gassed October 4, 1918.

Cartier, Joseph M – PVT, 373627, Plattsburg, NY.

Cassata, Anthony – PVT, 3323340, New York, NY.

Cateract, Charles – PVT, 373639, Redford, NY.

Catherman, Paul N – PVT, 3628776, Millmont, PA.

Clark, John J – PVT, 1257421, Fall River, MA.

Cole, Bert – PVT, 1257116, Honesdale, PA.

Colella, Nicklas – PVT, 1257114, Philadelphia, PA.

Collins, William P – SGT, 1257115, Peckville, PA, WIA August 17, 1918.

Condon, John B – PFC, 1257241, Port Clinton, PA.

Correll, Charles – SGT, 137037, Hamburg, PA.

Coulton, Leonard F – PVT, 1775955, Morrisville, PA, Died of wounds on July 16, 1918.

Court, James T – PVT, 1776333, Bristol, PA.

Creel, Evan L – PVT, 98232, Boaz, AL, Gassed September 8, 1918.

Crow, Ralph C – CPT, Lemoyne, PA, Company Commander from October 17, 1917 to October 12, 1918.

Crowder, Emmett L – PVT, 3180118, Fincastle, VA.

Cullison, Calvin E – PVT, 1776189, McKnightstown, PA, Shell shocked August 12, 1918.

Dalious, Harold W – PVT, 1257116, Hamburg, PA, Gassed October 8, 1918.

Darasmo, Vito – PVT, 3526849, New York, NY.

Davidson, Edward J – PVT, 1566262, Ora, IN, Gassed September 7, 1918.

Dean, Dalarvin – PVT, 2870722, Subiaco, AR, Accident wound on November 11, 1918.

DeCoursey, Roy – PFC, 1776208, Hartsville, PA.

Degutis, Andrew M – PVT, 1257121, Priceburg, PA, WIA July 30, 1918.

Deitrich, Roy J – PVT, 1776207, New York, NY.

Devore, Benjamin L – PVT, Matamoras, PA, WIA September 5, 1918, Died of wounds March 25, 1919.

Diddock, Walter S – PVT, 1566266, Shell shocked September 5, 1918.

Dietz, Leonard – PVT, Howard, PA.

Dissinger, Raymond – PVT, 1257120, Auburn, PA.

Dodge, Frank A – 1257124, Torrey, PA, KIA August 16, 1918.

Dohner, Walter H – PVT, Lebanon, PA, WIA October 4, 1918.

Dorman, Samuel P – PVT, 3628790, Millmont, PA.

Driscoll, Richard F – PVT, 373298, Lenoxdale, MA.

Drulia, Anthony – CPL, 1257122, Scranton, PA, Gassed September 7, 1918.

Duffy, Edwin – PVT, 1257164, Philadelphia, PA.

Easton, Theodore W – 1LT, Norristown, PA, Gassed August 12, 1918.

Eggleston, Leslie J – CPL, 1257126, Dyberry, PA.

Eggleston, Clarence – PFC, 1257130, Dyberry, PA.

Eichelser, Philip F – PVT, 373318, Dolphin, PA.

Eithier, Henry V – PVT, 2069917, Detroit, MI, Gassed July 31, 1918.

Eldridge, William H – 1257128, Lebanon, PA, Shell shocked August 12, 1918.

Elliot, Roy A – PVT, 2047870, Battle Creek, MI.

Ernest, Irwin J – PVT, 1257056, Cresson, PA, WIA October 1, 1918.

Evans, George F – 1LT, Scranton, PA.

Falcon, William – PVT, 373628, Champlain, NY.

Fallon, Clarence – Bugler, 1257064, Philadelphia, PA, WIA July 30, 1918.

Farley, Ray D – PVT, 1257132, Williamsport, PA.

Feeley, James A – PVT, 137133, Hazleton, PA.

Fidler, Charles A – SGT, 1257036, Boyertown, PA, Shell shocked August 11, 1918.

Fish, Robert – SGT, 1257035.

Fisher, Claude – CPL, Auburn, PA.

Fisher, Larry – PFC, 1257129, Blandon, PA.

Fitch, William J – SGT, 1257032.

Flanagan, Owen L – SGT, Carbondale, PA.

Fonte, Alberta – PVT, 3322022, Brooklyn, NY.

Foster, McKinley – PVT, 1416667, Bethany, MO.

Frederick, Cecil – PVT, 1566270, Died of wounds September 28, 1918.

Frederick, James A – PVT, 2870567, Springdale, AR.

Frye, George D – PVT, 1257131, Cresson, PA, Gassed October 4, 1918.

Frye, William B – 2LT, Steelton, PA.

Gahagan, Thomas M – PVT, 3626058, Pittsburgh, PA.

Gardner, Ira H – SGT, 1257029, Alexandria, PA.

Gaudliosi, Arturo – PVT, 33255568, New York, NY.

Geddis, Harry – PVT, 373607, Amsterdam, NY.

Gessay, Andrew – Mechanic, Philadelphia, PA.

Gifford, William C – PVT, 3627852, Parkersburg, WV.

Gingrich, Walter H – PFC, 1257071, Lawn, PA, Died of wounds September 7, 1918.

Giordano, John – PVT, 1566209, Clinton, IN.

Good, Charles H – CPL, 1257049, Hamburg, PA, KIA September 7, 1918.

Good, Raymond L – CPL, 1257068, Hamburg, PA.

Goodman, Emil J – PVT, 362984, Pittsburgh, PA.

Gray, Joseph W – PVT, 1586965.

Green, Clarence L – PVT, 1566274, WIA August 13, 1918.

Greenwalt, Charles A – PVT, 1257136, Hamburg, PA.

Gritton, James A.S. – SGT, Franklin, IN.

Hagan, Joseph J – PVT, 1257075, Roxbury, MA, WIA September 30, 1918.

Hall, Charles – PVT, 2870369.

Hamilton, Charles – PVT, 1566277, Clinton, IN.

Hartwell, George P – PVT, 1257137, Schuylkill Haven, PA, Gassed October 4, 1918.

Hassenauer, Charles I – PFC, 1257073, Hamburg, PA.

Hathaway, Ray – PVT, 1566281, Winamac, IN, WIA October 4, 1918.

Heckman, Edward, PVT, 1257076, Temple, PA, WIA July 30, 1918.

Hehn, Robert W – PVT, 1257145, Pottsville, PA, WIA July 30, 1918.

Hein, Thomas – Cook, 1257061, Hamburg, PA, KIA August 12, 1918.

Helmar, Edward – PVT, 2870760, Paris, AR.

Hendricks, Louis – PVT, 1566282, Gassed September 7, 1918, WIA October 7, 1918.

Henry, William V – CPL, 1257140, Stroudsburg, PA.

Herring, Foster – PVT, 1257143, Hamburg, PA.

Herring, Joseph – CPL, 1257138, Auburn, PA.

Hoch, John H – PVT, 1257144, Kutztown, PA, KIA September 6, 1918.

Hoebener, Albert H – PFC, 1257077, Williamsport, PA.

Hopkins, David – CPL, 1257140, Scranton, PA.

Horn, Walter J – CPL, 1257044, Orwigsburg, PA, WIA July 30, 1918.

Howard, Orval M – PVT, 1563142, Cameron, WV.

Hubbel, Carl G – SGT, 1257047, Williamsport, PA.

Hughes, George B – PVT, 1257141, East Strandstown, PA.

Huige, Edward A – PVT, 373998, Newark, NJ.

Humphrey, William G – CPL, 1257139, Carbondale, PA.

Hunsinger, Sylvanua S – SGT, 1257142, Scranton, PA.

Hurt, Eugene W – PVT, 3180324, Pools Mills, MD.

Hutt, Frank J – Mechanic, 1257059, Pottstown, PA.

Ionata, Nazzario S – PVT, 3321756, Pittsburgh, PA.

Isett, George E – PVT, Hamburg, PA.

Itinger, John K – 1SG, 1257027, Alexandria, PA.

James, Edward N – CPL, 1257147, Reading, PA.

Jubis, Andrew – PVT, 1257147, Wilkes-Barre, PA.

Kauffman, James – SGT, 1257078, Auburn, PA.

Kein, Thomas – Cook, Reading, PA.

Keipper, John C – PVT, 373987, Liverpool, NY.

Kelchner, Jefferson W – PVT, Reading, PA.

Kemmeren, Charles A – PVT, 1257149, Blandon, PA, Shell shocked August 20, 1918.

Kerr, Ralph L – PFC, 1257152, Scranton, PA.

Kinchler, Michael J – PVT, 1257150, Gassed August 12, 1918.

King, Harold O – PFC, Sidney, NY, WIA October 5, 1918.

Kingman, Lawrence – 2LT, Brockton, MA.

Kinter, Russell A – 1LT, Lemoyne, PA, Gassed.

Kirchoff, Paul H – PVT, 1566294, Evansport, IN.

Kiser, Luke – PVT, 2117939, Maynardsville, TN.

Klippel, Clarence L – PVT, 374028, Buffalo, NY.

Knarr, Clarence L – PVT, 1257080, Reading, PA.

Koch, Charles D – PVT, 1257151, Auburn, PA.

Koch, George H – PVT, 1257156, Scranton, PA.

Koeninger, Frank T – PVT, 1569794, Huntsville, IN, Gassed September 7, 1918.

Kozicki, Joseph – PFC, 1257062, Ashley, PA, WIA July 30, 1918, DOW August 23, 1918.

Kuntz, George E – Cook, 1257081, Greensville, OH.

Lange, Oscar E – CPL, 1257082, Newfoundland, PA, WIA September 30, 1918.

Larson, Oscar L – PVT, Scranton, PA.

Learn, Wayne H – PVT, 1257158, Erie, PA.

Leiby, Paul – PFC, 1257083, Hamburg, PA.

Lipp, Glen R – PVT, 2053856.

Long, Harvey T – PVT, 1257154, Auburn, PA, WIA and Gassed August 14, 1918.

Long, John B – PFC, 1257084, Hamburg, PA.

Long, Paul – PVT, 1257159, Auburn, PA.

Long, Ray C – PFC, 1257089, Auburn, PA, Gassed August 12, 1918.

Long, William R – PVT, Auburn, PA.

Loon, Paul N – PVT, 1257041.

Loose, Paul N – CPL, Hamburg, PA, WIA July 30, 1918.

Loris, Henry W – PVT, 1257155, Newark, NJ.

McCarty, William H – 1LT, Philadelphia, PA.

McKenna, Henry – PVT, 1257160, Philadelphia, PA, Gassed September 7, 1918.

McLaughlin, Thomas D – CPL, 374105, Scranton, PA, KIA September 27, 1918.

McNarry, Milton – PVT, 3131824, Kingsburg, CA.

McNeal, Homer E – CPL, 1257088, Williamstown, PA.

Mathias, Bower – PFC, 1257085, Temple, PA.

Mest, Rufus D – PVT, 1257161, Topton, PA.

Meyers, Andrew H – PVT, 1257163, Philadelphia, PA, MIA September 6, 1918.

Miller, Irwin F – PVT, 1257162, Hamburg, PA, Shell shocked August 19, 1918.

Miller, Robert R – PFC, 1257086, Port Clinton, PA, MIA July 20, 1918.

Miller, Wirt E – SGT, 1257046, Hamburg, PA.

Moll, James F – PVT, 1257165, Shoemakersville, PA, Gassed October 3, 1918.

Moody, Erdie – PVT, 2870464, Fort Smith, AR.

Morford, Leland R – PVT, 126789, Highmore, SD.

Moskowvitz, Jacob – PVT, 3325725, New York, NY.

Moyer, Daniel H – CPL, 1257087, Temple, PA.

Moyer, Warren D – SGT, 1257034, Temple, PA.

Moyer, William C – SGT, 1257043, Orwigsburg, PA, Gassed September 7, 1918.

Mummert, Jein B – PVT, 3624936, Thomasville, PA.

Myers, Grant – PVT, 373958.

Nevil, Charles G – PVT, Stroudsburg, PA, Shell shocked August 19, 1918.

Nevil, Stewart K – CPL, 1257090, DOW August 12, 1918.

Newkirk, Frank – 1LT, Gassed October 1, 1918.

Nicolls, Willoughby F – PVT, 1257167, Camp Hill, PA, WIA August 21, 1918.

Ollon, Fred J – PVT, 3837707, Montgomery, WV.

Olsen, Henchald – PVT, 3324588, Brooklyn, NY, WIA September 6, 1918.

Pappodinitropoulas, Pangrotes – PVT, Syracuse, NY.

Pegram, Charles – PVT, 2870564, West Fork, AR.

Pehlman, Raymond C – Mechanic, 1257057, Temple, PA.

Pelcher, Roy – PVT, 373617, Mineville, NY.

Peel, William J – 2LT, New York, NY.

Perini, Dominico – PVT, 1685514, Pittsfield, MA.

Peters, Elmer L – SGT, 1257030, Kutztown, PA, Gassed September 7, 1918.

Peuscher, John – PVT, Hudsonville, MI.

Pickel, Owen G – PVT, 2870815, West Hartford, AR.

Polt, Alfred J – CPL, 1257168, Honesdale, PA.

Powell, John – PVT, 2870837, Fort Smith, AR.

Prostler, August – PVT, 373589, Schenectady, NY.

Quinn, George P – PVT, 3323269, Gassed September 7, 1918.

Rabenold, Edgar W – PVT, 1811601, WIA August 10, 1918.

Race, John C – SGT, 1257091, Forest City, PA.

Raines, Bernard – PVT, 3321322, New York, NY.

Ranich, Johnson M – PFC, 1257092, Fleetwood, PA.

Ranszys, Frydrych – PVT, 1811658, Summit Hill, PA, Gassed September 7, 1918.

Raul, Paul C – Bugler, 1257063, Hamburg, PA, WIA August 12, 1918.

Reber, Robert C – Wagoner, 1267095.

Redding, James H – Stable SGT, 1257095, Wimmers, PA.

Reeser, Robert W – SGT, Sidney, AR, WIA July 15, 1918.

Reifsnyder, Charles J – PFC, 1257096, Reading, PA, WIA September 7, 1918.

Reimert, Joseph A – PFC, 1257097, Kutztown, PA, MIA September 6, 1918.

Reinhard, Harold – CPL, 1257050, Hamburg, PA.

Reisinger, Lewis G – PVT, Carman, NY, Gassed September 7, 1918.

Rex, William F – PFC, 1257098, Philadelphia, PA, Gassed October 14, 1918.

Reynolds, James H – CPL, 1257051, Jermyn, PA.

Rhoads, Robert E – PVT, 125769, Mertztown, PA.

Rice, Dorsey S – PVT, 1811285, WIA October 8, 1918.

Richard Carl J – PVT, 3633998, Madera, NY.

Rignal, John C – PVT, 373305.

Riley, Oscar A – PVT, 412387, Dunlap, IA.

Roberts, George – PVT, 1811596, Bangor, PA.

Roberts, Hugh – PVT, 1811582, Wilkes-Barre, PA.

Roderick, William N – PVT, Scranton, PA.

Rodger, Edmund – PVT, 3636489, Sayre, PA.

Roggeri, Luigi – PVT, 1811663, Lansford, PA.

Rutter, William L – SGT, 1257045, Orwigsburg, PA, Gassed August 13, 1918.

Ryan, Martin – PVT, Philadelphia, PA.

Sabulsky, Herman – PVT, 1811160.

Sacalrides, Nick – PVT, 1811471.

Sawyer, Harry – PVT, Oswego, NY.

Schafer, Theodore, PVT, 1257172, Matamoras, PA.

Schollenberger, Howard – Saddler, 1257172, Hamburg, PA.

Schollenberger, Robert D – PVT, Hamburg, PA.

Sexson, Ernest A – PVT, 2870536, Baldwin, AR.

Appendix D

Seymour, George W – PVT, 2870437, Kingland, AR.

Shafer, Theodore T – CPL, WIA October 4, 1918.

Shea, Patrick - PVT, 373620, Mineville, NY, WIA October 4, 1918.

Shea, Peter L – PVT, 3322949, Holyoke, MA.

Shelly, Sebastian M – PVT, 2870863, Midland, AR, Gassed November 5, 1918.

Shnitman, Harry – PVT, Rochester, NY, Gassed November 1, 1918.

Shott, Russell R – PVT, 1257175, Lebanon, PA.

Simmons, Eddie C – PVT, 3256305, Elmo, AR.

Smith, Claude T – PVT, 2867806.

Smith, Clyde L – PVT, 1257099, Orwigsburg, PA.

Smith, Harvey B – PVT, Lebanon, PA.

Smith, Merton V – PVT, 1257179, Honesdale, PA, Gassed September 7, 1918.

Spicer, Bryant S – PVT, 3639154, Orange, VA.

Spicer, William R – PVT, Prairie View, AR.

Staller, Jeremiah – PVT, 1257199.

Staller, Paul A – CPL, 1257101, Auburn, PA.

St Clair, George W – PVT, 3634655, Pittsburgh, PA.

Sousley, Earl E – PFC, 1257100, Hamburg, PA, Gassed September 7, 1918.

Stephens, Hollis – PVT, 2870818, Hackett, AR.

Stevens, Alfred – PVT, 376066, Central Valley, NY, Gassed September 7, 1918.

Stewart, Harvey T – PVT, Center, AR.

Strausser, Albert J – PVT, 1257177, Reading, PA.

Street, Arthur W – PVT, 3180407, Skeggs, WV.

Strope, Edward B – PVT, 1257180, Troy, PA, WIA August 12, 1918.

Strunk, Reuben E – PVT, East Stroudsburg, PA.

Sulzer, Edward A – PVT, Philadelphia, PA.

Sunday, Frank C – Mechanic, 1257058, Hamburg, PA, WIA August 10, 1918.

Sweigert, John E – PVT, 1257182, Tremont, PA, MIA August 14, 1918.

Swingle, Ernest A – CPT, Ariel, PA, WIA August 11, 1918.

Swingle, Howard – CPL, Scranton, PA, WIA September 30, 1918, DOW October 5, 1918.

Swingle, Simon L – 2LT, Ariel, PA, WIA September 5, 1918.

Tenney, Paul B – PVT, 363579, Pittsburgh, PA.

Terpening, Earl P – PVT, 3735579, Schenectady, NY.

Timman, Charles R – PVT, 1257054, Matamoras, PA.

Toomey, Arthur A – CPL, 1257054, Scranton, PA.

Torrey, Kenneth W – PVT, 373382, KIA October 2, 1918.

Turner, William A – 1LT, New York, NY, Gassed.

Underkoffeer, Tolbert – PFC, 1257104, Lebanon, PA.

Vidurges, Paul – PVT, New York, NY, WIA September 7, 1918.

Wagner, Clarence J – PFC, 1257110, Hamburg, PA, WIA July 30, 1918, DOW August 1, 1918.

Wagner, Horace – CPL, 1257105, Bethel, PA.

Wambaugh, Ernest E – PVT, Wrightsville, PA.

Wampler, John E – PVT, 3626159, Mt Solon, VA, Gassed November 5, 1918.

Wannesmacher, Sylvanus L – PVT, 374956, Arlington, NY, Gassed October 4, 1918.

Wehr, Leroy M – PVT, 125788, Hamburg, PA.

Weidner, Floyd E – PVT, 1256106, Oley, PA.

Wengert, Darius D – PFC, 1257106, Bernville, PA, WIA August 18, 1918.

Wengert, Walter – CPL, Bernville, PA, Gassed September 7, 1918.

White, George F – Bugler, Chelsea, MA.

White, William C – PVT, 3636880, Clarksburg, WV.

Wike, William B – PFC, 1257107, Auburn, PA, WIA September 30, 1918.

Williams, Frank – PVT, 1257187, Kutztown, PA, Gassed September 7, 1918.

Williams, Lemont A – PVT, 1257187, Elmhurst, PA.

Williams, Orlando – PVT, 375785, Waverly, NY.

Wojeck, Lewis – CPL, WIA September 30, 1918.

Wolfe, Clarence J – PVT, 1257189, Williamstown, PA.

Yanney, Charles R – PVT, 3636525, Elmira, NY.

Yeager, Clayton A – Horseshoer, 1257055, Orwigsburg, PA.

Zellers, Howard – PVT, 1257186, Maiden Creek, PA, Gassed July 15, 1918.

Company D (Truck), 103rd Quartermaster Regiment:

December 1940

PVT Ahrensfield, Herman E
2LT Baver, James M
PVT Berger, Raymond
PVT Borkey, Floyd W
SGT Casper, Harold C
PVT Chattin, Harry L
PVT Correll, Edward V
PVT Degler, Guy C
PVT Dietrich, Marvin A
PVT Dreibelbis, Leon E
PVT Eckroth, Reynold I
SGT Fisher, LaMar O
PVT Freese, James P
SGT Gwynn, John E
PVT Heck, Edwin J
PVT Heffner, Paul H
PVT Henninger, Osville K
PVT Kauffman, Lawrence W
CPL Krieger, Henry C
PVT Lindermuth, Robert W
PVT Long, Howard F
PVT Machemer, Gerald B
PVT Miller, Charles L
PVT Miller, Russell S
PVT Phillips, Edward F
SGT Rollman, Adam N
PVT Schwenk, Marvin L
2LT Shollenberger, Allen E
PVT Wiliams, Franklin

SGT Bachman, Nevin R Jr.
1LT Beck, Peasron A
PVT Binner, Walter E
PVT Bressler, Harry M
CPT Casper, Raymond E
PVT Chattin, Paul H
CPL Daniels, Marlin A
PVT Deisher, Daniel H
SGT Dixon, Albert C
SGT Dunkelberger, John J
PVT Eyer, Raymond S
SGT Fisher, Lester M
PVT Gehringer, Elmer M
PVT Hage, Richard J
PVT Heckman, James B
PVT Henn, Lester D
PVT Hepner, Samuel B
CPL Ketner, Wellington R
PVT Kunkel, Alton P
CPL Long, Floyd R
PVT Long, Luther J
PVT Mellon, Paul W
PVT Miller, Randall W
PVT Moyer, Richard L
PVT Rex, Stewart A
PVT Schappell, Earl A
CPL Shoener, Roy A
PVT Shollenberger, Karl A
PVT Williamson, George E

PVT Williamson, Norman W   PVT Wuchter, Roland M
PVT Yoder, Lloyd S

World War II

121st Quartermaster Car Company:

Adamek, John – Hamtramack, MI.
Adams, William K – KIA.
Ahrensfield, Herman E – PVT, Orwigsburg, PA.
Alberding, Conrad A – Washington, D.C.
Albright, Robert H – Iowa.
Allen, Russel A – Center Hall, PA.
Anderson, Earl A – Almont, MI.
Anderson, Jesse L – Los Angeles, CA.
Ankney, Merle L – Norvelt, PA.
Antelope, George W – Killed in auto accident near Hamburg, Germany, 1945.
Anthony, Mark M – KIA.
Antol, Steve – Washington, PA.
Arneson, Joseph T
Augustine, John L – Ardmore, PA.
Bachman, Nevin R. Jr. – 1LT, Hamburg, PA.
Bajnoci, Alex J – Bethlehem, PA.
Baltz, Clair M – Nazareth, PA.
Barder, Joseph P – Lykens, PA.
Barshinger, Robert O – Red Lion, PA.
Barrett, Eugene J – Kingston, PA.
Bartlett, Joah C – Mineral Wells, TX.
Basarab, Joseph – Philadelphia, PA.
Basel, Ernest J – Plymouth, MI.
Bateman, Woodrow W – Paris, TN.
Baver, James M – 2LT, Hamburg, PA.
Beck, Pearson A – 1LT, Hamburg, PA.
Belin, George – Utahville, PA.
Berger, Raymond C – PVT, Hamburg, PA.

Bergschneider, Werner J – Springfield, IL.
Binder, Allen H – Macungie, PA.
Binner, Walter E – MSG, First Sergeant, Hamburg, PA.
Blais, Roland – River Roque, MI.
Blaney, Edward D – Philadelphia, PA.
Blank, Christian J – Easton, PA.
Bockino, Ralph J – Mount Vernon, NY.
Bork, Cyril G – Wisconsin.
Borkey, Floyd W – PVT, Leesport, PA. Major (Retired).
Bosserman, Earl G – Spring Grove, PA.
Bowersox, William E – Lewistown, PA.
Boyd, George H – Pittsburgh, PA.
Bozman, Floyd G – Steubenville, OH.
Brady, Sherald P – KIA.
Brandel, Louis J – Niagara Falls, NY.
Bratz, Joseph A – Bridgeport, CN.
Bredbinner, Harold L – Freeland, PA.
Breen, Matthew – East Rutherford, NJ.
Bresin, Emil C
Bressler, Harry M – SSG, Mess Sergeant, Auburn, PA.
Bressler, Luckey W – York, PA.
Briggs, Harold D – Centerville, LA.
Brodbeck, Theodore S – York, PA.
Brouillette, Joseph A
Brown, Harold D – Uniontown, PA.
Bryan, Daniel C – Philadelphia, PA.
Bryan, James W – New Brauntels, TX
Buchanan, William S – Pickerington, OH.
Burch, J. Albert – Paw Creek, NC.
Burkhart, John G – Jersey Shore, PA.
Butkiewicz, John L – Claremont, NH.
Byerley, Albert R – Chicago, IL.
Byrnes, Frank L – Green Bay, WI.
Cain, Joseph J
Cain, William G – Prarie Monroe, MS.
Candella, Jerry – SSG, Polpeville, NY.

Cannon, Grady C – Jay, FL.
Capalong, Andrew M – Scranton, PA.
Capko, Peter J – Cleveland, OH.
Carlson, Elmer S – 2LT
Carriper, John H – Corpus Christie, TX.
Carter, Allen W – Wilmington, OH.
Casper, Harold C – 1SG, Hamburg, PA.
Casper, Raymond E. Sr. – CPT, Hamburg, PA.
Cauthon, Virgel A – Hattiesburg, MS.
Cella, James J – Brooklyn, NY.
Cesaro, Michael D – Detroit, MI.
Chattin, Harry L – PVT, Hamburg, PA.
Chattin, Paul H – Pottsville, PA.
Chesney, Edward C – Detroit, MI.
Chesser, Billie M – Tampa, FL.
Chop, John Jr. – Cleveland, OH.
Chornock, George – Lowellville, OH.
Ciccarelli, George J – Darby, PA.
Clark, Edward A – Grahamsville, NY.
Cleveland, Alexander, Jr. – Milwaukee, WI.
Cline, Edgar J. Jr. – Suffolk, VA.
Cloeren, Matthew J – Philadelphia, PA.
Cobb, Norman D – West Chesterfield, NH.
Cochran, Forrest
Colosurdo, Victor V – Detroit, MI.
Corner, Howard M – Dayton, OH.
Correll, Edward V – CPL (85th Infantry Division), Hamburg, PA.
Coverstone, James M. Jr. – Front Royal, VA.
Crawford, Earl W – Buffalo, NY.
Cretton, Robert L
Czaplicki, Raymond P – Bridgeport, CN.
Dalton, Charles W – Cyclone, PA.
Daniels, Marlin A – CPL, Orwigsburg, PA.
Dean, Melvin G – Ohiopyle, PA.
Degler, Guy C – CPL, Port Clinton, PA.
Deisher, Daniel H – PVT, Shoemakersville, PA.

Appendix D

Delninger, Earl
DeSanta, John
Des Jardin, Thomas E – Detroit, MI.
Desseau, Glidden E. Jr.
Dietrich, Marvin A – PVT, Slatington, PA.
Dixon, Albert C – SGT, Hamburg, PA.
Dixon, Quentin D
Donahue, Charles M
Donathan, George – Saline, MI.
Doubet, Raymond A – Meadville, PA.
Dowling, Willard H E – Oswegatzhie, NY.
Dreamer, Daniel M – Crow Agency, MT.
Dreibelbis, Leon E – PVT, Hamburg, PA.
Dunkelberger, John J – T-SGT, Alexandria, VA.
East, Robert L – Spray, NC.
Eckroth, Reynold I – TECH-5, Hamburg, PA.
Edelman, Sidney
Eline, Elroy A – McSherrystown, PA.
Elliot, Loren L – East Detroit, MI.
Elliott, Alfred B – Norfolk, VA.
Ellis, Thomas W – Alexandria, IN.
Elsis, Joseph G – Queens, NY.
Eye, Stelman R – Ruddle, WV.
Eyer, Raymond S – MSG, Carmaster, Hamburg, PA.
Fail, Benjamin P
Feagans, Robert E – Indianapolis, IN.
Fendt, Harry E. Jr. – Philadelphia, PA.
Ferguson, William J – Philadelphia, PA.
Figurniak, Stanley B – South Janesport, NY.
Fike, Harry – Uniontown, PA.
Fisher, LaMar O – SGT, Pottsville, PA.
Fisher, Lester M – SGT, Orwigsburg, PA.
Foreman, Gordon K – Reading, PA.
Fourniew, Adelard V – Manhattan, NY.
Freese, James P – PVT, Reading, PA.
French, John C – Jackson, MS.

Fricker, George F – Cincinnati, OH.
Fritts, Harry D – CPT, New Canaan, CN.
Frost, Turner F – Kite, GA.
Frye, Clyde H – Bridgeville, PA.
Galloway, Ernest F – Kenova, WV.
Gausman, Raymond E – St. Mary's, PA.
Gehringer, Elmer M – CPL, Lenhartsville, PA.
Germanton, Elwood S – Allentown, PA.
Gibson, Thomas D
Gilbertson, Alfred C – Madison, WI.
Ginther, James W – Pottsville, PA.
Gise, Earl G – York, PA.
Goffredo, Antonio – Cambridge, MA.
Goodling, James R
Gould, Gordon G – Dorchester, MA.
Graef, Paul – Harrisburg, PA.
Grant, Henry R – Manchester, NH.
Gray, Fay H – Fordyce, AR.
Greene, Harold E – East Williamson, NY.
Greenhalgh, Ray E – PCF, POW, Bronze Star, Layton, UT.
Greenwalt, Robert J – Ozone Park, NY.
Greer, Aggy L – Shiner, TX.
Gregg, Arlington C – Royal Oak, MI.
Gregorich, John – Gilbert, MN.
Greminger, James F – Chester, PA.
Gret, Walter H
Gromlich, Charles C – Hamlin, PA.
Gwynn, John E – SGT, Hamburg, PA.
Hage, Richard J – PVT, Hamburg, PA.
Harris, Raymond C Jr. – Wilmington, DE.
Hartel, Gilbert J – Portage, WI.
Hartlaub, Charles A – McSherrystown, PA.
Hartman, Ralph E D – Wilmington, DE.
Hartman, William R – Chicago, IL.
Hayes, Ray J – Milwaukee, WI.
Hebbeler, Raymond M – Cincinnati, OH.

Heck, Edwin J – SSG, Hamburg, PA.
Heckman, James B – PVT, Shoemakersville, PA.
Heffner, Paul H – PVT, Hamburg, PA.
Heiser, Donald H – Davenport, IA.
Heller, Lester G – Alma, WI.
Heller, Willard L – KIA 1943.
Hendricks, Kenneth P – Columbus, IN.
Henn, Lester D – SGT, Hamburg, PA.
Henninger, Osville K – CPL, Kempton, PA.
Hepner, Samuel L – SSG, Platoon Sergeant, Temple, PA.
Higgins, George T – Ashland, NY.
Hillding, Edward – Grand Rapids, MI.
Hinckley, Herschell A – CPT, Monroeville, PA.
Hoiland, John W – Cheybogan, MI.
Holloway, Kenneth O
Horine, Earle A – Baltimore, MD.
Horton, Raymond L – Grand Rapids, MI.
Howlin, Charles A – Washington, D.C.
Hubler, Arthur K – Pine Grove, PA.
Huesman, Robert B – Cincinnati, OH.
Huff, Clarence C – Raton, NM.
Humberd, Paul R – Delphi, IN.
Ilyes, Paul E – Seven Valleys, PA.
Immacolato, Rosario – Richmond Hill, NY.
Ingalls, Roy M – Escanab, WI.
Jakimowicz, Matthew – Philadelphia, PA.
Johns, Edward – Jacksonville, FL.
Johnson, Ralph J – Sanford, ME.
Jones, Frank H – Lynchburg, VA.
Jones, Russell D – 1LT.
Junktis, Albert J – Philadelphia, PA.
Jusczcyk, Xavier, J – Jackson, MI.
Karwoski, Theodore – KIA.
Kauffman, Lawrence W – PVT, Hamburg, PA.
Kaufman, Ward R – Green Bay, WI.
Kell, Arthur C

Kelly, Robert E – Brighton, MA.
Kessce – TECH-5.
Ketner, Wellington R – CPL, Hamburg, PA.
King, Edward C
Kinnes, William G – Northfield, NJ.
Knaub, Clarence R
Koers, Donald – Detroit, MI.
Konfesky, Manuel – Philadelphia, PA.
Koons, George D – Pine Grove, PA.
Kopec, Joe H – Grand Rapids, MI.
Kraszewski, Edward – Flint, MI.
Kreiger, Henry C – SGT, Shoemakersville, PA.
Kunkel, Alton P – PVT, Hamburg, PA.
Kushner, Nathan – Philadelphia, PA.
LaPoint, Leo A – Scotia, NY.
Lawrence, John H – Littletown, PA.
Lazur, Andrew J – Rahway, NJ.
Leapley, John L D – Washington, D.C.
Leas, Harry W – York, PA.
Leipensberger, Arthur W – Philadelphia, PA.
Leone, Rudolph M – Camden, NJ.
Levine, Harry – Brooklyn, NY.
Lewis, Donald E – Portland, OR.
Lindermuth, Robert W – PVT, Reading, PA.
Linders, Raymond E – Manchester, CN.
Lippman, Burt B – Newark, NJ.
Lisowski, Joseph P – Arcadia, WI.
Little, James M – Baltimore, MD.
Long, Floyd R – CPL, Dispatcher, Shoemakersville, PA.
Long, Howard F – TECH-4, Mechanic, Shoemakersville, PA.
Long, Luther J – PVT, Hamburg, PA.
Longton, Raymond A – Lincoln Park, MI.
Loughlin, Robert A
Loy, Franklin L – CPT, Middletown, PA.
Ludwig, Henry S – Ephrata, PA.
Lugli, Michael J – New Britain, CN.

Macaluso, Vincent J – Brooklyn, NY.
Machemer, Gerald B – SSG, Supply Sergeant, Cressona, PA.
Maday, John D – Jersey City, NJ.
Mahan, William L – Kilbourne, IL.
Maloney, Harry – New York, NY.
Mann, Robert D – York, PA.
Mantyck, Leo – South Bend, IN.
Marchand, Raymond E – LaGrange, IN.
Massaro, William – New Haven, CN.
Matina, Peter F – West New York, NY.
Maxwell, John S – Hartford, KS.
May, Alex F
McConnell, William F – Bristol, VA.
McCord, Robert J – Detroit, MI.
McDaniel, Warren D – DeVine, TX.
McGee, John V – Indianapolis, IN.
McKenna, James F – 1LT
McNabb, John J
Mead, Robert F – 2LT, Glenview, IL.
Melen, Henry C
Mellon, Paul W – PVT, Orwigsburg, PA.
Merrill, Donald – Owl Creek, WY.
Metrick, John – St. Clair, PA.
Michalczyn, Peter P – Trenton, NJ.
Middleton, Harry H – Detroit, MI.
Mikulskie, John – Wilmington, DE.
Millan – 1LT.
Miller, Charles L – MSG, Orwigsburg, PA.
Miller, Charles R – Sonora, TX.
Miller, Delmar R – Irwin, PA.
Miller, Frank – Newark, NJ.
Miller, Lawrence H – Killed in auto accident in North Africa, 1943.
Miller, Randall W – PVT, Laureldale, PA.
Miller, Russell S – PVT, Hamburg, PA.
Minerchak, Joseph – Winfield Park, NJ.
Moose, Kenneth L

Moran, William P – Jersey City, NJ.
Moscatelli, Samuel – Chisholm, MN.
Mosley, Lloyd T – Poplar Bluff, MO.
Moyer, Richard L – PVT, Hamburg, PA.
Mumma, George J – 2LT, Villanova, PA.
Murray, Edgar F – Greensboro, NC.
Napolitano, Dominick A
Naylor, Theodore C
Nelson, Carl O – Spooner, WI.
Nelson, Frank A
Nerney, William E – Brooklyn, NY.
Neuhaus, Peter J – Detroit, MI.
Nezezon, John J
Nichols, William E – Dukecenter, PA.
Nickless, Harland U – Terre Haute, IN.
Nolen, Edward J – Floyd, VA.
Northup, Lawrence E – Nodaway, IA.
Norviel, Noah N – Lakeview, OH.
O'Brien, James F – 2LT, Pittsburgh, PA.
O'Hara, Gerald L – New Castle, PA.
Olson, Leonard D – Strum, WI.
O'Neal, Alvin J – Saginaw, MI.
O'Neill, Thomas J – Brooklyn, NY.
Onsrud, Clarence H – Arcadia, WI.
Oxley, Lawrence W – Cedar Creek, NE.
Pankow, Fred J – 1SG.
Paster, Hyman W – Bronx, NY.
Patton, William A – Belton, SC.
Peacock, Sidney H – Lexington, MS.
Perkins, Donald H – Granite City, IL.
Perry, Clyde M – Parkton, MD.
Peters, Grady B
Peterson, Edward S – Minneapolis, MN.
Pettit, William S – San Antonio, TX.
Phillips, Edward F – PVT, Pottsville, PA.
Phillips, Gordon H – Erie, PA.

Pope, William S – Bluff City, TN.
Prosser, Paul E – Dillsburg, PA.
Ramage, William J – Port Huron, MI.
Reed, Eugene M – Richmond, CA.
Reed, Richard E – Piqua, OH.
Resnick, Frank J
Rex, Stewart A – PVT, Hamburg, PA.
Richburg, George O – Manning, SC.
Riggs, Charles J – McSherrystown, PA.
Ritter, Don R – Janesville, WI.
Riverburgh, Kenneth
Robertson, W. J – Wiville, AR.
Robinson, Jerome T – Decatur, IL.
Rock, Robert F – Harrison, NJ.
Rollman, Adam N – SGT, Hamburg, PA.
Romanos, John A – Detroit, MI.
Rosenthal, Charles J – 2LT, Harrisburg, PA.
Rotegliano, Paul F – Renova, PA.
Rothstein, Seymour – Brooklyn, NY.
Roulston, Joseph A – Philadelphia, PA.
Rowlier, Francis A
Ruggieri, Robert J – 1LT
Rushatz, Stephen J – Coplay, PA.
Scampome, Joseph E – Williamsport, PA.
Schappell, Earl A – SGT, Shoemakersville, PA.
Schmidt, Howard E – Baltimore, MD.
Schomburg, Carl F – Columbus, OH.
Schwab, Henry
Schwalm, Joseph A – 2LT, Pine Grove, PA.
Schwenk, Marvin L – PVT, Orwigsburg, PA.
Scott, Burgess M
Seebaugh, Herbert M – Mineral Wells, WV.
Seybole, Herman F – Crawfordsville, IN.
Shafer, Clyde E – Morgantown, WV.
Shoener, Leroy A – SFC, Orwigsburg, PA.
Shollenberger, Allen E – 2LT, Hamburg, PA.

Shollenberger, Karl A – PVT, Port Engineer, Hamburg, PA.
Shoulders, Ernest S
Silsby, Orville D – Swedeboro, MO.
Simonds, Howard F – Salina, NY.
Sincavage, Joseph J – West Wyoming, PA.
Sine, Lonnie J – Fairview, WV.
Small, Norman F – Gettysburg, PA.
Smerdell, James
Smith, Burl H – Hemlock, WV.
Smith, Edward C
Smith, Henry D – KIA near Seblia, Tunisia, 1943.
Smith, Ralph H
Smith, William – New York City, NY.
Smoot, George W – Lynchburg, VA.
Snopkosky, Walter W – Scranton, PA.
Spillane, John J – Astoria, NY.
Splan, Richard G – Sault St. Marie, MI.
Stanco, Lawrence A – Glen Cove, NY.
Standill, Otis G – Dayton, OH.
St. Clair, Forrestt – Pipesten, WV.
Stein, Oscar J
Steinhaus, Walter - Cheybogan, WI.
Stemple, Lester E – Aurora, WV.
Stepien, Joseph P – 2LT, Norfolk, VA.
Steuber, John W
Stevenson, Keith H – Port Huron, MI.
Stickney, Leonard Jr. – Davison, MI.
Stockman, Perry A – Duluth, MN.
Stover, Harvey E – Dover, PA.
Stubble, Leon A – Harmonsburg, PA.
Taber, Donald E – Albion, MI.
Tate, George E – Gettysburg, PA.
Taylor, Carl S
Taylor, Clare H – Birmingham, MI.
Taylor, Jessie – Kayford, WV.
Teets, Ellis H – Eglon, WV.

Texter, Clavin J – Cincinnati, OH.

Theodore, Joesph – TECH-5, WIA near Saarbracken, Germany, 1945.

Thomey, Harold J – Chicago, IL.

Thompson, Charles L – Martin, TN.

Tomaszewski, Louis B – Chicago, IL.

Tompsett, Richard J – Dent, MI.

Tonglet, Gerlad J – 1LT.

Treanor, Bernard J – Philadelphia, PA.

Triplett, Arduth M

Van Geldemen, Samson H – Cincinnati, OH.

Vdoviak, John

Vognetz, Norman A – Danville, PA.

Wambaugh, George W – Detroit, MI.

Weaver, Rudolph H – Apollo, PA.

Webb, Clyde W – Elkton, MD.

Weiland, Jack M

Weinheimer, Howard E – 1LT

Weldon, William E – Cordele, GA.

Wemmer, Robert H – Indianapolis, IN.

West, Gilbert G

White, William J – New Rochelle, NY.

Wilder, Willie R – San Antonio, TX.

Williams, Earl – Grand Rapids, MI.

Williams, Franklin – TECH SGT (90th Infantry Division), Schuylkill Haven, PA.

Williams, Walter – Remsen, NY.

Williamson, George E – PVT, Hamburg, PA.

Williamson, Norman W – Hamburg, PA.

Windsor, Herbert A – Cincinnati, OH.

Wood, Cyril – South Seattle, WA.

Wooton, James M – Combs, KY.

Wowak, John C – Shenandoah, PA.

Wuchter, Roland M – PVT, Chauffer and Clerk, Reading, PA.

Yates, Herschel – Sunnyside, WA.

Yoder, Lloyd S – PVT, Hamburg, PA.

Zicovage, John – Selinsgrove, PA

Zierer, Stanley – Garnerville, NY.
Ziombkowski, Anthony – Grand Rapids, MI.
Zonge, John S – State College, PA.

Korean War

Battery D, 337th Anti-Aircraft Artillery Battalion:
(Roster of men mobilized on May 1, 1951)

Adam, Irvin C – CPL, NG33840111
Bachman, Richard A – PVT, NG23879092
Bainbridge, James W – CPL, NG23879019
Bainbridge, John G – CPL, NG23879018
Balthaser, Norman W – CPL, NG23879034
Baver, Alfred E – CPL, NG23879069
Becker, Kenneth D – CPL, NG23879069
Becker, Norman L – CPL, NG33840173
Beitler, Richard E – PVT, NG23879047
Berger, Floyd C – SGT, NG33839144
Bohn, Floyd H – CPL, NG23879022
Bordner, Clarence W. Jr. – PFC, NG23879059
Budden, Clarence R – PVT, NG23879094
Calnan, William H – CPL, NG23879001
Christman, Stanley P – PFC, NG23879057
Correll, Ellis J – PVT, NG43013189
Coyle, James W – CPL, NG23887061
Dietrich, Walter F – PVT, NG23879097
Dougherty, Arthur M – CPL, NG33772212
Dunkel, Carl J – PFC, NG23879075
Dunkel, Floyd D – SGT, NG23879012
Dunkle, Ray A – PVT, NG23879090
Eyer, Clifford M – PVT, NG23879089
Faust, John A – PVT, NG23879091
Faust, Lester L – CPL, NG23879020
Fister, Harvey L – MSG, NG33079493
Fryer, Kenneth G – PVT, NG23879095

Graeff, Robert C – CPL, NG23879058
Greenawalt, Franklin A – PVT, NG23879084
Greenawalt, Herbert A – PVT, NG23879082
Grill, Stephen F. Jr. – SFC, NG33618127
Haas, Wayne C. Jr. – PVT, NG23879079
Heckman, William C – PVT, NG23879071
Heffner, Lester A – SFC, NG13029627
Henne, Charles W – PVT, NG23879087
Herber, Lee W – CPL, NG23879017
Hess, Harland H – PFC, NG23879024
Hummel, Lee F – PVT, NG23879096
Hunsicker, Forrest A – PVT, NG23879088
Kautter, William J – 2LT
Keller, Raymond J – PVT, NG23879093
Kelly, Earl W – CPL, NG23879054
Kershner, Curtis L – PVT, NG23879086
Kershner, Leroy P – PFC, NG23879080
Ketner, Wellington R – 1LT, 0-1595620
Kieffer, Lawrence W – NG23879065
Kleinsmith, Merryl J – SGT, NG13243509
Kline, Carl E – PVT, NG23879072
Loeb, Paul E – PFC, NG23879085
Loeb, Raymond A – SGT, NG33489951
Loeb, Wayne H – PFC, NG23879061
Lonergan, Melvin S – CPL, NG23879043
Madtes, Lester L – CPL, NG33984321
Meck, Stuart T – CPL, NG13147682
Noecker, Forrest J – 2LT, 0-971005
Oswalt, William H. Jr. – PFC, NG23879064
Peters, Ralph P – PFC, NG23879074
Rhoads, Paul H – PFC, NG23879083
Rickenbach, Earl E – SGT, NG13194012
Ruth, Robert G – CPL, NG23866016
Schaner, Vernon C. C – PVT, NG23879072
Schappell, Mylan L – PFC, NG23879068
Schrepple, Lee S – SGT, NG33489919

BLUE MOUNTAIN LEGION

Seigfried, Ernest G – PFC, NG23879015
Shollenberger, Clyde S – PFC, NG23879036
Smith, John D – CPL, NG13210730
Smith, Norman F – CPT, 0-358280
Spease, Floyd A – PVT, NG23879077
Stewart, Harvey M – CPL, NG23879006
Trabosh, John C – PVT, NG23879070
Varner, Charles F – PFC, NG23879033
Wagner, John G. Jr. – CPL, NG23879037
Wanner, Roy L – CPL, NG13052377
Wink, Walter N. Jr. – PVT, NG23879098

Abbreviations

MUSC – Musician
QM – Quarter Master
PVT – Private
PFC – Private First Class
SPC – Specialist
CPL – Corporal
SGT – Sergeant
SSG – Staff Sergeant
SFC – Sergeant First Class
PSG – Platoon Sergeant
MSG – Master Sergeant
1SG – First Sergeant
ENS – Ensign

2LT – Second Lieutenant
1LT – First Lieutenant
CPT – Captain
MAJ – Major
LTC – Lieutenant Colonel
COL – Colonel
BG – Brigadier General
MG – Major General
LTG – Lieutenant General
DOW – Died of Wounds
KIA – Killed in Action
MIA – Missing in Action
WIA – Wounded in Action

Awards

Unit Awards

1958:   337th Anti-Aircraft Artillery Battalion Award for Highest Attendance.

1958:   337th Anti-Aircraft Artillery Battalion Award for Highest Qualification.

1959:   213th Anti-Aircraft Artillery Battalion Award for Best Firing Battery.

1959:   213th Anti-Aircraft Artillery Battalion Award for Highest Small Arms Qualification.

1959:   213th Anti-Aircraft Artillery Battalion Award for Highest Annual Training Rating.

1960:   213th Anti-Aircraft Artillery Battalion Award for Best Air Defense Firing Battery.

1960:   213th Anti-Aircraft Artillery Battalion Award for Highest Attendance.

1960:   Awarded the "First Defender Trophy" for Highest Possible Score with 90mm AAA guns. Presented at Camp Perry, Ohio by the 51st Anti-Aircraft Defense Brigade.

1961:   213th Anti-Aircraft Artillery Battalion Award for Best Firing Battery.

1965:   3rd Battalion, 103rd Armor Commander's Trophy for Best Company at Annual Training.

1966:   3rd Battalion, 103rd Armor Commander's Trophy for Best Maintenance at Annual Training.

1967:   3rd Battalion, 103rd Armor Commander's Trophy for Best Maintenance at Annual Training.

1968:   3rd Battalion, 103rd Armor Commander's Trophy for Best Company at Annual Training.

1970:   3rd Battalion, 103rd Armor Commander's Trophy for Best Company at Annual Training.

1970:   56th Brigade Material Readiness Award.

1974:   The Adjutant General of Pennsylvania Retention and Recruiting Honor Roll streamer.

1975:   3rd Battalion, 103rd Armor Commander's Trophy for Outstanding Performance at Annual Training.

1976:   Adjutant General of Pennsylvania Honor Roll for attaining 106.5% of Authorized Strength.

1979:   Awarded the "Liberty Bell Award" for achieving the Most Outstanding Record of Enlistments, Reenlistments, and Extensions in the Pennsylvania Army National Guard for the period of January 9, 1978 to June 30, 1978.

1987:   First Cavalry plaque for Outstanding Support during "Operation Certain Strike" REFORGER-87.

1987:   7th Support Command Citation for Outstanding Support during "Operation Certain Strike" REFORGER-87.

1988:   213th Area Support Group Award for Best Rifle Team.

1988:   Third Place Rifle Team in the Adjutant General of Pennsylvania Rifle Trophy Match.

1988:   Military Assistance Command, Region II Trophy for Second Place Rifle Team.

Individual Awards

1965:   PSG Floyd A. Spease – Battalion Trophy for Best Instructor at Annual Training.

1968:   PSG James M. McDonald - Battalion Trophy for Best Instructor at Annual Training.

1978:   SSG William C. Bandholz – 165th Military Police Battalion Soldier of the Year.

1981:   PSG Michael W. Werley – LTG Milton G. Baker NCO Leadership Award as the Most Outstanding NCO in the Pennsylvania Army National Guard.

1981:   PSG Michael W. Werley – 1st U.S. Army NCO of the Year.

1983:   SP4 Michael A. Peters – Pennsylvania Army National Guard Soldier of the Year.

1983:   SSG Donald G. Erway - 165th Military Police Battalion NCO of the Year.

1984:   SP4 Paul H. Shollenberger - Military Police Battalion Soldier of the Year.

1984:   SSG Wade E. Heilman – 213th Area Support Group NCO of the Year.

1985:   PFC Robert D. Wessner Jr. – 165th Military Police Battalion Skills Competition Winner.

1986:   PFC Michael D. Macluskie – 165th Military Police Battalion Soldier of the Year.

1986:   SFC Craig A. Kleinsmith - LTG Milton G. Baker NCO Leadership Award as the Most Outstanding NCO in the Pennsylvania Army National Guard.

1987:   SP4 Mark S. Rizzardi – 213th Area Support Group Soldier of the Year.

1987:   SGT Robert D.Wessner Jr. – Pennsylvania Army National Guard NCO of the Year.

Annual Training

August 1953	Fort Miles, Delaware
August 1954	Fort Miles, Delaware
July 1955	Camp Perry, Ohio
July-August 1956	Camp Perry, Ohio
July 1957	Camp Perry, Ohio
July-August 1958	Camp James Parke Postles, Bethany Beach, Delaware
June 1959	Camp Perry, Ohio
July 1960	Camp Perry, Ohio
July-August 1961	Camp James Parke Postles, Bethany Beach, Delaware
July-August 1962	Fort Indiantown Gap, Pennsylvania
August 1963	Fort Indiantown Gap, Pennsylvania
August 1964	Fort Indiantown Gap, Pennsylvania
May-June 1965	Camp Pickett, Virginia

THE BLUE MOUNTAIN LEGION

July-August 1966	Camp Pickett, Virginia
May-June 1967	Fort Indiantown Gap, Pennsylvania
August 1968	Camp Drum, New York
July-August 1969	Camp Drum, New York
August 1970	Camp Pickett, Virginia
August 1971	Camp Drum, New York
June 1972	Eastern Pennsylvania – Flood Duty
August-September 1972	Camp Drum, New York
July-August 1973	Camp Drum, New York
July-August 1974	Camp Drum, New York
May-June 1975	Fort Stewart, Georgia
July 1976	Fort Meade, Maryland
June-July 1977	Fort Pickett, Virginia
July 1978	Fort Meade, Maryland
August 1979	New Cumberland Army Depot, Pennsylvania
May 1980	Fort Drum, New York
March-April 1981	Fort Ritchie, Maryland
June 1982	Fort A.P. Hill, Virginia

July 1983	Fort Drum, New York
June 1984	Fort Indiantown Gap, Pennsylvania
May 1985	Fort Indiantown Gap, Pennsylvania
June 1986	Fort A.P. Hill, Virginia
September-October 1987	Trauen and Munster, Germany
July 1988	Fort Drum, New York

Bibliography

Adjutant General, PA. *Annual Report,* 1875.

Adjutant Generals Office. *Statistical Exhibit of Strength of Volunteer Forces Called into Service During the War with Spain,* Washington, Government Printing Office, 1899.

Alger, Russell A. *The Spanish-American War,* New York and London, Harper, 1901.

Anderson, James S. *The March of the Sixth Corps to Gettysburg,* War Papers, IV, 77-84 (Commandery of the State of Wisconsin, Mollus), Milwaukee, 1914.

Bannan, Benjamin. *Memorial Patriotism of Schuylkill County,* 1865.

Bates, Samuel P. *History of the Pennsylvania Volunteers, 1861-1865,* Harrisburg, PA: B. Singerly, 1870.

Bosbyshell, Oliver C. *The 48th Pennsylvania Veteran Volunteers in the War,* 1895.

Clarke, William P. *Official History of the Militia and National Guard of the State of Pennsylvania,* 1909.

Fox, William F. *Regimental Losses in the American Civil War, 1861-1865,* Albany, 1898.

Gould, Joseph. *The Story of the 48th Pennsylvania Volunteer Infantry 1861-1865,* 1908.

Headquarters, 121st QM Car Company. *History of the 121st Quartermaster Car Company*, APO 772, U.S. Army, 1945.

Hyde Thomas W. *Following the Greek Cross: Or Memories of the Sixth Army Corps*, New York, 1894.

Johnston, Henry P. *The Campaign of 1776 Around New York and Brooklyn*, Brooklyn, Long Island Historical Society, 1878.

Martin, Edward. *The 28th Division, Pennsylvania's Guard in the World War*, 1923.

Military Commission Book (Militia Book). *Volumes 7, 8, 9, 10 & 11.*

Minutes of Blue Mountain Legion. *Company E, 4th Regiment.*

Montgomery, Morton L. *Statement of Men Supplied by the County of Berks in the Civil War*, 1905.

Nicholson, John P. & Beitler, Lewis E. *Pennsylvania at Gettysburg*, Harrisburg, 1914.

PA Militia. *Order Book A, Issue of Ordnance & Quartermaster Stores.*

Pennsylvania Archives. *6th Series, Volume 10, War with Mexico.*

Pennsylvania. Gettysburg Battlefield Commission. *Pennsylvania at Gettysburg: Ceremonies at the Dedication of the Monuments Erected by the Commonwealth*, Harrisburg, PA, William S. Ray, 1914.
Sedgwick, John. *Correspondence of Major General John Sedgwick*, New York, 1902-03.

Stevens, George T. *Three Years in the Sixth Corps*, New York, 1870.

Swinton, William. *Campaigns of the Army of the Potomac*, New York, 1866.

U.S. Army, Historical Branch, War Plans Division, General Staff. *Outlines of History of Regiments, U.S. Army*, Washington, 1921.

U.S. Army, Historical Section, Army War College. *Order of Battle of the U.S. Land Forces in the World War, American Expeditionary Forces*, Washington, Government Printing Office, 1931-1949.

U.S. Army, Military History Research Collection. *U.S. Army Unit Histories*, Special Bibliographic Series, No. 4, Carlisle Barracks, PA, 1971.

U.S. Department of War. *Official Army Register of the Volunteer Forces of the US Army for the Years 1861, 1862, 1863, 1864, 1865*, Washington, 1865.

U.S. Department of War. *The War of the Rebellion: A Compilation of the Official Records of the Union and Confederate Armies*, Washington, 1880-1901.

U.S. War Department. *Bibliography of State Participation in the Civil War.* 3rd Edition, Washington, Government Printing Office, 1913.

Wagner, A. E., Balthaser, F. W. & Hoch, D. K. *The Story of Berks County (Pennsylvania)*, Reading, PA, Eagle Book and Job Press, 1916.

Index

Adam, George, 23
Aisne-Marne, 140, 160
Algeria, 169
Ancona, John F, 118
Antelope, George, 173
Anti-Aircraft Artillery Group, 213th, 178
Antietam, 42, 81
Anzio, 170
Arndt, Charles, 77
Auburn, PA, 3

Balty, Christian, 24
Barnett, J.D., 30
Battery D, 2nd Gun Battalion, 213th Artillery, 184
Battery D, 337th Anti-Aircraft Gun Battalion, 177
Battery D, 337th Anti-Aircraft Artillery Searchlight Battalion, 177
Baum, Christian, 110
Baver, Alfred, 177
Behler-Hein Post No. 637, 157
Behler, Walter E, 157
Beitenman, Frederick A, 30, 31
Beitenman, Frederick E, 32
Beitenman, John A, 32, 33
Beitenman, John Alfred, 31

Berger, Floyd, 177
Berks County Rifle Rangers, 31, 33
Berlin, Germany, 174
Berstler, Roy, 201
Bethesda Church, 93
Billich, Anthony, 27
Billman, Neil, 185
Bloody Angle, 65, 67
Blue Mountain Legion, 109, 164
Bogart, Humphrey, 175
Braddock, 1
Breezewood, PA, 195, 197
Brobst, John, 23
Bronze Star, 173
Bull Run, Second Battle of, 39, 79

Camp Stewart, Georgia, 178
Cashman, Stephen, 185, 186, 201
Casper, Raymond E, 125
Champagne-Marne, 140, 160
Chancellorsville, 47, 50, 53, 62, 92
Chateau-Thierry, 138, 142, 160
Churchill, Winston, 175
Civil Air Patrol, 185, 186, 189

Cold Harbor, 68, 70, 94
Company A, 3rd Battalion, 103rd Armor, 184
Company A, 107th Machine Gun Battalion, 127
Company A, 108th Machine Gun Battalion, 127, 161
Company D, 3rd Medium Tank Battalion, 184
Company D, 48th Pennsylvania Volunteer Inf. Rgt., 74
Company G, 96th Pennsylvania Volunteer Inf. Rgt., 35
Cramptons Pass, 40, 41
Crater, Battle of, 95
Crow, Ralph C, 127

Dalious, Harold W, 162
Degler, Allen, 164
Deisher, William S, 33
Derr, Benneville, 31, 32, 33
Douden, James M, 35
Douty, Jacob, 101
Dumon, Levi, 34
Dunkel, Floyd, 178

Ebling, John, 185
Eckert, Valentine, 25
El Paso, Texas, 125
Emrich, Sebastian, 22, 23
England, 132, 133
Epler, Samuel, 164
Everett, Pennsylvania, 194, 195, 196, 197

Fesig, Arthur S, 31

Fisher, Edward, 185
Fismes Sector, 144, 160
Fister, Simon S, 30, 31
Flammer, Eugene, 185, 188
Fort Dix, New Jersey, 179
Fort Lebanon, 3, 4, 5, 7, 8, 13, 14, 17
Foust, Samuel, 33
Francis, Kay, 175
Frantz, Donald E, 204
Frantz, Jacob, 24
Fredericksburg, Virginia, 37, 43, 44, 45, 47, 48, 49, 51, 53, 54, 77, 78, 83
Fritts, Harry D, 167
Fryer, Kenneth, 178

Gable, Clark, 175
Gaines Mill, 38
Ganadenhuth, 24
Geehr, Baltzer, 21, 22, 27
Germany, 205, 206
Gettysburg, 57, 58, 59, 73, 101
Gilmartin, James, 186
Gladwyne, Pennsylvania, 180
Good, Charles H, 157
Greenhalgh, Ray E, 173

Hamburg Artillerists, 30, 31, 32
Hamburg Artillery, 30, 31, 32, 33
Hamburg Athletic and Military Association, 164
Hamburg, Germany, 173
Hamburg Light Dragoons, 30

Hamburg Volunteer Battalion, 31, 32, 33
Hamm, Darryl R, 194
Harris, Charles C, 164
Hartz, George, 107
Hein, Thomas, 157
Heinly, George, 33
Herbein, Jonathan S, 33
Hill, Jacob, 23
Hinckley, Herschell A, 168
Hower, George, 22

Ireland, 166
Isett, Chester, 164

Johnstown, 199, 201
Jolson, Al, 175

Kaercher, Martin, 22, 24, 27
Keel, Howard, 202
Ketner, Wellington R, 181
King, Randy, 201
Knoxville, Tennessee, 86, 87
Krause, Peter, 32
Kreusher, Simon, 27
Krick, Mark, 185, 187
Kutztown, 177

Leary, Dennis, 24
Lehighton, 24
Lewars, Clayton, 164
Lewars, Edward, 164
Lindenmuth, Michael, 21, 22, 23, 24
Lindermuth, Lee M, 185
London, England, 166, 169

Long Island, Battle of, 21
Loy, Franklin L, 165
Loy, Lewis A, 125

Malvern Hill, 38
Maryes Heights, 44
May, George, 21, 22
Mayfair, Mitzi, 175
McDonald, James, 189
McKenna, James F, 170
Mead, Robert F, 167
Meuse-Argonne, 147, 160
Mexican Border, 124
Military Police Company:
  723rd, 198
  1068th, 194
Miller, E. Newton, 164
Miller, Heinrich Gustav, 125
Miller, Joseph M, 33
Miller, Lawrence H, 169
Miller, William, 31, 33
Miller, William R, 32
Minnich, Conrad, 22, 23, 24
Moll, Edward, 33
Morgan, Jacob, 3
Morgan, Richard D, 185
Morris, Governor, 2
Mumma, George J, 167
Munster, Germany, 205

Nagle, Daniel, 76
Naples, Italy, 170, 171
Negman, John, 24
Newberne, 76
Nuremberg, Germany, 175

O'Brien, James F, 167
Oise-Aisne, 145, 160

Pas de Calais, 133, 159
Pegram's Farm, 105, 106
Peninsula Campaign, 37
Petersburg, 73, 94, 95, 108
Pistos, Marydel J, 199
Pleasant Valley Artillery, 33
Pleasants, Henry, 92, 96
Port Clinton, 3
Potteiger, George F, 124, 164
Pottsville, 35, 74, 89
Powell, Jane, 202
Prutzman, James F, 124
Puerto Rico, 120, 122

Quartermaster Car Company, 121st, 165, 167, 168, 169, 175, 177

Railroad riots, 111
Reber, George, 22, 27
Reese, Harry, 97, 100
Reeser, John F, 30, 31
REFORGER, 204, 206
Reilly, Vincent, 201
Reinhart, William, 164
Ritter, Ferdinand, 23, 24
Robinson, Edward G, 175
Rosenthal, Charles J, 167

Sandridge, Rodger, 201
Savage, E. S., 186
Schappell, Eberhard, 22
Schappell, Jacob, 27

Schappell, Jeremiah, 30, 31
Scotland, 166, 168
Scott, Winfield, 31
Schwalm, Joseph A, 165
Seaman, Charles F, 114, 116
Seaman, Harrison F, 125
Seaman, Jeryl, 185
Seaman, William F, 164
Seiberling, John, 31
Seidel, John S, 33
Seidle, Godfrey, 27
Seiger, Thomas, 31
Shadle, Jacob, 22, 23
Shartel, Jacob, 24
Shenandoah Valley, 56, 73
Shoemaker, Charles, 29
Shoemakersville, 29
Shollenberger, Benjamin E, 32
Shollenberger, Robert, 164
Shollenberger, Robert, 185,
Shomo, William, 31, 32, 33
Shraedel, Jacob, 22, 23
Sicily, 170
Siegfried, Charles, 22
Smith, Andrew, 27
Smith, Edward F, 109, 113
Smith, Harvey, 164
Smith, Henry, 169
Smith, John M, 164
Smith, Michael, 23
Smith, Norman, 177, 178
Smith, William, 109
Smith, William M, 164
Smith, William R, 33
Smoke Church, 2
Soder, John, 22

South Mountain, 40, 41, 59, 81
Spanish-American War, 119
Spease, Floyd, 184, 185, 201
Spottsylvania, 62, 65, 68, 91,
 92, 94
Stambach, Daniel M, 32
Stapleton, Jacob, 23
Stepien, Joseph P, 170
Strabel, Jacob, 24
Stalnecker, J. P., 33
Stitzel, John, 33
Strausstown, 3
Suicide Squads, 156
Sunday, J. Albert, 162
Swingle, Ernest A, 155

Talbot, John, 31
Tenant, Jacob, 23
Theodore, Joseph, 173
Thiaucourt, 153, 160
Trauen, Germany, 205
Tropical Storm Agnes, 184,
 193
Tunisia, 169

Udree, Daniel, 30
Umbenhacker, Francis, 24
Upton, Emory, 60

Vennerwaldt, William, 164

Villa, Pancho, 124

Wagner, Benjamin R, 33
Wagner, Clarence J, 157
Wagner-Good Post No. 216 of
 The Veterans of Foreign
 Wars, 157
Wagner, John R, 118
Wagon Company No. 106, 161
War of 1812, 29
War with Mexico, 32
Washington, D.C., 36, 37, 39,
 40, 52, 54, 70, 73, 74, 80, 81,
 99, 108
Weinheimer, Howard E, 170
Weiser, Conrad, 3
Werley, Michael, 201
Wetstein, Jacob, 22, 23, 24
Wilderness, The, 62, 90
Wilhelm, Carl, 163
Will, Daniel, 22, 23, 24
Williamson, Abraham, 164
Williamson, Levi, 34
Williamson, Levi, 164
Williamson, William, 22
Windsor Cavalry, 32, 34
Windsor powder magazine, 23
Windsor Rifles, 32
Windsor Township, 2

ABOUT THE AUTHOR

Craig A. Kleinsmith, Master Sergeant (retired), began his military career with the Hamburg unit in 1973, and retired from the military as the Transportation Supervisor for the 28th Infantry Division (Mechanized) in 1995. He is an avid student of history; particularly military history. He has participated as a re-enactor in Civil War battle reenactments and living history programs, and conducted military history lectures and demonstrations for local organizations. His extensive research of *The Blue Mountain Legion* includes official military records, governmental records, official muster rolls and orders, newspaper articles, and interviews with veterans of the unit. The research for this book took him approximately ten years to complete.